Life
Guidance
through
Literature

Life Guidance through Literature

Arthur Lerner
and
Ursula R. Mahlendorf

American Library Association
Chicago and London 1992

Cover and text designed by Charles Bozett

Composed by WordWorks in Goudy Old Style
   on Xyvision/Cg8600

Printed on 50-pound Glatfelter B-16, a pH-neutral
   stock, and bound in B-grade Arrestox cloth
   by Edwards Brothers, Inc.

The paper used in this publication meets the minimum require-
ments of American National Standard for Information Sciences
—Permanence of Paper for Printed Library Materials, ANSI
Z39.48-1984. ∞

Library of Congress Cataloging-in-Publication Data

Life guidance through literature / [edited] by Arthur Lerner and
   Ursula R. Mahlendorf.
        p.   cm.
   Includes index.
   ISBN 0-8389-0580-3
   1. Bibliotherapy.   2. Life change events in literature.
   3. American literature—20th century—History and criticism.
   I. Lerner, Arthur.   II. Mahlendorf, Ursula R.
   RC489.B48L54   1991   91-27499
   158—dc20

Printed in the United States of America.

96 95 94 93 92   5 4 3 2 1

Contents

Introduction

Life Guidance through Literature proceeds from the premise that insightful contemporary writers are keen observers of others, of their age, of their society, and of themselves. They are therefore eminently well qualified to advise us on our and our society's most pressing problems. If we learn to read them well, we can benefit from their insights. In the individual chapters of this book, experts in psychology and literature who use literature in their counselling and therapy with patients and clients help the reader learn to read well so that the reader can more fully understand works of fiction and learn from them to question his or her own life situation and its meanings. In their chapter annotations, the contributors suggest what additional readings on the chapters' problems the reader might do.

The dilemmas thoughtful persons face in twentieth-century America are different and more complex than those encountered even by the generation of their parents. In fact, social change after the 1960s, the end of the Vietnam conflict, and the 1960s information revolution has been so staggering and the problems it caused so many that it is impossible for any one person to comprehend them, either intellectually or emotionally. We live daily with such painful, perplexing, and fast-changing situations as the recent Gulf crisis and its economic impact that we all too easily lose sight of human concerns that remain beyond the hubbub of crises. Thoughtful and sensitive creative writers and film makers, working on the edge of the future, can help us—through their works—to experience and hence to gain deeper understanding of what it means, for instance, to live with AIDS, to face death as a soldier, to lose a profession because it is obsolete, to be a despairing Vietnam veteran, or to have a child commit suicide.

Organization of This Book

We have centered the beginning chapters and reading selections of this book on topics that shed light on problems dealing with, hopefully, short-term crises and decision making: What stresses in a rapidly changing society affect *marriages*, bring about crises? How are they resolved? What situations, opportunities, and liabilities do singles live with, and what does *being single* mean? How do people handle the emotional and financial ravages of *divorce and separation*? How do they bear the stress of caring for a terminally ill family member or friend for weeks, months, or years and cope with the tragedy of *death and dying*? How do people manage when *sudden and untimely death* strikes a loved one? How are they affected by and how can they come to understand the *suicide* of a family member or friend? How do they bear up under the catastrophes of war, cope with the loss of property and livelihood, overcome the sudden displacements caused by economic depressions and recessions, and otherwise face *man's inhumanity to man*? And on a lighter, but sometimes no less stressful note, how do people adjust to the unexpected turns of fame and fortune they might experience in our fast-moving world? How do they *face sudden success*? What in all these situations do people hold on to? How do they make sense of these events and how the events relate to themselves? These are the concerns of the first half of this book.

The chapters and reading selections of the second half deal with specific life and developmental phases, with long-term existential conditions, problems, and challenges. What does it mean to be a young person in America today, and what are the social and emotional dilemmas of *adolescence*? What are the challenges and tasks of an adult in this society, and how are *adult responsibilities* defined by writers? How do people manage these responsibilities or fail in them? What are *midlife crises* all about? What is particular about *men's experience* with men in urban America today? What human predicaments are encountered by the gay population? What about *women's experience* with each other, particularly within the family between mothers and daughters and sisters? How does men's experience differ from women's? What are the stresses, dilemmas, and agonies faced by different *ethnic minorities*? Finally, what are the difficulties and the rewards of *aging*? This book is equipped with a table of contents indicating the main problems and topics so that the reader can easily find a reading selection suitable to his or her interests and concerns. An author-title index assists in finding the works discussed and annotated.

Fiction as Instruction about Life

Why should fiction, whether in print or on film and video, be able to guide us in difficult life situations? Writers of fiction construct in each work a whole world, complete with persons and events, from their felt experience and observations, from their values, ideas, and world views. Recent research on the working of the human mind tells us that we all construct our worlds from our experience. Writers therefore can enrich each of our limited individual constructed worlds by wider and often more mature perspectives. Literature as instruction can provide positive models of behavior. It can also illustrate self-destructive or self-defeating behavior—if we can be helped to recognize the signs of such behavior. In this way, literature can change our ideas about life and make us more sensitive to those of others.

The Emotional Impact of Fiction

Such intellectual instruction is only a small part of literature's effect on us. Two other far-reaching and interlinked effects derive from the fact that a fictional work is a totality that portrays a changing human world. This totality involves us as total persons in a process of transformation, namely the transformation that is portrayed in the work of fiction itself as the characters interact and change. This transformation of the characters brings about a transformation in us as readers as we identify with and are emotionally moved by the events and characters of the narrative. It is our emotional involvement with fictional characters that causes them to influence us with lasting motivations.

How does a work of fiction reach our emotions? And is that safe? A carefully constructed fictional world is complete in itself, with a beginning, a middle, and an end; therefore, it is endowed with clear boundaries that separate it from reality. The fictional world follows conventions with which we are all familiar. Bruno Bettelheim, in his book about fairy tales, *The Uses of Enchantment* (1977), taught us that formulas which begin and end fairy tales (for example, "Once upon a time," "And they lived happily ever after") tell the child reader that it is emotionally safe within the fairy tale world to feel the events of the story, even if they are violent, gruesome, and frightening, for they are clearly separated from reality, in the past, and a *story*. In the end, everything will be fine. The child, for example, can identify with the anger of the bad witch, be bad in his imagination, and release the feeling without guilt. He can feel stupid with the simpleton, come to know that at times everyone feels dumb, and yet triumph in the end. We sometimes observe that during story telling small children become unsure about the boundaries between the real and the fictional and experience a frightening or an unacceptable feeling all too strongly. At such times, we see them reassure themselves by saying, "It's just a story, it's make believe, it's not real," and then return to the enjoyment of the story.

Most adult fiction has similar conventional boundaries, formulas that are variations of the "Once upon a time," familiar and trusted since childhood. For example, book covers and title pages announcing "a novel" or "a story" and the authorial comments or interruptions in narrative like "Did you ever, dear reader . . ." express to the reader, "You can put the book away if it frightens you too much." "This is fiction, not real," and "In case you forgot, I, the author, am manipulating your response." Similarly in film, titles, credits, flashbacks, framing, varying lengths of shots, and other techniques provide emotional distance so that the viewer is not overwhelmed. Yet surely we have all cried during movies or been frightened by a tale and felt the emotional impact of fiction. The trick for the writer or director is to find the appropriate aesthetic distance—that is, the right proportion between involving us and yet not overwhelming us.

Within the boundaries of novels and films, the writer or director can have characters experience the most harrowing emotions, the most tragic events. Characters' conflicts and motivations can be fully developed from beginning to resolution. If the fictional world is properly distanced, the reader or viewer can feel safe in vicariously experiencing the characters' feelings and the emotional impact of the story events. It is for the reason of emotional safety by proper distancing that literary works can do more than merely instruct us. By affecting us emotionally and intellectually, they allow us to feel, give us understanding of our and others feelings, and make us more sensitive to these feelings and ourselves. In this way, we gain an emotional awareness that transforms us and gives us the motivation to change ourselves.

In the beginning, we spoke of the reader needing to learn to read in a special way so as to profit from literary guidance. The teachers of literature, psychiatrists, psychoanalysts, and psychotherapists who wrote the chapter analyses and annotations are experts in understanding human behavior, and all use literature in their counseling work. They understand that a narrative, be it a movie, novel, story, or drama, is not a patient on a couch or a client facing a therapist. They have experience in using literature to locate, identify, define, and solve problems. Their purpose is to help individual readers actualize and enhance themselves as human beings capable of making serious choices or, at least, attempting to do so with a minimum of doubt, guilt, and hostility.

The Interpretation of Fiction

Let us now return to fiction as instruction. Though adults may be carried away by stories, unlike children they have also the capacity to deliberately examine and think through the successes and failures they read about. In fictional representation, just as in life, there are many alternatives to any course of action if we take the time to deliberate. A skilled writer, through complexities of character and event depiction, through subplot and minor characters, implies many roads not taken that could have been. Therefore, in a good work of fiction, there are always many ways of interpreting fictional events and characters. Serious fiction is always multidimensional. It can be read in a number of ways. Unlike in living life, in reading fiction about life and reflecting on it, we as readers have the time and composure to explore in our imagination alternative courses of action and to think through the choices an author attributes to characters. We can agree or disagree with both characters and authors. In fact, precisely because a work of fiction is multidimensional, we can experience and interpret it in many valid ways.

Aims of the Contributors

Each contributor selected from an overall listing of topics prepared by the editors that topic he or she found most congenial and useful in counseling work with patients or clients. From the contributors' experience with the clinical situation and from their knowledge of literature, they explain how they interpreted the works illustrative of their topics. They demonstrate how narrative events and images support the basic theme, how to understand the psychological motivations of characters, and how characters' interactions lead to either personal success or failure. And above all, the contributors teach the reader how to ask questions of a text by their own sample questions. The reader addressed by the contributors is the generally educated lay reader. But librarians of schools and communities will find this book helpful in recommending readings on life problems to their public. (Librarians have for a long time been interested in bibliotherapy.) Psychological counselors and therapists should find the analyses and the reading suggestions of assistance both for individual clients and patients and for therapy groups.

How to Use This Book

Readers might best turn to the table of contents and select from it that chapter of most personal concern. Each of the chapters analyzes a specific life problem as portrayed in a work of fiction; each stands by itself and does not presuppose knowledge gained in a preceding chapter. The analysis is followed by several questions about the work of fiction designed to guide the reader's reflections. Some twenty additional reading or film-viewing suggestions on the same problem, each with a brief plot summary and a statement of relevance, complete each chapter. The reader can profit most from an analysis if he or she first reads the literary work discussed. This should be a fast reading, caught up in the flow of the narrative. The reader might next peruse the chapter analysis while asking, "Does this analysis corroborate what I got out of the narrative?" Next, a critical reading of the analysis should lead to the reader's rereading those portions of the work of fiction on which there is disagreement. Here, a look at the questions the chapter author asks might be helpful in elucidating the differences of opinion. Finally, the reader should attempt to answer the questions and to formulate others that he or she finds important.

This method of working through a fictional piece becomes useful if the reader becomes a discussion leader. By knowing what questions to ask, the discussion leader will form—through the responses—an interpretation of the novel. In the process, the leader will, we hope, find out that there is no such thing as one correct interpretation; there are many. There are some that are more insightful than others; and there are some that ask better questions than others, just as some of us construct our world views based on more experience and better insight than others. But by questioning and paying attention to the constructions of others, we all can learn about our own constructions of the world, and by such learning come to lead wise lives. In the process of such reading, the editors hope that all users of *Life Guidance through Literature* will experience a sense of delight, along with the feeling that they are learning and gaining the age-old benefit of all great literature—to instruct and delight.

Acknowledgments

The editors of *Life Guidance through Literature* have benefited from the knowledge and skills of many individuals in the planning, follow-through, and completion of this work. We deeply appreciate the encouragement, professional expertise and help of Herbert Bloom, senior editor, and Mary Huchting, production editor, both of the American Library Association. We are also grateful to all the contributors for their patience, time, and effort in shaping and reshaping their respective chapters to meet the requirements of producing a unified, meaningful whole. Matilda Lerner assisted with bibliographical reference and we thank her.

1 Marriage:
John Updike's *Rabbit Is Rich*

By Marian I. Goldstein

Twentieth-century American literature increasingly reflects the harsh realities of marriages where the emotional needs of the partners remain unmet. The growing awareness of the difficult realities of marriage has affected cultural and social attitudes. The Judeo-Christian ethic that has long imposed sanctions governing marriage has been revised to accommodate the number of divorces prevalent in the twentieth century. It is difficult, if not impossible, to predict the outcome of a given marriage. There are many conditions that affect success: familial, interpersonal, and individual. The suitability of the partners, the support of family and friends, and the traditions of the community offer insight into the future course of the union. Of great importance are the traits of individuality and immaturity present in the personalities of one or both spouses. These tend to grow over time, often to the detriment of the union.

The Paradigm

The novel *Rabbit Is Rich* (Knopf, 1981) serves as a paradigm that illustrates how these early considerations influenced a marriage for the next two decades. Updike captures the inner and outer realities of the protagonist, whose emotional growth has been stunted by circumstance and chance. Too immature to act in his own behalf, he is propelled into a marriage for which he is unprepared. This sets in motion a pattern of drifting through life reacting to situations and impulses, and of failing to develop a sense of inner control whereby he could plan and create his own destiny rather than have it imposed upon him. Revealed are the frustrations, forsaken dreams, and personal hardships wrought on the individual as well as the family, through the relinquishing of oneself to circumstance. The novel subtly offers resolution and hope as the reader enters into the struggle with the protagonist as he begins to reclaim his life and find the voice to influence events rather than to simply and passively react to them.

This novel illuminates the pitfalls of marriage in the context of early influences on the relationship and highlights areas of concern that may predict a troublesome union. It stunningly validates the small events that constitute struggles in an ordinary life and illustrates how these very struggles also can be vehicles for personal growth.

Rabbit Is Rich, written by John Updike in 1981 and awarded the Pulitzer Prize for Literature, is the story of a tumultuous marriage and how it survives in middle-class America. It is the story of Harry Angstrom, 46 years old, married 23 years, and ready to enjoy life at last. A crisis ensues when his son Nelson, a sulky and disenchanted only child, unexpectedly returns from Kent State College and announces his intention to quit school and work in the family-owned Toyota dealership. Several weeks later, when his girlfriend Pru arrives, Nelson informs the family that not only is he going to marry this girl, but also that she is five months' pregnant. Harry's response to his son's plans for the future sets in motion a retrospective view of his own marriage, one that began under similar circumstances and was subsequently beset by tragedy and grief. A series of angry conversations between Harry and his son reveals that Harry was not ready for marriage, as became apparent from events that followed his own "shotgun" wedding. The unresolved conflicts of his own life and the feeling aroused by the prospect of a new baby in the family compel Harry to revisit the failed and tragic aspects of his marriage. These include the accidental death of an infant daughter for which Harry has borne the guilt, a series of affairs that nearly ended the marriage, his hostile relationship with his son, and his failure to relinquish a passive, dependent, and immature role in his career and marriage. Based on his own experience, Harry predicts unhappiness and failure for Nelson, but the wedding takes place in spite of his protest. The tragic patterns seem destined to repeat themselves as Pru nearly loses her unborn baby as a result of an accident involving Nelson. When, after months of prodding by his father, Nelson abruptly decides to return to school, there is a glimmer of hope that the marriage of the son will fare better than the marriage of the parents. As the story unfolds, the crisis of Nelson's return becomes a catalyst for change in Harry. Finally, in a rare act of independence, Harry and his wife Janice buy their own home. Alone for the first time, they begin a new phase of their marriage as Pru and the baby take over their old room in Grandmom's house.

The spectre of his son's marriage precipitates in Harry an onslaught of memories involving his own wedding. He recalls how at Nelson's age he, a high school basketball hero full of dreams, fantasized about leaving his small Pennsylvania town and marrying a girl from another town. That dream was aborted. His family was too poor to send him away to college, a situation much different from that which he offers his son years later. Stuck in the small town, his horizons limited by lack of money and, in his own words, lack of sense, Harry found himself with a pregnant girlfriend. Her family, in response to their daughter's pregnancy and intent upon upholding the tarnished family honor, orchestrated his wedding. Harry passively acquiesced to what others expected of him. He and Janice were married in a traditional church ceremony with family and friends present to witness the event. With Nelson's announcement, Harry re-experiences his own sense of entrapment, of having no choice, and of being unable to say no to the marriage in which he has felt stuck for as long as he can remember.

How has Harry been stuck in his marriage throughout the years? For one thing, he never fulfilled his dream of leaving that small town. He still lives in the house owned by his mother-in-law Bessie, the house in which his wife grew up and the place where he could most easily leave her should he ever again decide to run from the marriage—an indication that he is still ambivalent about his "choice." He vies for his own space. The barcalounger, which both he and Bessie covet, has become a territorial symbol, and mostly it is Bessie who rests in it while Harry seethes with resentment. He works in the family-owned Toyota dealership, in a job that his now-deceased father-in-law created for him. Although he now owns half of the dealership, Bessie owns the other half, and he is unable to make changes without her approval, an emasculating situation that frustrates and angers him. For instance, she will have him fire his old friend, a long-time employee, to make room for Nelson in the business. Even his lovemaking is constrained by the knowledge that Bessie sleeps on the other side of the paper-thin wall that separates their bedrooms. Harry continues to live as a victim of his marriage and has never made the transformation to become co-creator of it.

In the early years of his marriage, Harry's sense of entrapment and anger manifested itself in a series of tragedies not uncommon in marriages with such fragile roots. Harry was unable to take the responsibilities of husband and father and escaped into numerous sexual affairs that wounded his wife and son and laid the foundation for the anger and disrespect that still undermines his relationship with his son. Nelson remembers sitting in a car with his distraught mother watching his father leave the love nest he shared with another woman. Nelson remembers his mother's eventual revenge, which took the form of an affair with a man who, unfathomable though it is to the boy, was then and still is his father's best friend. Then there was an infant baby sister who drowned

while Harry was on one of his all-night trysts. And Nelson holds his
father responsible for the death of a young girl named Jill whom he loved
and who burned to death in his father's house during the years his
parents were separated. Another piece of unfinished business in this
marriage is the longing Harry feels in these mid-life years for the daughter
he never raised. Upon meeting the teenaged daughter of his former lover
when she comes into his dealership, Harry begins to fantasize that this
young woman is truly his daughter. He becomes obsessed with confirming
what he wants to be the truth—that there is a daughter, a love child that
he has never known.

Harry finds it impossible to talk to Nelson, and Janice has become
the buffer between them, mediating Harry's anger by offering reasoned
explanations on explosive subjects. She has carved out a niche for herself
on the tennis courts and spends her days playing tennis before returning
home to the evening round of drinks on which she has come to rely.
Because the Toyota dealership—and therefore the money—belongs to her
family, Janice holds the power. In her quiet way, she uses it to support the
son whom she feels they have failed.

Harry's immaturity is further evident in his response to the present
crisis. Initially, unable to feel for his son, his main concern is that his life
has been disrupted. He is persistent in his attitude about not hiring the
boy. He suggests an abortion without considering the repercussions on
the two people involved. He offers Nelson money to run away. He is
desperate to have Nelson return to college and in essence leave Harry
to his life of small pleasures and even smaller responsibilities. Drifting
through life in a hit-and-miss fashion, Harry is rarely committed and
reacts to events impulsively. His goals are limited, with his chief goal being
to improve his golf score. His view of the world is formed solely by
Consumer Reports, which he reads avidly and exclusively. As evidenced by
his angry outbursts at his son, he seeks only immediate gratification of his
impulses. Although he is no longer acting out his sexual urges, in many
ways Harry is still the adolescent he was when he married. His mental life
is fueled by a perpetual series of sexual fantasies that include just about
every female he encounters. His preoccupation with the sex lives of his
friends prompts him to sneak into their bedrooms, open drawers, and
help himself to private material in search of evidence that will support his
fantasies about them, behavior more typical of adolescence than mid-life.

Although Harry is vehemently opposed to Nelson's decision to
marry, he finds himself alone in his opposition. He tries to get his wife to
align herself with him by suggesting the girl might be marrying his son to
get a foothold in the revered family business, and Janice sarcastically
reminds Harry that he did the very same thing. Janice, whose relationship

with her son was cemented years ago as they suffered together at Harry's indiscretions, empathizes with her son and is steadfast in her support. Grandmom is openly antagonistic toward Nelson at first. Old wounds regarding her embarrassment at Janice's premarital pregnancy are reopened. However, Grandmom comes around, and this feisty matriarch orchestrates, once again, a proper wedding. Nelson capitulates to her insistence on a church wedding, as did his father before him. Traditions, still important to Bessie and Janice, are upheld. The wedding ritual underscores recognition of a need for continuity and cohesion within the family, which remains an essential part of our human heritage. Family and friends are invited to witness, and during the ceremony—in a flood of emotion that surprises even him—Harry is awash with tears as he gazes at the vulnerable neck of his son taking marriage vows. One wonders if the tears are for himself or his son as the duty-induced wedding of the father is reenacted. At the reception in her home, Grandmom toasts the couple with a Pennsylvania Dutch phrase that she translates for Nelson as "You are now one," and in a warning born from the tragedies this old woman has witnessed in her daughter's family, she admonishes them to keep it that way.

The "honeymoon" period for the young couple seems to further suggest that, as Harry feared, history is repeating itself. Grandmom has given them the house in the Poconos for a week, and the newlyweds find themselves bored. Within a month, Pru has forsaken all the activities that made her attractive to Nelson and sits around watching soap operas on television. Nelson starts to enumerate the things he cannot stand about his new wife. He is annoyed with her sleepiness and prods her to go to parties with him. Leaving one party after just having argued about the possible mistake of having gotten married at all, Pru—perhaps inadvertently, perhaps willfully—bumps his hip with hers. He considers a little shove back, but suddenly Pru, seven months pregnant, tumbles down the stairs. She does not lose the baby, merely breaks her arm. Yet what has been narrowly averted for Nelson is the near recreation of the central tragedy of Harry's life—that of being indirectly responsible for the death of his infant daughter.

Grandmom, still the matriarch of the family business, is determined to have Harry hire Nelson and continues to use her position to get her way. And so it happens, Nelson steps into the family business just as his father did before him. When Janice and Harry decide to move out of Grandmom's house, Nelson and Pru move into the vacated bedroom of Nelson's parents. Once again, Nelson repeats a pattern of his father's life.

Although Harry, reevaluating his life, is aware of his many losses, Nelson views his parents' present life as one of comfort and even excess.

But he sees only the surface: the ready-made job at the Toyota dealership, a nice car, enough money, the country club set, the vacations. Observed from this perspective, it is not surprising that Nelson would choose to take the same route that Harry took by default. After all, in Nelson's boyish view his father now has it all, regardless of how bad the past might have been. However, when Harry was thrust into marriage, the family did not support his feelings of entrapment, nor could his father offer him the option of leaving town for college. In offering this to his son, Harry is fighting back against his own past and trying to make it possible for Nelson to have more options than he did.

How has Harry managed to sustain himself within the marriage? His fantasy life of the last ten years has replaced the sexual acting out that wreaked so much havoc earlier in his marriage. Over the years, Harry has learned to take small pleasure in the splatter of rain in the copper beech outside his bedroom window, in his tomato garden, in his jogging, in memories of glory as an adolescent on the basketball court, in his *Consumer Reports*, and especially in his golf game. He has some money now and invests in gold coins and becomes like a child reveling in the gold. His friends, the country club group, are a source of company, entertainment, and stimulation for his sexual fantasies.

There exists for Harry a great number of mistakes to live with, yet as he explains to Nelson in perhaps the pivotal point of the novel, he has not lain down and died. He has not given up. Underneath his immaturity, his excesses, and his lack of responsibility, he is a survivor. He is a man who is starting to feel capable of loving his wife and his son in sudden small rushes and whose goal is self-preservation, a task he has managed in spite of himself. The crisis precipitated by Nelson's return has caused Harry to take a long, hard look at his life and consider the legacy he has left his son. When he learns that his son did in fact suggest his girlfriend get an abortion, he begins for the first time to feel empathy for him. He begins to recognize that his wife, the woman he has called his "mutt," is his treasure. He resolves the unfinished business of a previous affair and the nagging question of a love child. He fights with Bessie to retain his friend as an employee on the car lot instead of passively accepting her dictate. He listens when his friend prods him into making a life with Janice away from his mother-in-law's home. He does not stop urging his son to go back to school. He is beginning to make some choices and take action, evidence that there is a subtle sense of maturing that is taking place.

Resolution to the crisis is suggested as Harry continues to prod his son to return to college. Although his motives are partly selfish, experience has taught him to want more for his son than he had for himself.

However, the lot seems to have been cast for Nelson to step into patterns established by his father, and this is further reinforced when Nelson, in an act reminiscent of his father, runs away from home. However, the cycle is interrupted when it is discovered that unlike Harry, who on the fateful night his daughter drowned had run to the bed of another woman, Nelson ran away to college. Symbolically, a daughter is born during Nelson's absence. Rather than the death of an infant girl, as in Harry's case, there is new life. Nelson will complete his degree. Harry wins. The pattern of acting on impulse or choosing to not act at all is interrupted, and it seems as though the son might just be capable of putting some thought into his life.

At the novel's conclusion, Harry and Janice are frightened and unsure as they begin, for the first time in their 23-year-old marriage, to make a life for themselves in their new and unfurnished home. They are finally growing comfortable with and accepting of one another, and they will continue to survive in this marriage. Janice introduces the topic of giving up the wife-swapping country club set with whom they have been involved. As Janice shows the new house to her mother, Pru enters Harry's den and quietly places on his lap that which he has been waiting for—the infant granddaughter born just one week ago. This simple act fulfills Harry's unacknowledged longings, which have been held in abeyance for almost a quarter of a century.

Summary

This novel illuminates the disastrous effects of immaturity on marriage as evidenced by a spouse's inability to sustain fidelity or to accept responsibilities. In particular, it illustrates the effects of such a union on the children. It offers a view of the dynamics that lead a child to follow the patterns set by the parents, while at the same time hating the effects of those patterns on him. The novel demonstrates how difficult it is to break patterns set in the family tradition because the experience, albeit painful and unprofitable, is *familiar* to the offspring and thus comfortable and easy to adapt to and maintain. The novel clearly illustrates the difficulty in sustaining a marriage that is not entered into freely and the curtailment of the emotional growth of individuals in such a union. In its resolution, it offers hope for a better future as Nelson relinquishes his passive stance and returns to college. There is also in the older generation the potential for a more mature relationship as Harry and Janice start out on their own, ready to rely on each other at last. The fulfillment of longing, through the birth of a granddaughter, offers joy from the most unlikely circumstance. Harry, an ordinary man, becomes a hero in refusing to give up and finally, in beginning to grow up, offers this same challenge to the reader.

Questions for Discussion

1. What are the conflicts that lead Harry Angstrom to oppose his son's wedding?
2. What is the evidence that Harry Angstrom's emotional growth was curtailed during his marriage?
3. How did Harry serve as a role model for his son?
4. What are the indications that unsuccessful patterns of behavior will be repeated in a family?
5. What are some of the strategies Harry Angstrom used to survive in his marriage?
6. How has the event of Nelson's marriage served as a turning point for the family?
7. Does *Rabbit Is Rich* realistically portray the consequences of an early marriage? If so, how? If not, why not?

Annotated Bibliography

Print

Adams, Alice. "Alternatives." In *Prize Stories of the Seventies from the O'Henry Awards*, selected by William Abrahams. New York: Doubleday, 1981.

   This short story revolves around the affair and second marriage of a couple who marry twenty years after first being infatuated with each other while each was married to someone else. This story chronicles the reaction of the spouses and children to the long-standing affair and finally the culmination of the affair in marriage. Bereft upon the death of her husband ten years later, the wife returns to the site of their first meeting, where in a ritual of remembering she reminisces about that first attraction and tells herself she would not have altered anything. However, the very fact that she feels compelled to recreate their first meeting suggests that she has regrets for having waited twenty years to marry.

Auchincloss, Louis. *Portrait in Brownstone*. Boston: Houghton, 1962.

   While courting Ida Dennison, Derrick Hartley meets and falls in love with her beautiful cousin Geraldine. She refuses his proposal of marriage in order to comply with her socialite New York family's desire and expectation that he marry Ida. Family obligation and tradition drive the actions of this extended family, whose members allow their needs for human closeness and love to be held hostage to what they consider good manners. The novel offers a view of the false self generated by the need to conform to society's expectations and the empty and shallow marriages such a self breeds.

Connell, Evan S. *Mr. Bridge*. San Francisco: North Point, 1969.

Content with his law practice, home, marriage, and children and ever unyielding in his convictions, Mr. Bridge is a man who desperately loves his wife, but who lacks the capacity to express that love in other than materialistic ways. Themes in this novel revolve around the subtle escape from intimacy that the workaholic can achieve in the guise of duty and the sadness inherent in the need of a man to repress his emotions for unexamined and unknown reasons. Told from a man's perspective, this novel offers insight into a life where the tight control of emotions leads to a marriage that never achieves true joy.

Connell, Evan S. *Mrs. Bridge*. San Francisco: North Point, 1959.

Unremarkable though she found him, India—without much fore-thought—slips into marriage with a man she can count on to give her a beautiful home, children, membership in a country club, and a trip to Europe. However, he is incapable of giving of himself. The novel is written from the wife's perspective, and themes deal with a marriage devoid of passion, intimacy, and personal growth. The story is an intimate journey with a woman who not only never quite finds herself, but who really does not know for what she is searching. It subtly portrays the insidious relinquishing of one's self to one's partner in a marriage and the personal cost extracted by such acquiescence.

de Hartog, Jan. "The Fourposter." In *Best American Plays*, edited by John Gassner. New York: Crown, 1958.

This drama revolves around a series of conversations that take place in or around the fourposter bed that the couple have shared (or not shared) since their wedding night. These conversations highlight the major events and turning points of the marriage. Explored are the joy and undying commitment of the wedding night, the birth of their first child, the pathos of the other woman, the other man, the strains created by raising children, boredom with each other, and a final resolution. These crises allow the reader to witness, often in a humorous way, the re-linquishing of wedded bliss and the confrontation with the realities of sharing one's life. The play provides a rationale for working through the inevitable problems that arise in a marriage.

Gardner, John. *Nickel Mountain*. New York: Knopf, 1973.

Unlikely and illogical a union as it seems, the marriage of Henry Soames, a thinking man, grossly obese, middle-aged, and dying, and Callie Wells, a seventeen-year-old pregnant farm girl, serves as a vehicle for themes concerned with existential questions. Henry, whose weak heart continues to tick away like a time bomb, refuses to take care of his failing body. Attitudes dealing with courage, violence, death, God, and love are explored through Henry's involvement in his marriage and through his interactions with the plain country people in this novel. Henry finally becomes capable of loving—first Callie, the girl who is in many ways transformed by his love, and subsequently her illegitimate son Jimmy, to whom Henry becomes a father. The story offers love within marriage as an antidote to the inevitability of death.

Gordon, Noah. *The Rabbi*. New York: McGraw-Hill, 1965.

In this novel, a nervous breakdown by the seemingly happy wife of Rabbi Michael Kind serves as the precipitating event for examining circumstances of their life and marriage. Themes dealing with religious heritage, the relationship of adult children with their parents, conversion as a factor in marrying, and repressed guilt are explored through events that span a quarter of a century. There is resolution as Leslie Kind confronts the guilt inspired by her conversion from Christianity to Judaism and makes peace with herself. The novel calls attention to the many problems that need be addressed when deciding whether to convert and the devastating effects of unacknowledged feelings.

Gurganus, Allan. "A Hog Loves Its Life." In *White People*. New York: Knopf, 1991.

This short story, told by the grandson of a couple whose marriage flourished for 60 years, is an exquisite love story that reverberates through future generations. At age ten, sitting on his grandfather's lap, listening to his fantastic tales about "dead people," young Willie is a student of his grandparents' marriage. He learns how their verbal dueling was an excuse to initiate intimacy and how outward impatience was a cover-up for admiration and pride. After the death of his wife, Willie's grandfather begins his slide into senility and finally death. Years later, as Willie considers his own ex-wives, he observes that his grandparents were "just really happy." This not-so-simple concept is stunningly offered to the reader.

Lindbergh, Anne Morrow. *Dearly Beloved*. New York: Harcourt, 1962.

In this novel, the marriage ceremony of a young couple is the catalyst for a reassessment of the lives of family members who are in attendance. Written in stream of consciousness technique, each chapter offers the perspective of a wedding guest. Represented, among others, are the mothers of the bridal couple and the grandfather of the bride. The movement of their thoughts, precipitated by the actual words of the ceremony, leads these individuals to a deeper understanding of themselves and their role in marriage. In its conclusion, the novel encourages relinquishing the fantasy that a perfect marriage exists and further suggests that life be viewed as a creative act of community that has its highest potential in marriage. Thus, this novel offers the reader two inspirational views of marriage.

Lurie, Allison. *The War between the Tates*. New York: Random, 1974.

Brian Tate, bored with himself and his inability to achieve an illustrious career in academia, succumbs to the advances of one of his graduate students, precipitating a marital war. This novel explores the dynamics of a male mid-life crisis. In addressing the attraction of the older male for the younger woman, it highlights some of the ensuing disenchantment. It also addresses the reaction of women coping with the unpredictable behavior of their husbands. Themes dealing with abortion, teenage children, and feminism make brief appearances. In its resolution, the novel suggests that a brief hiatus from fidelity need not terminate a marriage.

Myrer, Anton. *The Last Convertible*. New York: Putnam, 1978.

Unrequited first love, as a source of unremitting influence on the future, is examined through a retrospective look at a group of men and women who met at college and still affect each other 25 years later. Divided loyalties as a result of marrying one's second choice, obsession with an individual, the sadness inherent in being the second choice, and eventually falling in love with one's second choice are themes that emerge from the lives of the characters. Because the outcome in terms of marital happiness for each character runs the gamut—a ruined life, stoic acceptance, and actual fulfillment—the book offers several perspectives for considering one's choice of partner.

O'Neill, Eugene. *Long Day's Journey into Night*. New Haven, Conn., and London: Yale Univ. Pr., 1965.

This drama, which takes place on a single August day, offers a retrospective view of a marriage that has been doomed from its inception, when Mary, the wife, mistakes a schoolgirl's infatuation for love and embarks on a marriage with only this as its underpinnings. It portrays the devastation wrought by unremitting dissatisfaction within a marriage. Avoidance and denial as means of coping, along with addiction and its destructive effects on a family, are explored. There is no hope offered for resolution of the problems that will continue to plague these characters as Mary, in witnessing the ruined lives of her adult children, continues to cope with her unhappiness by using drugs and as her husband continues to deny her addiction. This drama provides insight into the dynamics that cause family members to enter a conspiracy of silence rather than confront addiction.

Paley, Grace. "Distance." In *Enormous Changes at the Last Minute*. New York: Farrar, 1960.

This short story is narrated by Dolly, the self-righteous, domineering, sarcastic, possibly alcoholic mother of John, her only child. It exposes the havoc wrought by Dolly's reaction to her son's desire to marry a girl whom Dolly views as a whore. As a result of his mother's hysterical reaction, John capitulates to her wishes and eventually marries someone else. There are immediate and long-term negative repercussions of this decision. Dolly's own marriage deteriorates and then ends as a result of her husband's inability to tolerate her meddling. John's marriage is fraught with infidelity because he is unable to let go of his first attraction. This short story provides the reader with a rationale for allowing one's children to make their own choices regarding whom they will marry and highlights the unpredictable consequences of meddling.

Roth, Philip. *Letting Go*. New York: Random, 1961.

The involvement of protagonist Gabe Wallach in the marriage of his friends, the Herzes, is the vehicle for exploring an interfaith marriage. The negative response to the union by both their families results in emotional and physical hardship for the couple. Themes explored include the effects of changing one's faith as an accommodation for marriage and the search for meaning or for God that arises in the face of the subsequent unhappiness. A recurring theme that questions the right of an individual, however well meaning, to interfere in another's life is interwoven throughout the protagonist's long-term involvement with the unhappy couple. Although the novel provides no definitive answers, it highlights the negative repercussions of an interfaith marriage and exposes the fragility of intimate relationships both within and outside of marriage.

Sarton, May. *Anger*. New York: Norton, 1982.

The initial infatuation and subsequent marriage of Ned Fraser, a 40-year-old business executive, to Anna Lindstrom, an accomplished

concert singer, is the subject of this novel. Indications of their tempera-
mental incompatability are present from the earliest days of their
relationship. Once married, they struggle to resolve the conflict produced
by the inevitable personality clash of the spontaneous, emotionally
expressive Anna and the closed, uncommunicative Ned. Anger as a way
of coping and the influence of past experiences on present behavior are
addressed. The survival of the marriage as a result of the efforts portrayed
offers the reader support and incentive for addressing similar personality
differences in his or her own marriage.

Smiley, Jane. "The Age of Grief." In *The Age of Grief.* New York: Knopf,
1987.

Totally committed to his wife and three small daughters, Dave comes
to the conclusion that his wife is in love with another man and is
planning to leave him. As he deliberately avoids having his suspicions
confirmed, the reader experiences with Dave the anguish of living with
such fears. Themes involving the demise of love although loyalty and
caring persist, the effects of a strained relationship on children, and the
sheer energy called upon to keep oneself together in the face of impending
loss are explored. Although Dave's worst suspicions are eventually
confirmed, his wife does not leave the marriage. The novella suggests that
in every marriage there is an age of grief and that if you can hold on long
enough you might just survive it.

Taylor, Peter. "The Old Forrest." In *The Best American Short Stories 1980,*
edited by Stanley Elkin with Shannon Ravanel. Boston: Houghton, 1980.

This short story, developed around an automobile accident that
occurs one week before the wedding of the prospective bridegroom,
spotlights the groom's unacknowledged involvement with other women.
The subsequent handling of this revelation by the groom and his fiancée
blends themes dealing with a marriage that is influenced by parental and
societal expectations, the inclination of men to sow their wild oats before
marriage, fears associated with being found out, and qualities of manipulation, power, fear, jealousy, and dependence in women. The successful
resolution of the incident, as the couple confront the unpleasantness
together, portends how they will resolve conflicts throughout their
married life and offers this insight to the reader.

Tyler, Anne. *Accidental Tourist.* New York: Knopf, 1985.

This novel chronicles the events that lead to the second marriage of
Macon, the protagonist. Tormented by grief and loneliness after the tragic
death of his child and the emotional and physical separation from his

wife, Macon barely manages his daily life. A chance meeting with an eccentric young woman, the mother of a frail and needy son, who imposes herself on his life provides the catalyst for reevaluating his marriage, his rigid lifestyle, and the lack of spontaneity within his marriage. This woman is as unpredictable, emotional, and joyful as Macon is controlled, emotionless, and joyless. The relationship enables him to access parts of himself that have been inhibited all his life. The novel illustrates how one's personality and the quality of one's life can be influenced by the person one marries.

Van Slyke, Helen. *The Mixed Blessing*. New York: Doubleday, 1975.

Toni, the mulatto daughter of a white woman and her black husband, is the mixed blessing of this novel. Unaccepting of his own heritage, Toni's father urges his grown daughter to pass as white. As Toni falls in love and plans for marriage, her attempt to honor her father's wish gives rise to themes that deal with the difficulties of a mixed marriage, the influence of early life on feelings of prejudice, the dangers inherent in lying, and the difficulty in eradicating prejudice on intellectual, emotional, and physical levels. Ending with a happy albeit contrived resolution, this novel provides a view of some of the dynamics of a mixed marriage.

Wilder, Thornton. *Our Town*. New York: Harper, 1938.

This drama, composed of three acts, spans a quarter century of life in a small New Hampshire town. By focusing on the children of two neighboring families, it depicts a relationship that develops between the offspring. Initially playmates, Emily and Wally evolve through a series of stages, including adolescent attraction, courtship, love, marriage, parenthood, and death. Themes dealing with the fleetingness of time, the need to embrace life, and the sorrow inherent in doing so are beautifully portrayed through the actions of the characters. The play shows how fleeting happiness can be due to the limits imposed by time and impels the reader to attend to the details of his life and loves.

Wilson, Sloan. *A Summer Place*. New York: Arbor, 1958.

Teenagers John and Molly are thrown together when his mother and her father meet and rekindle their own teenage romance. Themes revolving around the effects of a marriage based on convenience, the repercussions of alcohol abuse on a marriage, parent-child relationships, and the effects of being overprotective of one's child are interwoven throughout the novel as it expands on both the parents' and the children's relationships. Culminating in the untimely teenage marriage of John and Molly, the book provides insight into factors that contribute to impulsive acts by teenagers and the long-term negative consequences of those acts.

Film

About Last Night. Tri-Star Picture. 1986. 113 min.

This film depicts the struggles of a relationship that progresses from a sexual attraction and a one-night stand, to becoming roommates, through living together, separating, and eventually recognizing that love has developed. Modern in its approach, the film explores such themes as the fear of intimacy, the fear of marriage, the reluctance to relinquish sexual freedom (as commitment requires), and the influence of friends on the course of a relationship. In the end, each partner changed by the experience of a torturous breakup, the couple begins a reconciliation. Thus, the film offers the viewer insight into the effects of contemporary lifestyles on the decision to marry.

Betsy's Wedding. Touchstone Pictures. 1990. 94 min.

Betsy, the younger of two daughters, casually announces that she is getting married, and this is the catalyst for a series of events that eventually culminate in her wedding. Themes examined include family reactions, sibling jealousy, the working out of problems that arise when families are of different socioeconomic means, the stress family involvement can put on the prospective bride and groom, and the examination of differences as an asset to a marriage. Depicted in a humorous way, this film offers a lighthearted approach and solution to events that have the potential for causing long-term repercussions if taken too seriously.

Chapter Two. RCA/Columbia Pictures Home Video. 1979. 127 min.

Preoccupied with thoughts of his recently deceased wife and riddled with grief, protagonist George is resistant to matchmaking attempts by his well-meaning brother. However, through a comedy of errors, George meets a woman, quickly falls in love, and despite family warnings that he is acting impulsively, marries her. The film depicts the struggle that begins a few days into the marriage as the two must work through his still unresolved grief and attachment to his deceased wife. The film offers a perspective for letting go of the past and allowing oneself to continue to live fully in the present after the death of one's mate.

The Creator. Thorn EMI/HBO Videos. 1985. 108 min.

This film, a fantasy, concerns itself with letting go of one's spouse in the face of death. Thirty years after the death of his wife, a Nobel scientist, thought insane by some, is still trying to recreate her in a test tube. His reluctant assistant is a graduate student who good humoredly belittles this endeavor. When the woman whom the assistant is planning to marry becomes ill and falls into a coma, the fantasy is juxtaposed to reality as the young man refuses to allow tubes to be disconnected and devotes his days to keeping her alive. In the young woman's recovery, the film depicts the extremes to which a spouse is driven in grappling with the loss of his mate.

Crossing Delancey. Warner Bros. 1988. 97 min.

After accommodating her matchmaking Bubba (grandmother) and reluctantly agreeing to meet the neighborhood pickle salesman, Isabella, at age 33, sees no possibility for the development of a relationship that will lead to marriage and tries to make this point clear to her grandmother. Themes dealing with the liberated woman who is unwilling to relinquish her successful single life are interwoven with themes contrasting down-home values with New York chic. At the film's conclusion, Isabella comes to terms with the fact that she has grown to love the persistent pickle salesman. Thus, the film delightfully conveys the message that cultural and family values regarding marriage can be temporarily forgotten, but are not relinquished. These values, having served as a foundation for marriage in the family, remain viable options for consideration once a child is reintroduced to them.

2 Being Single:
Alison Lurie's *Foreign Affairs*

By Marjorie Marks-Frost

Singleness as a socially acceptable lifestyle choice in American society is a rather recent development, at least for women. Historically, single women have been the object of pity. Fiction about singleness written earlier in the century portrays this stereotype—that is, single women as spinsters, old-maid teachers, and nannies—while earlier fiction portrays single men as dashing or rakish figures. Even now, women older than 30 experience strong pressure to conform to the mainstream of society. The culture has been kinder to men, for whom there exists no equivalent word for "spinster" to describe male singleness. This double standard is pervasively challenged in contemporary fiction about women, much of it written by women, in response to the awareness and empowerment provided by the women's movement. (It is worth noting here that the modern feminist movement was catalyzed by the invention and widespread use of the birth control pill; in other words, when women gained control over reproductive choice, they gained control over all kinds of choices, including whether and when to have children and as a result whether to marry or remain single.)

Although singleness for men generally has not been regarded in the same negative sense as it has been for women, single men too have suffered under society's stereotypical macho expectations of bachelorhood. As a result, men who do not conform to that image have likely felt miscast in society. On a more subtle level, the real loneliness and fear that both single men and women at times may feel because they are not married or in a committed relationship are increased in a society insensitively focused on stereotypes rather than on the real needs of those who never marry, marry late, or become single through death or divorce. And perhaps most important, the positive aspects of singleness—and there are many—remain unexplored and inaccessible in a culture that is unsupportive of that possibility.

The challenge, of course, is to remain single or marry for the right reasons—that is, consciously chosen reasons that enhance one's way of being in life. Both options may be either positive or negative. Fortunately for both life and literature, singleness finally is recognized as having positive attributes for both men *and* women.

The Paradigm

In *Foreign Affairs* by Alison Lurie (Random, 1984), both Vinnie and Fred represent the problems and challenges of singleness experienced by women and men in our society. Being single can present a problem for the individual on two levels: the outer life and the inner life. In a coupled society, the single individual may be regarded as odd, eccentric, or uninteresting, and this is particularly true for the single woman. As a result, single people can feel out of the mainstream of society and unsupported in their loneliness. It is extremely difficult for an individual to hold an image of self that is at odds with society's values; that is, low self-esteem can result from being viewed negatively by society.

Vinnie Miner, a 54-year-old small, plain, unmarried professor at an Ivy League university in upstate New York—the novel's fictional American heroine in this book—gives the reader an opportunity to gain a deeper understanding of the struggles of the single person. Although the likelihood of a novel based on such an unconventional character popularly succeeding in the past would have been slim, the fact that this book was written at all, and then published to much acclaim, is a measure of how far society has progressed in its acceptance of the single older woman not only as an interesting character, but as a multidimensional, dynamic, and sensual person. It also indicates the gradual acceptance by society of how much—for many individuals—reality differs from the persistent image of the intact nuclear family as the norm.

The novel's finely wrought plot is balanced in alternating chapters between the lives of Vinnie Miner and her colleague Fred Turner. Vinnie, who feels more at home in London than in the United States and more at ease in literature than in life, is a confirmed Anglophile on sabbatical to do research for a book about the folk rhymes of school children. She is looking forward to her annual vacation in London, where she can replenish her spirits and her friendships with the more literate, worthwhile kind of people with whom she has a natural rapport. Unfortunately, on the flight over she finds herself seated next to Chuck

Mumpson, a retired sanitary engineer from Tulsa, estranged from his wife, and Vinnie's opposite in every way; he is large, crude, and by her standards, uneducated. He represents everything she detests in Americans.

Coincidentally, her young, tall, extremely handsome colleague Fred also is in London doing research, although he does not share Vinnie's adoration for either London or the British. Recently separated from his wife, he feels as dismal and claustrophobic as he perceives the London weather to be. The only connection between Vinnie and Fred is that they are both members of the English department at the fictional Corinth University. And they both embark on unsuitable affairs that are interwoven in alternating chapters.

Vinnie cannot help feeling that life owes her a little something. When things are not going well, she makes small "annexations" to her life. She pilfers towels from hotels, napkins and coasters from restaurants, and the like. Highly critical of tackiness in others, Vinnie avoids consciously focusing on these habits in herself. But a relentless, critical inner voice constantly nags her about these shortcomings. It is a voice she would rather not hear, another facet of herself that she refuses to explore.

A central image in *Foreign Affairs* is the invisible Welsh terrier that follows Vinnie around and represents her demon—self-pity. Despite her self-sufficiency and professional accomplishments, Professor Virginia Miner finds herself silently dogged by this dirty-white, long-haired animal, particularly in her vulnerable moments, such as when she reads an article disparaging her life's work. (Vinnie also is surprised sometimes at her own violent thoughts.) Meanwhile, she must refrain from discussing with anyone her feelings about the attack on her in print because it would cause her fellow academics to view her as weak and undignified. She feels ashamed for taking the criticism so hard in the first place because she realizes that her reaction indicates how little identity she has outside her career. She remembers that during her brief marriage professional setbacks were offset by the more balanced life she led, a time when her entire identity was not based on the vicissitudes of career. Now, despite her many friends Vinnie trusts none of them enough to confide her pain.

Since childhood, Vinnie has relied on English literature, her passion, for the truth of what she might do, think, feel, desire, and become—and what it has taught her is that single women of her age rarely have a sexual or romantic life, and if they do it is either vulgar or comic. It is not surprising then that Vinnie becomes increasingly uncomfortable and untrusting of her own erotic impulses that erupt from time to time. Vinnie's inability to trust and her overreliance on literature have disconnected her from fleshly reality. She lives a removed, cerebral life that manifests itself in an effete snobbery.

Vinnie's coincidental encounter with Mumpson on the plane does not end with their arrival in London. With his good ol' boy demeanor (and against Vinnie's better judgment), he manages to finagle one meeting after another with her. Each time, Vinnie struggles mightily with her critical self, who cannot believe she would be seen with this oaf. But gradually, insidiously, he pierces her armour of superiority by doing what she has never been able to do herself—he accepts her unconditionally. She is disarmed and touched, yet still unbelieving of her own desirability. She remains ever critical of him and embarrassed at the thought of her friends' reactions if they knew how intimate their relationship had become.

Vinnie becomes extremely confused, but gradually accepts how much he means to her. Yet still she holds back, still she is unable to travel with him, to give in fully to the passion that has engulfed her. She cannot understand Mumpson, who seems not to need her reciprocation in order to love her. He expects nothing from her. But there is one thing he would like her to do.

Mumpson has decided to travel to another part of England in pursuit of answers regarding his ancestry, particularly one intriguing legendary character who seems to hold secrets about his identity. Through his quest, he begins to explore a riskier, more sensitive side of himself. Since his wife back in Texas has lost interest in him, Mumpson has no rooted reason to return home. While there, he repeatedly invites Vinnie to come join him. She keeps putting it off. Because Vinnie rejects Mumpson's invitation to be together, he continues his solitary research, which ends after he climbs three long flights of stairs on a hot day despite his heart condition.

Vinnie finally realizes that if she had not been so afraid to express her love for Mumpson, he still might be alive. If she would have gone to him and accepted his invitation that fateful weekend of his death, things might have turned out differently.

Summary

Vinnie's inability to trust her inner feelings of love for Mumpson led to mistaken priorities that will haunt her forever. Mumpson is the first man who ever loved her unconditionally. His fleeting presence in her life, she begins to realize, finally frees her to be herself rather than the inflated individual who rejected the great love of her life. Now she can be alone, but less frightened and rigid in her attitude toward life. Ironically, she must admit that she has learned more about herself from the man she initially scorned as a buffoon than from all the erudite books and effete fools of her acquaintance. She will miss Mumpson terribly because everything reminds her of him, including Fido, the transformed dog who is now eagerly wagging his tail, looking up at her as if to say, without pity, "What now?"

Questions for Discussion

1. Do you believe *Foreign Affairs* is an insightful work on the issues faced by single people? If so, why? If not, why not?
2. What are some of the ways in which it is clear that Vinnie Miner feels isolated?
3. How important do you think the social networks of both Fred and Vinnie are? How did a lack of social and family support affect Mumpson?
4. What positive aspects of being single did Vinnie, Fred, and Mumpson experience, and what compensations did they make?
5. Did Vinnie and Fred change their attitudes about themselves and being single in the course of the novel? If so, how?

Annotated Bibliography

Print

Bellow, Saul. *Seize the Day*. New York: Viking, 1956.

This work is an unusually vivid psychological portrayal of the lonely journey of a man who is so estranged from his own feelings that he and his family are helpless to stop his decline into hopelessness and self-destructiveness. It is the story of one day in the life of blond, big-shouldered, fortyish Tommy Wilhelm, a man in crisis who feels that he is about to be crushed by his obligations. He is without a job, separated from his wife and children, estranged from his sister, and angry at his aloof and wealthy father, who is ashamed of him. Yet it is through Tommy's solitary anguish that he begins to reconstruct his life, this time based not on the conventional reality of marriage (even a bad marriage), but on an instinctually based, guilt-free view of life. Singleness was a requirement for attaining emotional survival. A psychologist and fellow resident at Tommy's boarding hotel helps him understand the need to live in the present: "The past is no good to us. The future is full of anxiety. Only the present is real—the here-and-now. Seize the day."

Forester, C. S. *The African Queen*. New York: Little, 1935. (Film: *The African Queen*. IFD/Romulus-Horizon. 1951.)

Set in 1915, this is the story of a hard-drinking river trader and a prim missionary forced by circumstances to become companions on a long and perilous trip down a dangerous African river during World War I. It is this journey, with its many hardships, that brings together these opposite characters. The tension created by their strong mutual attraction, which conflicts with the fierce independence of each of them, provides one of the great romantic liaisons of fiction. This classic story represents a still-relevant literary paradigm of female independence in conflict with the magnetism of an attractive but domineering male, centering on the question of singleness versus matedness.

Freeman, Judith. *The Chinchilla Farm*. New York: Norton, 1989.

Verna Flake is at the crossroads of her life. She is fleeing Utah, a failed marriage (her husband has left her for another woman), and the constricted Mormon way of life. Yet as much as she needed to leave, she finds that being alone is not easy. Striving to attain a balance between the pain of leaving and the pain of staying keeps this collection of characters uprooted and on the run, always musing over the meaning of it all. Deep worry leads to ruminations such as: "Is it possible to love someone if your first interest is always yourself? You've got to wonder. Does it mean you're just using them? Because, you know, you can't face the idea of being alone." The point is not whether to be single or to be married, but whether to be conscious.

Godwin, Gail. *The Odd Woman*. New York: Knopf, 1974.

Jane Clifford is a single woman in love with a married man. In the broader sense, however, the story is about loneliness and faithfulness in and out of marriage and the ways in which people compensate for what is amiss. The novel contains a beautiful soliloquy by the main character on the nature of singleness, in which she says that living alone spoils you and makes it harder to get together with someone, if you ever do, because you have become your own only child—that is, you have found a kind of self-sustaining centeredness that excludes others.

Godwin, Gail. *Violet Clay*. New York: Knopf, 1978.

This is the story of a 32-year-old woman with a failed marriage and many lovers behind her. She came to New York City to be a painter; instead, she has become a Gothic romance book cover artist, afraid of her authentic self and the serious work she wants to do. It has become her pattern to take on new lovers to assuage "the bitterness of uninspired work." The death of a beloved uncle propels her to settle not just his affairs but her own by facing up to the risks she must take in order to fulfill her soul. It is only when she makes a decision to isolate herself for months in a mountain cabin with "the thing that had lived with [her] longer than anyone in [her] life," her painting, that she finally becomes who she is meant to be.

Gordon, Mary. *Final Payments*. New York: Random, 1978.

Thirty-year-old Isabel Moore has lived in nearly total isolation for the past eleven years caring for her invalid father after he suffered a stroke as a result of finding her in bed with one of his students. As she stands at his open grave, she realizes that she has no idea of how to proceed as a person alone, only that she must invent a new existence. Support from two treasured women friends from childhood helps her make the precarious passage from dutiful daughter to autonomous adult. Frightened at her aloneness, she engages in an impulsive love affair, followed by a relationship with a married man that isolates her once again until she finally is able to let go of the past. This book is an exploration of the nature of friendship, desire, family love, and guilt. The importance of women to each other and the meaning of singleness in contemporary society are explored.

Jong, Erica. *How to Save Your Own Life*. New York: New Amer. Lib., 1977.

This novel brings more adventures of the madcap, liberated Isadora Wing, whom readers met in *Fear of Flying*. Author Erica Jong writes for and about the trailblazing liberated woman. In this incarnation, Isadora is a best-selling novelist who manages to conquer her fears, jettison her guilts, and plunge into a new series of feckless love affairs. She learns to handle fame and success and survives both a lesbian affair and a group orgy on the way to finding deeper meaning in the love of a younger man. Erotic and witty, funny and brave, this story offers support and healing for feminist-war survivors who are struggling to save their own lives.

Lamott, Anne. *Rosie*. New York: Viking, 1983.

This is a story that deals with the fears of loneliness, the joys of solitude, and the need for balance. Young widow Elizabeth Ferguson lives in an old Victorian home just outside San Francisco. Her husband has been dead for some months, and she is left to carry on a single life. Although her existence is cushioned by a trust fund and her glorious home, the loneliness is something else. Elizabeth savors much about her life, including her four-year-old daughter Rosie. But increasingly her despair over her own inability to get on with her life is assuaged with too much wine and too many wasted days. Eventually, she meets a wonderful man, but she is unable to act on their relationship or anything else until Rosie has a frightening encounter with her best friend's father that finally jolts Elizabeth out of her irresponsible reverie and causes her to finally realize how close she has come to derailing their lives.

McCullough, Colleen. *The Ladies of Missalonghi.* New York: Harper, 1987.

Set in the early 1900s in a tiny Australian town, this is the story of 33-year-old "spinster" Missy, who lives an impoverished existence because of an inheritance law that gives all power and assets to the male members of families. When a spunky divorced cousin comes to visit, Missy begins to realize that she can actually refuse to accept the victimhood imposed on her.

Michaels, Leonard. *The Men's Club.* New York: Farrar, 1981.

These stories are of seven men at an informal Berkeley get-together, which at first seems to be primarily a wine and marijuana fest. But gradually, perhaps accidentally, the revelations begin. They share humor, resentment, and brutality in attempts to make sense of their lives with women and in the process reveal what women know but always find surprising: men share many of the same fears, frustrations, and needs as women.

Parent, Gail. *Sheila Levine Is Dead and Living in New York.* New York: Putnam, 1972.

Thirty-year-old "fat, single, suicidal" Sheila Levine has spent ten years of her life desperately trying to get married, and she is tired. She has come to realize that it is just not going to happen for her—at least not in a country that "lost more Jewish boys to homosexuality than it did in any major war." This "life story" is in the form of a farewell note, but amounts to a hilarious compendium of New York cliches: singles bars, the Fire Island summer, the East Hampton summer, creepy men, illegal abortions, and neverending diets. This overanxious, overweight heroine whose life is one long black joke nevertheless is able to offer equally weary readers some kind of hope.

Parent, Gail. *A Sign of the Eighties.* New York: Putnam, 1987.

This acerbic comment on loneliness, as personified by the baby boomers, is principally represented here by Shelly Silver, a successful New York caterer who has reached age 35 without snaring a husband. Her former passions, which included militant feminist braless campaigns and the like, have not helped her find a suitable mate. Therefore, she launches a personal campaign (or is it a vendetta?) to achieve matrimonial supremacy, an endeavor replete with all the wackiness of a Lucille Ball rerun, updated for contemporary readers, whether single by default or by choice.

Pesetsky, Bette. *Midnight Sweets*. New York: Atheneum, 1988.

This is an ironic parable of the life of a woman pursuing an elusive goal: making the perfect life and the perfect cookie. After two failed marriages and five children, Theodora Waite's desire to succeed has not dissipated. Before becoming quite sure of the author's intent, the reader might find herself sneering at Pesetsky's plot line: a throwback, conventionally domestic woman setting out to turn her little cookie business into a real career. However, the reader quickly realizes that she has fallen into a clever trap because Pesetsky's finely and intensely wrought novel deals profoundly but hilariously with the whole shopping list of domestic and feminist issues.

Pym, Barbara. *Excellent Women*. New York: Dutton, 1978.

This bleak, brilliant, witty comedy describes the complications of being a spinster in England in the 1950s. Such excellent women had no lives of their own and so became embroiled in the lives of others. As one of them says, "We, my dear Mildred, are the observers of life." Main character Mildred Lathbury, thirtyish and already relegated to spinsterhood, uses up her days on small things: church, flowers, dinner with the bachelor vicar and his sister, brief encounters with neighbors. During a crisis, Mildred faces the risk of radically changing her life, but finally decides on singleness, an ultimately satisfying state for herself, but perceived mercilessly by others as an essentially meaningless way of life.

Pym, Barbara. *Quartet in Autumn*. New York: Dutton, 1978.

This story examines the deep rewards of friendships for older single people. Edwin, Norman, Letty, and Marcia are four elderly single people who work in the same office. Their work is their chief point of contact with each other and with society in general. Then the two women retire, an act that threatens the lives of all four. The author satirically but poignantly guides the reader through the lives of the four protagonists and describes the facade they erect to defend themselves from the facelessness of the welfare state. Seemingly hopeless, their story is actually optimistic in its portrayal of the triumph of human dignity over the threat of loneliness and the importance of supportive friendships throughout life.

Rhys, Jean. *After Leaving Mr. Mackenzie*. New York: Harper, 1972 (first published by Knopf, 1931).

This is a study of the gradual breakdown of a kept woman who is no longer kept. The parting from Mr. Mackenzie marks the downward turning point in Julia's life, a bleak one at best, though one with few illusions. It is the loss of her illusions that Julia is not able to face. Spiritually isolated and lacking a means of support, she attempts unsuccessfully to return to her family.

Sarton, May. *The Magnificent Spinster*. New York: Norton, 1985.

Jane Reid is a beautiful and wealthy Boston Brahmin who is pursued by men, yet has many women friends. The essence of the novel is its expression of the many possible aspects of friendship between women and the ways in which single women can lead full lives serving the less fortunate. The question for the individual is whether the role fulfills or oppresses.

Smiley, Jane. *Ordinary Love, a Novella*. New York: Knopf, 1989.

Rachel Kinsella's current contentment with her life has an unpleasant underside: it is built on her bold but cruel leavetaking from her pediatrician husband and four children twenty years earlier. This summer she has staged a reunion with all four of her children, who have lived away from her for a good many years. Traumas resulting from her abandonment of them are brought up for the first time, and Rachel is forced to weigh the pain and survival of her children against her need to escape a suffocating and insufferable relationship. She sees now that the thing that made her feel most guilty about leaving—her husband's enthrallment with his family—was really the "passion of an egomaniac." Rachel concludes that while a person can make room for anything she wants if she wants it enough, she must pay the price. Her reasons for destroying her nuclear family have come to her only lately. Perfect happiness, she concludes, must be accompanied by the inevitable pain of knowing it cannot last.

Weldon, Fay. *The Heart of the Country*. New York: Viking/Penguin, 1989.

With wit, irony, and consummate skill, author Fay Weldon again delves into her favorite subject: the foibles of the human spirit in the context of the snug, suburban dream. This story is about the painful education of Natalie Harris, whose husband has left her for another woman. Although she too has been unfaithful, she feels wronged and helpless. A less affluent single mother of her acquaintance, whom Natalie has previously scorned, becomes her ally and tutor in this new reality that reveals the depths of human resiliency.

Film

Manhattan. United Artists. 1979. 90 min.

This Woody Allen film captures the angst of young, single cosmopolites keening for mates as the only known way out of loneliness. Despite their sophisticated attire and pretentiously funny patter, their clumsy social strivings touch the viewer. Main character Isaac Davis, played by Allen himself, is a successful comedy writer whose life is anything but funny. His wife has left him, not for another man, but for a woman, and in addition she is writing a book about their failed marriage. Defensively, he commences a sexual relationship with a seventeen-year-old schoolgirl.

When Harry Met Sally. Columbia. 1989. 96 min.

This exceedingly well-written screenplay by Nora Ephron tells the story of two previously unacquainted college students who drive from Chicago to New York and en route debate the merits of male-female friendship. Harry says it is impossible for men and women to just be friends because of the "sex thing." Sally disagrees with this and just about everything else Harry has to say. Their simultaneous repulsion and attraction for each other resonates down through the years as they and their friends variously marry, divorce, and remarry, always attempting to get it right and never fully understanding why they cannot. The problem seems to be the one stated early on during the trip from Chicago to New York: the polarity in how the sexes look at the world is both the cause and the demise of male-female relations.

3 Divorce and Separation:

Anne Tyler's *Breathing Lessons*

By Ronald W. Pies
Owen E. Heninger

Separation and individuation are normal and inevitable processes in human development. All forms of separation—including that of the infant from its parents—carry the potential for both enrichment and impoverishment of the self. While we often regard marital separation as exceptional or aberrant, the potential for such dissolution exists in every marriage—indeed, in every relationship. Thus, the struggle against separation is also a struggle against basic human separateness, and as such, touches us all. But while these issues are in one sense universal, they raise complications in the case of the married couple—particularly when children are involved.

The Paradigm

What is the nature of the bond between man and wife? What makes up the "emotional glue" that holds a marriage together? Conversely, what are the forces that weaken and ultimately rend the marital bond? These are some of the questions Anne Tyler grapples with in *Breathing Lessons* (Knopf, 1988).

Tyler's book is extraordinary in its sympathetic understanding of the ordinary. Its characters are not movie stars or neurosurgeons, but everyday people struggling with painful choices and losses. While *Breathing Lessons* focuses on marital discord, it is more broadly concerned with the human struggle itself—the struggle against disorder and meaninglessness. Anne Tyler is not sentimental in her portrayal of this endeavor, but neither is she fashionably cynical. She intimates that with sufficient good will and effort a man and a woman may together surmount the forces that threaten their union. Thus, while *Breathing Lessons* is a kind of user's guide to all that can go wrong in a marriage, it is also a revelation of those mundane things that can go miraculously right.

Summary

Maggie and Ira Moran—a married couple in their late 40s—are preparing to leave for the funeral of Maggie's best friend's husband. But before they are under way, Maggie hears a radio show dealing with what makes an ideal marriage. To Maggie's astonishment, the young woman revealing herself on the air sounds remarkably like Fiona, the estranged wife of Jesse, Maggie and Ira's wayward son. Fiona reveals her intention to remarry—this time not for love, but for "security." Maggie is so bowled over at this, she manages to run their newly repaired car smack into an oncoming truck. But the car is drivable, and eventually Maggie and Ira set off, Maggie still preoccupied with Fiona's revelation.

It is this singular event that propels Ira and Maggie through the rest of the book's action with, of course, many physical and temporal detours along the way. At one point early in the journey, Maggie has one of her famous (infamous, to Ira) heart-to-heart talks with a waitress at a roadside diner. In the space of a few minutes, Maggie manages to reveal the whole saga of Fiona and Jesse, blaming Ira for Fiona's leaving the marriage. Ira and Maggie argue over this, and Maggie suddenly asks Ira to let her out of the car. She feels "pleased in a funny sort of way . . . almost drunk with fury and elation." She begins to spin out a fantasy of living on her own, imagining herself as a clerk or even a cashier. Maggie also recollects her many years as an aide in a home for the elderly, where she was complimented as "capable and skillful and efficient"—in painful contrast to Ira's view of her as a "scatterbrain." But Ira comes back to find Maggie, and eventually they make it to the funeral. Thanks to Maggie's friend Serena—a most unconventional widow—the plot takes a number of comic turns. But most centrally, we learn through flashbacks of Maggie's courtship with Ira—in the days when he was still a "long, dark shape," someone so mysterious and foreign looking "he could have been Asian."

After the funeral and its many complications, Ira and Maggie head back home to Baltimore—back, it seems, to their "normal" lives. But Maggie has something else in mind—couldn't they just swing by Cartwheel and "stop by Fiona's just for an instant. A teeny, eeny instant"? Ira knows that his fate is sealed. Ostensibly, Maggie wants to offer her baby-sitting services while Fiona goes on her honeymoon; after all, Fiona's daughter by Jesse, Leroy, would need someone to look after her while Mother was away. But Maggie is hatching grander schemes, as Ira suspects. Ultimately, Maggie succeeds in luring Fiona back to Baltimore in a desperate attempt to get her and Jesse back together. (From Maggie's point of view, they should never have parted; from Ira's, Maggie is once again trying to run people's lives.) Fiona and Jesse are ultimately reunited, though only fleetingly. In the intervening (and interlacing) segments of the book, we learn about Jesse and Fiona—how they courted, loved, married, bore a daughter, and ultimately came to grief. We also learn that, indeed, Ira did play a role in driving the young couple apart and that his intercession stemmed from inner forces quite beyond his understanding. Maggie too—though seemingly more benign—is driven by needs that go well beyond the wish to reunite Jesse and Fiona.

With this outline in mind, we are now confronted with a number of questions pertaining to separation and divorce. First, what is it about Ira and Maggie's marriage that allows it to "hold together," despite its myriad problems? How does it differ, in this respect, from the marriage of Jesse and Fiona, which appears doomed to fail? Second, what does the book teach us about the effect of separation on the families and children of the separated couple? Finally, what do we learn about the ways in which parents may unconsciously subvert or overcontrol their children's marriage?

At first glance, Maggie and Ira's marriage seems deeply troubled. Much of the time, Maggie and Ira seem to talk past, rather than to, each other. This problem is compounded by Ira's innate reticence. Indeed, when Maggie really wants to know what Ira is thinking, she ignores his words and listens to the tunes he whistles. For his part, Ira feels scorned by Maggie. He cannot comprehend her often fuzzy logic and is constantly irritated by what he sees as Maggie's meddling in other people's lives. Maggie too feels misunderstood and unappreciated. She sees herself as having "so much to offer, if only someone would take it." And yet, despite these difficulties, Ira and Maggie endure as a couple. There is a core of strength to their marriage that allows it to survive the slings and arrows of daily fortune. Ira sees his marriage as "steady as a tree; not even he could tell how wide and deep the roots went." Maggie and Ira are able to call upon a storehouse of "jokes and affectionate passwords . . . abiding loyalty and gestures of support." Thus, when Maggie temporarily abandons Ira on their way to the funeral, Ira remains steadfast. He finds Maggie in a roadside grocery and sidles up to her, saying, "Hey, babe, care to accompany me to a funeral?" Maggie and Ira survive as a couple because they are able to comfort one another in moments of shared vulnerability.

In contrast, Jesse and Fiona seem to lack this simple but critical faculty. At best, each is able to satisfy the infantile longings of the other.

At worst, each is trapped in a kind of petulant selfishness that eats away at their marriage. Thus, after an argument with Jesse, Fiona snatches up the ailing infant, Leroy, and disappears. When Maggie urges Jesse to go after her, he replies, "Why should I? She's the one who walked out." At a family outing, Jesse disappears, leaving Fiona to cope with the irritable Leroy. When she finally sights him, Fiona yells—very publicly—"Jesse Moran! You get your ass on down here!" The puerile petulance of this couple is evident to Maggie, who tries in vain to mediate. "You don't have to shout at me," Fiona says to Jesse. "I'm not shouting," he replies. The subsequent exchange ("Yes you are," "Am not," "Are too") prompts Maggie to protest, "Children! Children!" She was pretending to joke, but only pretending. At bottom, Jesse and Fiona *are* children—playing at marriage, playing at raising a child. They allow the infant Leroy to sleep in a bureau drawer. When Fiona asks Jesse when he is going to build a cradle, he replies with a kind of torpid innocence, "Any day now." Jesse's reason for wanting a baby in the first place sounds like a young boy's justification for owning a puppy: "It's exactly what I've been needing: something of my own."

Unlike Maggie, Fiona views her marital problems with a despairing fatalism. As symbolized by the name of the town she inhabits—Cartwheel—Fiona tumbles through cycles of marital discord. She says of her problem with Jesse, "I mean, it's bound and determined to go wrong. The whole cycle [will] just start over again." Maggie replies, characteristically, "Oh, Fiona, isn't it time somebody broke that cycle?" Perhaps it is this sort of optimism that allows Maggie and Ira to survive as a couple.

Breathing Lessons makes clear that the ripples of a broken marriage spread far beyond the sundered couple. Maggie, for one, cannot accept the separation of Jesse and Fiona, nor her own estrangement from her granddaughter. She makes "spy trips" to Cartwheel, during which she observes the infant Leroy from afar. Maggie is horrified by the slipshod care Leroy receives from Fiona's mother, Mrs. Stuckey. When Maggie happens to meet up with Mrs. Stuckey at Fiona's house, the confrontation is both bitter and poignant. When Fiona suggests to her mother that Leroy should "get to know her daddy," Mrs. Stuckey replies, "Anyone whose daddy is Jesse Moran is better off staying strangers." When Maggie overhears this remark, she feels her face grow hot. She wants to say to Mrs. Stuckey, "You think there haven't been times I've cursed your daughter? She hurt my son to the bone." More wrenching still is Leroy's inability to recognize Maggie after several years' absence. Maggie laments, "It was crazy to have to introduce herself to her own flesh and blood . . . what a sad, partitioned life they all seemed to be living!" For Maggie, "what's past is never past; not entirely." The cartwheel of pain turns again and again, until someone with enough strength steps forward to stop it.

Whereas Maggie emerges as such a figure, Ira functions as a destructive force in Jesse and Fiona's marriage. At two critical junctures, Ira reveals things about Jesse that drive Fiona away from him. Tragically, the destruction of his son's marriage is Ira's most dramatic achievement; otherwise, in 50 years, "he had never accomplished one single act of consequence." One wonders if, by destroying Jesse, Ira was also destroying some hated part of himself. And while Maggie's attempts at rescuing Jesse's marriage seem altruistic, they too may be motivated by more complex forces. In many ways, Maggie seems overly identified with Jesse. Both mother and son embody a sweet, befuddled vulnerability—"the triumph of sheer fun over practicality." Perhaps in rescuing Jesse, Maggie is acting out a need to save herself. Or does Maggie see in Jesse some scruffy incarnation of Ira? When she phones her son, Maggie notices that "his voice was Ira's voice, but years younger." Is Maggie's frantic attempt to rescue Jesse a way of reinvigorating her love for Ira—the Ira she once knew as a figure of mystery and romance? These rhetorical questions are raised to highlight an important issue in divorce and separation—namely, the complex feelings that may motivate apparently well-intentioned family members.

Breathing Lessons also adumbrates the damage done to the children of divorced or separated parents. While Fiona is scarcely an objective commentator, we may take her remarks about Leroy as paradigmatic: "And when [Jesse] hasn't laid eyes on his daughter since her fifth birthday? Try explaining that to a child. . . . Here she keeps wondering why all the other kids have fathers. Even the kids whose parents are divorced—at least they get to see their fathers on weekends." And though we do not learn a great deal about Leroy, she seems a rather gaunt and taciturn child. Her face is "so thin it [is] triangular, a cat's face, and her arms and legs [are] narrow white stems." Frowning "[gives] her forehead a netted look." When Maggie offers to buy Leroy a Frisbee that glows in the dark, the child thinks a moment, then replies, "Why would I want to play Frisbee in the dark?" Through such glimpses of Leroy, we take away the impression of a quiet and joyless child.

After all this, it may seem surprising that the closing image in *Breathing Lessons* is decidedly hopeful—a lovely paradox in which Ira's game of solitaire draws Maggie magically close to him. She feels "a little stir of something that came over her . . . she lift[s] her face to kiss the warm blade of his cheekbone." If Anne Tyler's novel has taken us down the road of marital dissolution, it has also pointed us toward a brighter path—though, as Maggie and Ira would attest, a path full of pitfalls for the unwary.

Questions for Discussion

1. What maladaptive strategies do Jesse and Fiona use to cope with their marital problems? How do these differ from those of Maggie and Ira?
2. Are some marriages not worth saving? Why or why not?
3. What does Maggie mean when she says that we are not given training in marriage? How might such training have helped Jesse and Fiona?
4. Do men and women perceive and communicate in different ways? If so, how might these differences contribute to marital strain?

Annotated Bibliography

Print

Armstrong, Charlotte. *The Balloon Man*. New York: Harper, 1968.

In this novel, a couple's marriage is driven to the breaking point by the husband's taking a hallucinogenic drug (LSD) and becoming violent. His young wife becomes terribly frightened and upset by this. She takes her child and leaves her husband for the safety of a boarding house. She then starts divorce proceedings. Aggravating her situation, her father-in-law tries to obtain custody of his grandson from her. He hires an unscrupulous and unsteady young man to ferret out defamatory information on her so he can have her declared an unfit mother. Violence and murder follow. With the summation of all these stresses, the mother is pushed to the brink of madness. This illustrates some of the forces that promote marital discord and the accumulation of aftereffects that may follow separation.

Barthelme, Frederick. *Tracer*. New York: Simon & Schuster, 1985.

This novel throws light on the emotional complications that may accompany separation. In the midst of the stress and loneliness of his marital separation, a man being divorced goes to his wife's sister for solace. They are attracted to each other and soon become lovers. Then his wife appears and makes love to him also. This forms a love triangle within the family as he finds himself in the predicament of divorcing one sister and sleeping with the other. This situation steps up his discomfort, and he soon finds himself at odds with both women. Unable to deal with the intensification of his troubles, he takes flight.

Cheever, John. "The Swimmer." In *The Stories of John Cheever*. New York: Knopf, 1979. (Film: *The Swimmer*. Image Entertainment Inc. 1968. 94 min.)

This short story depicts the accumulation of provocations that have led to a marital separation. The story is told through following a middle-aged man's adolescent antic of going from friend's pool to friend's pool and swimming his way home, eight miles away. As his allegorical trip unfolds, a continuous array of the self-delusions that have disrupted his marriage are exhibited. By doggedly denying reality and insisting on trying to maintain a macho image of virility and youth, he takes a journey to melancholy, bewilderment, and alienation. In his hubris, he tries to ignore the many effects of aging and becomes a vacuous and ridiculous figure who is finally no longer able to conceal the painful facts of his life. In contrast to the integrity and dignity of several of his aging neighbors, he is quite unprepared for his middle years and cannot avoid stagnation and despair.

Ford, Jesse Hill. *The Liberation of Lord Byron Jones*. Boston: Little, 1965. (Film: *The Liberation of L. B. Jones*. RCA/Columbia Pictures Home Video. 1970. 101 min.)

Lord Byron Jones, undertaker and respected member of the black community of Summerton, Tennessee, is forced to consider shedding his young wife because he has discovered that she is having an affair with a white policeman who is married. This adds the tension of both discrimination and miscegenation to his motivations. Jones is also under family pressure to divorce by an expatriate southern nephew and the nephew's wife. Though the case should be open and shut, the young wife refuses to cooperate. She contests, forcing the opposition to name her white lover in court. This threatens to project the attendant distresses of the divorce out into the larger society.

Guest, Judith. *Ordinary People*. New York: Viking, 1976. (Film: *Ordinary People*. Paramount Home Video. 1980. 124 min.)

This story demonstrates how unresolved grief and bereavement can lead to marital estrangement. The family recently has suffered the death of one of the two sons and the suicide attempt of the other son, Conrad. Much of the story focuses on Conrad as he returns home after eight months in a mental hospital. Although a psychiatrist helps Conrad unlock his feelings and move toward recovery, it is his mother who does not recover from these two traumatic events. She remains in a state of denial and numbing and emotional rigidity, unable to accept or resolve the tragedy of it all. Her unfortunate and fixed state plays havoc with her marriage and eventually destroys it.

Guest, Judith. *Second Heaven*. New York: Viking, 1982.

This novel has to do mainly with the aftermath of divorce and postdivorce relationships that do not turn out all bad. We learn that the

40-something Cat's husband has left her for a younger woman, and she is depressed. Her divorce lawyer is also in his 40s, and he too suffers emotional aches from his own divorce. Gale, a sixteen-year-old runaway boy, is taken in by Cat, but his parents petition the court to have their son jailed for stealing. Cat and her lawyer join forces to expose the child abuse that led Gale to leave home. During this process, which is helpful to each participant, they develop a new understanding of their lives, learn to trust one another, and eventually join as a new family.

Highsmith, Patricia. *Edith's Diary*. New York: Simon & Schuster, 1977.

This story illustrates how postdivorce distress can lead to serious mental illness. Edith and Brett move from New York City to a small town in Pennsylvania to escape the urban crowds of the 1950s. They realize their dream of living in the country and publishing their own newspaper. After ten years there, Brett divorces Edith to marry a younger woman, leaving Edith to care for Brett's invalid uncle George and their problem son Cliffie. As the realities and pressures of this new life become more intolerable, Edith retreats into the fantasy world of her diary, in which Cliffie is a successful engineer with a wife and children.

Lewis, Sinclair. *Dodsworth*. New York: Harcourt, 1929. (Film: *Dodsworth*. Image Entertainment Inc. 1939. 90 min.)

This story presents some of the irreconcilable differences that can lead to marital separation. Samuel Dodsworth is a rich automobile manufacturer in the midwestern city of Zenith. He retires and goes to Europe with his blatantly frivolous wife Fran. While in Europe, Fran becomes involved in several love affairs with European adventurers. Dodsworth, lonely, unhappy, and at odds with his wife's unfinished ways, meets Edith Cartwright, an American widow. She teaches him to appreciate the traditions of Europe and brings joy back into his life. He eventually leaves Fran for the more mature companionship of Edith.

Miller, Sue. *The Good Mother*. New York: Harper, 1986. (Film: *The Good Mother*. Touchstone Pictures Video. 1988. 104 min.)

This story throws light on some long-lasting effects of divorce on both parents and children and illustrates the powerful influence that a single parent's sexual behavior can have on the issue of child custody. Newly divorced Anna is ordering her life around her three-year-old daughter, when a new love interest sparks a sexual responsiveness that is refreshing to Anna. Her daughter appears to feel safe with and soon becomes fond of the new man, and it is easy for Anna to view them all as a loving family unit until her ex-husband sues for custody of their daughter. Anna's new love affair is irrevocably changed as her ex-husband alleges that Anna's lover has molested his daughter.

Simon, Neil. *The Odd Couple*. New York: Random, 1966. (Film: *The Odd Couple*. Paramount Home Video. 1968. 157 min.)

This account of two men who live together though they bicker constantly gives ample evidence of how they demolished their marriages. It is the story of two men estranged from their wives who eventually become estranged from each other. One of them, Oscar, an amiable slob who is bleary eyed and grumbling, dresses in unkempt clothes and wrecks the apartment. The other is fussy Felix, meticulous and fastidious to a fault, a weepy hypochondriac who is compulsively neat and wears an apron. Whereas Felix is defiantly domestic and wildly emotional, Oscar takes pleasure in creating untidiness and disarray. Their irreconcilable character traits give constant reason for the dissolution of their relationships.

Thayer, Nancy. *Nell*. New York: Morrow, 1985.

The difficulties of reestablishing a love life after a divorce are demonstrated in this story of the aftermath of Nell's divorce. Nell goes through an emotional roller coaster series of courtships and breakups. Her first lover, Steve, is a handsome young construction worker. He is good with her kids, but his strong commitment to dirt bikes and his earnest attachment to television reruns leaves Nell unfulfilled. Another lover, Ben, is affluent and deluges her with fine theater productions and dinners, but she feels no flicker of passion. Finally, she finds a man she can fully love. She sorts out her priorities and emerges with an honest enthusiasm for life.

Thayer, Nancy. *Three Women at the Water's Edge*. New York: Doubleday, 1981.

This story follows the urges felt and acted upon by three women in various stages of marriage and separation. It shows how much family members can be influenced by what happens to others in the family. Daisy, already the mother of two children, is pregnant again. Her stress is amplified when she must suddenly cope without her husband, who has left her for another woman. To make matters worse, Daisy's mother, Margaret, has left her husband to find a new life. And Dale, Daisy's sister who has recently fallen in love, is ambivalent about her feelings lest they move her into an unhappy marriage like those of her sister and mother. These women have shed their old roles and must come up with ways to face the changes that have occurred.

Wakefield, Dan. *Starting Over*. New York: Doubleday, 1973. (Film: *Starting Over*. Paramount Home Video. 1979. 105 min.)

This story chronicles the ways one man attempts vainly to avoid feelings of misery after his divorce. After Phil Potter fails as an actor, he becomes a successful New York City public relations executive. When his four-year marriage to a lovely model and closet alcoholic fails, he gets a divorce. Phil is frequently told how lucky he is, but being alone, he finds, can be as miserable as a distressing marriage. He starts a new life in Boston, where he teaches communications and has sexual encounters with every available New England divorcee and matron as the ineffective healing agent to his own painful isolation.

Wharton, Edith. "The Other Two." In *Collected Short Stories of Edith Wharton*, edited by R. W. B. Lewis, 2 v. New York: Scribner, 1968 (first published in 1904).

There are adjustments to a new family and a tolerance of former husbands in this story about the aftermath of divorce. Waythorn marries a twice-divorced Alice. When Alice's twelve-year-old daughter, Lilly, becomes ill, they cut short their honeymoon to be with her. Alice's first husband, Haskett, continues his weekly visitations to Lilly at the Waythorns' home. Then Alice's second husband, Varick, asks Waythorn's help in business. Waythorn sees the humor when all three men end up being served tea by Alice. The unwanted baggage of past relationships has to be dealt with, and Waythorn begins to see his bride as no longer uniquely his, but as "a shoe that too many feet [have] worn."

Film

The Color Purple. Warner Home Video. 1985. 154 min. (Print: Walker, Alice. *The Color Purple*. San Diego: Harcourt, 1982.)

In this chronicle, a chain of traumatic events sets off a separation. This story is set in impoverished rural Georgia and focuses on the life of the elder of two sisters, Celie. It shows her early life as a poor, shy, unattractive, and uneducated girl who is raped by a man she thinks is her father. She has the two children from that union taken from her and is then given to a brute of a man as his wife. His cruel treatment retraumatizes her, and for a while she numbly endures many indignities at his hands. But rather than being fixated, and by virtue of a special relationship with another woman, she works through her symptoms and begins to feel loved and valued. She develops self-worth and the gumption to leave her husband. She resolves her past traumas by reinvesting in a new life of mastery that is a personal triumph.

First Born. Paramount Video. 1984. 90 min.

In what might be called a cautionary tale, this film concerns a young divorcée who struggles to make a good life for herself and her two sons. In her search for love and support, she gets involved with an intense man who deals in cocaine, and he moves into their house. This man puts the entire family in danger. The woman, first in denial and then nearly paralyzed with fear, seems helpless to do anything about it. Her elder son shows exceptional courage and maturity in facing the danger and rescuing his mother from her disastrous relationship.

Peggy Sue Got Married. CBS/Fox Video. 1986. 103 min.

This film follows a long series of marital stresses that set in motion the breakup of a marriage. Like insight-oriented psychotherapy, it uses the device of reliving the past with the aid of present knowledge and experience. Peggy Sue attends her 25th high school reunion, passes out, and awakes in her teenage body with her 42-year-old mind. She finds herself in the early days of dating and loving the teenage boy she will later marry and still later separate from. By the end of the film, Peggy Sue is able to integrate both her past and her present to gain a new awareness and start on a better informed relationship.

See You in the Morning. Warner Home Video. 1989. 119 min.

The major emphasis of this film is on the longer term aftermath of marital dissolution and the difficulties in starting new filial relations with stepchildren. It starts with the termination of two marriages: one ends in divorce and the other by the husband's suicide. Then the divorced man and the widow marry. He is still wrestling with ambivalence and the aftereffects of his divorce; therefore, he cannot devote his full energies to being stepfather to her two children. As if to demonstrate his vacillation, he tries to make love to his first wife, but his vacillation prevails and he founders.

Shoot the Moon. MGM/UA Home Video. 1981. 124 min.

This story exposes agonizing episodes caused by a variety of emotions in a dissolving marriage. It also illustrates the fallout effects on the large family. A man desperately wants to keep his family and be with another woman at the same time. Eventually, his thinly disguised anger and infidelity sour the marriage. He leaves but he cannot abide another man working on the house he himself built. He performs a "moonlight flit," or "shoots the moon," by breaking into his own house at night to try and get what he thinks are his personal belongings before someone else can get them. When he beats his daughter because she will not love him, his wife reacts with an affair that smacks of revenge. Then she and her husband demonstrate their shared wavering by sharing with one another elusive feelings of love and passion.

Sweethearts Dance. RCA Home Video. 1988. 101 min.

This film explores some reasons for separation—taking one's spouse for granted, the lack of romance in a marriage—but it tells more about the trials and tribulations during separation. A hard-working man who has had children and a long marriage with his high school sweetheart finds his marriage slowly coming apart. At the same time, in contrast, his best friend is falling in love. He moves into a trailer and struggles to keep his emotional balance and understand his family relationships. He shows vital concern about how his leaving home is affecting his children. Of particular interest is the stress-driven reaction of the oldest son to his father's moving out and the help given the father by the father's best friend.

Twice in a Lifetime. Vestron Video. 1985. 117 min.

An apparently stable marriage is pulled apart by the husband's attraction to a barmaid and his desire for what he sees as a second chance at life. He is excited, rejuvenated, and fully caught up in his middle-age love for this beguiling younger woman. His fascination overpowers his good sense. When he decides to leave his wife and move in with this woman, it sets off upheaval throughout his family. His wife is distraught and tries to replace old routines with new ones, and his oldest daughter, whom he sincerely cherishes, develops a bitter resentment toward him.

An Unmarried Woman. CBS/Fox Video. 1978. 124 min.

The immediate, distressing effects of divorce on a woman and her anguish and effort in trying to start a new life are the subject of this film. When her marriage is broken up by her husband's leaving her for a younger woman, the protagonist becomes consumed with anger, grief, uncertainty, and fear. She begins a journey back to being single. She gets support from three friends and tries to make sense of what is happening to her. She talks things over with her daughter and goes to a woman psychiatrist for help. Eventually, she bravely begins a new life by starting to date.

The War of the Roses. CBS/Fox Video. 1989. 116 min.

This film begins in a lawyer's office, where the attorney narrates a cautionary tale of what can happen in a divorce. The lawyer tells the story of a couple who, on the surface, seemed to have a perfect life and marriage. The man was a successful lawyer, and the wife an accomplished caterer. They had a great house, great cars, great art, and great children. When the wife sued for divorce, a set-to began and escalated in malevolence, fury, and destructive force to a veritable free-for-all. Though many divorcing people have intense hatred for each other, they usually try to keep it in check. This story reveals the many vengeful impulses that can be unleashed during a divorce. It presents an object lesson that illustrates what a couple might do if they were to fully act out their strong urges to get even with or destroy each other.

4 Death and Dying:

William Faulkner's *As I Lay Dying*

By Aaron Kramer

The pioneering work of Elisabeth Kubler-Ross and others has helped clarify the experience shared by the terminally ill. Before arriving at acceptance of their reality, it is typical for them to pass through the painful phases of denial, isolation, anger, and depression. In their interaction with the terminally ill, the survivors can help satisfy the needs of the dying for comfort and for an openness leading to acceptance. But the survivors have needs as well: to express grief, to accept loss, and to find the strength to endure. The terminally ill can play a major role in satisfying these needs if their final weeks or months are a period of full communication and if in their preceding years of good health a habit of expressiveness and a candor toward death were established. Once acceptance is achieved, the time remaining can be spent valuably, with a maximum of dignity and togetherness. Afterward, the survivors can benefit from the consolations of ritual and community caring.

The Paradigm

Almost none of this takes place in *As I Lay Dying* (Cape, 1930). If art criticizes life, more often dramatizing the consequences of wrong than right behavior, this novel stands as a classic example. Even in its years of physical health, the Bundren family was emotionally crippled. Although each member performed his or her chores well, and on that level their farm ran smoothly, the valves of their hearts and minds were locked against one another and against the outside world. No genuine communication occurred. Their somber home was inhabited by rejection, favoritism, secrecy, guilt, suspicion, and alienation. These conditions intensified when the crisis came—the time of fatal illness. Burrowing even further into herself, the mother welcomed and supervised her death, giving instructions and assigning family chores to the end—allowing absolutely no room for a summing up, an expression of feeling, a farewell; such words she had always held in contempt. Thus, instead of the family coming together, each member withdrew into wordless, often destructive and self-destructive, activity. Utterly unprepared for their mother's death and for death in general, the younger children did not know how to grieve, while the older ones grieved by means of ferocious doings—often heroic, often incoherent—with tragic consequences.

No work could be more revealing of a family's interaction through the death experience than Faulkner's. He allows us the privilege of entering fully the thought processes of all involved, and through their differing perceptions, he chronicles in excruciating detail a slowly unfolding nightmare, allowing us to develop our own insights and draw, if we care to, lessons on a life disastrously lived, leading to a disastrous death.

Summary

Addie, the wife of hill-farmer Anse Bundren, is dying. Many years back, Anse promised to bury her not locally, but with her kinfolk in Jefferson, 40 miles away. She is holding him to that pledge. Intimidated by and beholden to no outsider, she wants a coffin made of wood from her own land, constructed—within sight and sound of her window—by her beloved eldest son Cash, a master carpenter. He toils incessantly and, trained to share her contempt for words, shows her instead each plank as it is finished. Incessantly too, and silently, her daughter Dewey Dell sits fanning Addie. Anse allows the two middle sons, Darl and Jewel, to deliver a load of lumber miles from home, although a storm is brewing and the plan is to head for Jefferson as soon as Addie has died. Without a word to his mother, Darl comes to her door and silently predicts she will be dead before he and Jewel return.

A neighbor perceives Darl's visit as an act of love and condemns Jewel for not saying goodbye; but in fact, Darl's life has been poisoned by Addie's rejection, whereas her adored Jewel refuses to believe she is dying and cannot bear to see her. Instead, he fiercely immerses himself in other matters. He resents the buzzardlike presence of outsiders, considers his sister's fanning a discomfort, and sees his brother's sawing as a torment to his mother.

Vardaman, the youngest child, is robbed of a farewell and given no preparation for his loss; instead, he is sent fishing. His father even forbids him to show the dying woman his splendid catch, but rather orders him to wash it and cut it up.

For Addie, the doctor's coming signals her welcome death. She raises her face to the window one last time, and Cash shows her how well the planks fit together. As she did through most of their marriage—detestable for her and emasculating for him—she ignores Anse. But into the eyes of her last-born boy, her eyes send forth one last mysterious spurt of flame; then the light goes out, as it went out in the eyes of Vardaman's fine fish.

Much later we learn that Addie, in those final hours, is occupied with far more than the progress of her coffin. Though her family desperately needs for Addie to speak to them, in silence she uses her dying to survey and assess her life, to confront—if not to unburden herself of—the venomous secrets in her keep. We find out that she had hated her father, who called life a preparation for a long death. She came to cherish her aloneness and resented her first-born for violating it by capturing her heart. Enraged by a swift second pregnancy, she wanted to murder Anse; but deciding he was already dead, she instead rejected him for many years. With the unwanted birth of Darl, Addie came to accept her father's grim view of life and made Anse promise to bury her with her kin in Jefferson, thus divorcing herself from him forever. For words like "love," she had only contempt; reality needed no words. (The reader can imagine a household active, but silent, in which the communication of ideas and feelings was minimal.)

Addie intends to carry to the grave her greatest secret: the child sired a decade after Darl by Preacher Whitfield. Like Cash, Addie loves Jewel; she also hates him for making her love him so. Addie coldly assigns Anse the final pair of children, Dewey Dell and Vardaman, as compensation for her having had Jewel. It has been suggested that this central section of the novel, Addie's only inner monologue, places her like a spider whose web of control radiates through the narrative; the web binds in its grip the whole family, from first to last, making the phases of their loss, from grief through acceptance and healing, a pathetic mess and nearly destroying them in the process. But this is an oversimplification. It would make Addie responsible for even the flood caused by the storm raging outside their house; it would make Anse responsible for nothing.

Perhaps she can, in part, be held responsible for the situation in which Dewey Dell finds herself because she has chosen to withhold her motherly role from the girl and has imposed on her the isolation that is so dear to Addie. Desperately fanning Addie now (which is the utmost of involvement permitted her), the girl—like all the others—has thoughts beyond her mother's dying. She relives her sexual intercourse with a farmhand and the promise of secrecy she silently extracts from Darl, whom she hates for knowing.

Dewey Dell and Vardaman are the first to experience Addie's death. Dewey Dell hurls herself onto the body, keening not only for her loss but also for the fact that her love has fled, leaving her ten dollars for an abortion. Vardaman rushes down to the barn, where he cannot stop crying and vomiting. Not mother or father has prepared either of them; she does not know how to cry, and he cannot reconcile the body on the bed with his mother. Confused, Vardaman equates Addie with his fish, so vital an hour ago, now cut up.

Informed that Addie is dying, the adulterer-preacher Whitfield sets out on horseback for the farm, but by now the bridge is down. Against great odds and buffeted by floating logs, Whitfield crosses the ford, determined to ease his own soul and save Addie's by confessing their sin before Anse. Merely imagining the scene is enough to absolve him; he sees his victory over the flood as a sign of God's acceptance. By the time Whitfield arrives, Addie is dead. Telling Anse nothing, he conducts a hypocritical service that reassures himself and the community, but not the family.

Stuck for three days miles from home with a mud-wrecked wagon, Darl punishes Jewel for being Addie's favorite and having a horse to love: he taunts his already tormented brother, declaring that Addie Bundren is dead, that Jewel's mother is a horse, and that he himself has no mother. As soon as the brothers return home, the family sets out for Jefferson, though the bridge is down and the river is still rising. Somehow, Jewel single-handedly gets the unwieldy coffin into the wagon.

For Vardaman, Jefferson means more than a burial: a miniature railroad is displayed in a store window; bananas are on sale. For Dewey Dell, it means a pharmacy to abort her pregnancy. Cash hopes to buy a "graphophone." And although Anse loftily insists he must fulfill his pledge to Addie (who appears to govern him still) and to her family, Jefferson for him means a new set of teeth, and perhaps more.

Anse and his two youngest children cross the partly submerged bridge by foot. The other three, attempting to cross what was once a ford, are confronted by a floating log that overturns the wagon, drowns the mules, and nearly drowns Cash, who cannot swim. It is Jewel who saves the wagon and its passenger—"her," as the coffin is now called. Thus, he fulfills the first half of Addie's prophecy that, though he is her cross, Jewel (not Jesus) will be her salvation past death through flood and fire. Because Cash has suffered a broken leg, Jewel again risks death by diving repeatedly to save his brother's beloved tools.

Through ordeal after ordeal, with the smell from the coffin worsening and the number of buzzards increasing, they move uncomplainingly ahead. Anse, however, utters not one word of praise for his children's efforts, but rather accuses all five of not loving their mother. None of them disputes this, nor could they be expected to; they have been brought up with no such word as "love," with no outlet but mute action for a grief they have not been trained to deal with and cannot even name.

At each of their catastrophes, Anse whines of his misfortunes, further excluding his children, as he has from the start of the journey (except when their practical help is required). Refusing the loan of a mule team to complete their mission—because dramatizing his devotedness and proud independence matters most—Anse insists on buying one. Without asking their permission, he barters away the most precious possessions of Addie's favorite sons: Cash's tools and Jewel's horse. Jewel delivers the horse personally to its new owner and, without a murmur, catches up to the wagon on foot. Cash, also acquiescent, rides atop the coffin in silent agony at each jolt of the wagon. Instead of seeking a doctor as he promised, Anse has Darl set the fractured leg with cement, though it is likely to cripple his son permanently. Cash and Jewel's stoic heroism is the way they honor Addie and express their love.

Darl, who has studied Jewel carefully since birth and has noted their mother's special devotion to him, his unique tallness, and his affinity for horses, chooses this worst of moments to twit him: "Your mother is a horse, but who is your father?" Jewel's rage at the question suggests that he too has wondered.

Still focused on the coffin, with its unmotherly stench, Vardaman is now obsessed with the buzzards, wildly driving them off. Darl believes he hears his mother within the box asking for rest and convinces Vardaman he hears her too.

Granted lodging on the last night of their journey, the Bundrens are roused by a barn fire from which the mules, the cow, and the coffin are barely saved by Jewel's single-handed efforts. Thus, the second half of Addie's prophecy is fulfilled. When Vardaman tells Dewey Dell he saw Darl set the fire, she instructs him to keep the secret. Why did Darl do it? It was more than a final snapping of his always frail equilibrium, an act of insanity expected by the community. It was done partly to end the horror of the journey and his mother's and Cash's agony. After the fire, Vardaman finds Darl lying on the coffin, protecting it, crying. Perhaps under the veneer of uncaring, of taunting cruelty toward Jewel, he has hidden a lifelong ache for the oneness between mother and child enjoyed by Cash and Jewel, but denied him. Of all her children, perhaps he alone has found the tears with which to mourn her.

As the family enters Jefferson, all the tensions of the trip break their enforced forward-moving unity. Other matters now dominate their thinking. If not for Darl's intervention, Jewel would be knifed by a stranger he attacks for commenting on the wagon's overpowering smell. Darl finally criticizes his father for not bringing a shovel and for failing to phone ahead so that the grave would be ready; he suggests too that, before the burial, they should get Cash to a doctor. When Darl is out of earshot, the family agrees that, as soon as Addie is buried, he will be tied up and shipped to an asylum rather than risk being sued by their host whose barn he burned. Anse knows exactly at whose house to stop for a shovel. He stays a long time, and Cash is enamored of the gramophone music coming from the house.

Interestingly, Faulkner (through the mind of Cash) devotes not one sentence to the actual burial. Swiftly, still in the cemetery, Darl is seized by his father, his sister, and Jewel, along with the two guards assigned to accompany him to the asylum. Dewey Dell, hating Darl for knowing her secrets, claws at him savagely, while Jewel, hating Darl for having asked who his father is, urges the guards to kill him. Addie has truly been left at peace in her grave, rid of her family, alone at last. Now Cash can have the cement removed from his leg, along with 60 square inches of skin. Dewey Dell and Vardaman can eat bananas, and Vardaman can look (in vain) for the miniature railroad. Dewey Dell, in her quest for an abortion, can take drugs that may be lethal and be raped by a clerk in a pharmacy basement. Anse can return the shovel to the house with the music, wheedle his daughter's bit of money, go off that night freshly shaved, hair slicked, smelling of perfume, and in the morning rejoin the coffinless wagon looking a head taller, with a set of new teeth and a new Mrs. Bundren, bringing a gramophone to liven their winter evenings.

What can this improbable tale (whose aim is not to teach) teach a family faced with the loss of an apparently indispensable member? At the very least, Faulkner assures us that, even under the most adverse circumstances, even led by the weakest of men, even with its members facing crises of their own and filled with submerged resentments, the family can survive its loss, although in a seriously fractured form and with the future of each member uncertain. One lesson the novel shares is the degree of self-reliance the children have been forced to achieve, growing up on a lone hilltop farm. All have shouldered considerable responsibilities, in all weathers and at all moments of unexpected calamity, developing wills, skills, and strengths that are called upon throughout their nine disastrous days on the road.

What many families experience during the predeath period is demonstrated here: a denial of illness by the mother herself; a denial by those around her; a fatal delay in seeking medical attention; a desperate escape to inappropriate activities (such as Vardaman's fishing and Jewel's riding) when the truth becomes too painful to face; and an excessive, therapeutic zeal by those assigned tasks (Cash sawing planks, Dewey Dell fanning her mother). That Addie has mapped out her burial makes the grieving period bearable, though the trip to Jefferson is itself a nightmare. The episode becomes an extended ritual, as satisfying (yet without the life-renewing magic usually granted by ritual) as the funeral singing and preaching was not. Again and again, challenged by hospitable but misjudging outsiders, the family must reassert that together, unbeholden, willing to endure discomfort and even risk death, they are bringing their loved one to the rest she has asked for.

More than perhaps any other crisis, a major death brings out the strongest and weakest elements in the family unit. Festering jealousies and resentments, temporarily controlled, can explode at any time and usually will once the period of respect for the dead is over. Strangers as well as kin can be victimized when passion has been contained too long (such is the case with Jewel on the Jefferson street).

Perhaps Faulkner not only honors Addie for her iconoclasm and forthrightness, but also questions her view of life as preparation for death and her suspicion of words like "love." Perhaps her dying is made easier for her by its being long sought and welcome; but what a bitter life it is that "flashes before her eyes" at its close—a life of hatred, contempt, isolation, and carcinogenic secrets: hating two children because she loves them too much; allotting the other three to their father like bookkeeping entries; needing no words to express her love for the lucky two; emotionally crippling at least Darl to the point of madness by withholding her love from him, as he of all her children needs no words to realize; and giving none of her five children the power to speak their grief at her death.

Outsiders judge her husband harshly, and in truth he is an unappealing figure, functioning under her rule for thirty-odd years, all at once forced to make fateful decisions, yet clinging to her burial wish as if to a living presence. Toothless, unshaven, stooped—whining, wheedling, sly—he is her product as much as their children are. How poor their marriage—for him to be declared dead with her second pregnancy, for him to be ignored for three decades as her eyes ignored him at the end. Cash rightly endorses his father's sprucing up. Outsiders say Addie's reward is being free of Anse. But, as at the end of many marriages misjudged by others, Anse also is free of her. No longer is he a dead man. We can see why he seems a head taller. He deserves a new set of teeth and a new Mrs. Bundren who will not greet his word "love" with contempt.

Questions for Discussion

1. What values can a family derive from the loss of an indispensable member? To what degree do Addie and her loved ones derive those values?
2. How do Addie's character and philosophy determine the way this story unfolds?
3. How would this story have changed if Anse had told his sons not to deliver the load of lumber at the beginning? If Whitfield had arrived before Addie's death? If there had been no storm and no flood?
4. Were the events after the interment justified or unjustified? Queer or understandable? Explain.
5. Faulkner withholds judgment. Do you think there is a right way to prepare for and deal with a death? In what ways do Addie and her family deviate from your standard? In what ways do they think and act as they should, according to your standard?

Annotated Bibliography

Print

Anderson, Sherwood. "Mother," "Death," "Sophistication," and "Departure." In *Winesburg, Ohio*, introd. by Ernest Boyd. New York: Modern Library, 1919.

At age 41, Elizabeth, hiding in a rented hotel room, hopes her son can escape his surroundings and add something beautiful to the world. Slowly dying, she occasionally sparks to life in the office of her doctor, a kindred spirit who moves from sympathy to love. But to elude her gross husband, she sees death as her ultimate lover, for which she hungers in her final months. She talks often with her son, but neither prepares him for her death nor tells him of the money she has hidden for his escape from Winesburg. Paralysis soon increases the agony of her frustration; she becomes mute and unable to tell him. At first he resents her death for spoiling a rendezvous. Death leads him through violent stages of feeling. Then shame grips him, followed by an overwhelming grief. Finally with the acceptance of her death, his boyhood ends. He leaves Winesburg, but it will be the stuff of his art; through him she will be heard and her dream fulfilled.

Bellaman, Henry. *Kings Row*. New York: Simon & Schuster, 1940.

Parris' mother died at his birth, her husband some months later. Therefore, Parris was raised by his grandmother, who arranges her grandson's future without consulting him. The whole town knows she is dying of cancer; but for Parris, immersed in his studies, she and her household feign an aura of health and cheer. Wracked with pain, she somehow always manages a smile and almost survives to his departure for medical school in Vienna. They have only each other, and their love is deep; but she has given Parris no chance to intimately share her dying or say goodbye.

Bellow, Saul. *Mr. Sammler's Planet.* New York: Viking, 1970.

Elya's vast, tainted wealth cannot save him from—and perhaps guarantees—a mean and lonely death, tormented by a vulturelike son and a daughter whose latest sex scandal helped cause Elya's aneurism. She vows vengeance on Uncle Sammler, Elya's brother, for condemning her loud attire and urging her to make peace with her father. Elya has made these children what they are; now he misuses his final hours, still absorbed in the *Wall Street Journal,* still talking stocks with his lawyer. When Sammler visits, the dying man assures him of a financially secure future, but postpones the long-yearned-for conversation about their family roots, which might have comforted him. Sammler returns too late; feigning the need for further tests in order to avoid insincere good-byes, Elya has been wheeled off to die alone. Bursting with sorrow and guilt, Sammler forces his way into the death room and pays the corpse the tribute he did not pay the man.

Cather, Willa. *My Mortal Enemy.* New York: Knopf, 1926.

Nellie comes across an old couple who acted as her hosts ten years ago, when they had a circle of actors and writers. Even then, their marriage was flawed by Myra's jealousy. Now, poor and friendless, they are wracked by Myra's deepening but unmentionable illness. Instead of letting her death serve as a rapprochement, she rages at her husband and her dependency on him. She challenges his recollection of a happy past, accuses him of having torn her from her Church, damns a marriage that disinherited her, and rejects Nellie, her last friend, for daring to defend him. Hatred of her life helps her leave it. Religion provides the impersonal structure and consolation of ritual. In a supreme gesture, she flees and dies unattended at her beloved cliff, facing the sunrise.

Cheever, John. *The Wapshot Scandal.* New York: Harper, 1964.

Honora insists on being as independent and munificent in death as she has been in life. Banishing the friends who want to nurse her and the doctor who wants to operate, she faces death boldly, combating her physical agony with favorite books and hard liquor. She also takes pleasure in Coverly, a younger cousin who has always relished her spirit.

Now he promises to let her die at home and to play host at her post-humous Christmas party. His wife resents attending, as does his brother, who sulks at being torn away from a motel orgy. But for Coverly, the event is a revelation that soothes his solitary mourning: Honora's dinner guests are eight blind people bussed from their communal home. In death, the essence of her life is being sustained and honored.

Dos Passos, John. *Manhattan Transfer.* Boston: Houghton, 1925.

Had Jimmy's overprotective mother not minimized her illness and robbed him of that final intimacy, had his aunt not lied near the end that her sister was out of danger and forbidden him entry into the room, he might be less stunned when her death comes. Now, summoned to Uncle Jeff's ritzy club for lunch, the bereaved lad expects some ritual solace; instead, he is given the cold legalities of his uncle and aunt's powers as guardians and executors. Offered a place in their stiflingly opulent world, Jimmy rejects it in honor of his mother, who long since rejected it. He chooses instead a life that will be true to her free spirit: he will attend not Princeton but Columbia, become a city reporter, and surround himself, as she did, with exciting friends from the real world.

Dreiser, Theodore. "The Lost Phoebe." In *Best Short Stories*, edited by James Farrell. Cleveland: World, 1956.

This story represents the extreme to which an obsessed aloneness can lead a mourning person with no caring network to keep him whole. After 48 years of marriage, Henry loses his wife. Though lukewarmly invited by family and neighbors to resettle and put the past behind him, he remains at home, near her grave, his own life ebbing. Slowly, he loses control of reality. Imagining he sees her one night, Henry convinces himself that a loving ghost can return. Next, he decides she did not die, but merely fulfilled a threat spat out during a quarrel to leave him and hide where he would not find her. This fantasy sustains his eerie, hermitic existence. For seven years, in ever-widening circles that eventually embrace three counties, he pursues her in sun and storm, barely subsisting. One night, seeing her just ahead—not as she looked before she died, but in her early beauty—he reaches a cliff. The long search is over; with joy, he leaps to join her.

Fitzgerald, F. Scott. "Babylon Revisited." In *Taps at Reveille*. New York: Scribner, 1935.

It was understandable that, before dying of a heart attack, Helen would ask her sister, Marion, to serve as Honoria's guardian in the case of Helen's death. Stuffily bourgeois, Marion at least offered stability; whereas Charles, Honoria's father, bankrupt since the stock market crash, sat drying out in a sanatorium. Helen's playmate in the old Paris binges, Charles had been guilty of maddening flirtations and had once locked her out in a blizzard. How could their child be entrusted to him? But now, prosperous again and sober, he wants his daughter. The power lies with Marion, who sees Charles as her sister's murderer. Believing that Helen would have wished her child and husband to be united does not suffice. Months, if not years, of contrition will pass before he can overcome the punishing arrangements made by his dying wife, whose dying is punishment enough.

Kramer, Larry. *The Normal Heart.* New York: New Amer. Lib., 1985.

Stricken with AIDS, Felix angrily implicates Ned, his only homosexual lover. But they remain together through chemo treatments, excruciating experimental drugs, and hospitalizations. As the disease progresses, it is Ned's total solidarity that makes dying bearable. Felix insists on getting his own affairs in order and on helping Ned meet the future without him. To accomplish both goals, he summons Ned's lawyer-brother, Ben, to make Ned his legal beneficiary, thus reconciling the brothers, who had broken on the AIDS issue. He also yearns to bid his son good-bye, but is thwarted by his vengeful ex-wife. At his deathbed, with Ben as witness, a wedding ceremony is performed by Felix's doctor.

Gresham, William Lindsay. *Limbo Tower.* New York: Rinehart, 1949.

At age 24, Ben is dying of tuberculosis. A year ago, the specialists gave him six weeks; his survival amazes them. Clearly, more than physical factors are involved: his fellow patients rally his depressed spirits, and he rallies theirs with a dream of social justice; he expresses himself in poems of increasing power; he loves his nurse and lives for her visits. One night, she lets him kiss her, and he hemorrhages and dies in her arms. But the ferocity of his caring has not only extended and deepened his own life; it has transformed others. He has unlocked the nurse's childhood trauma, freeing her to love a resident doctor, and has inspired that doctor to revise his career. One patient will now dedicate himself to the publication of Ben's poems; another will return to the mines and fight to unionize them, as Ben urged.

Gunther, John. *Death Be Not Proud.* New York: Harper, 1949.

Surgery removes only half of Johnny's brain tumor. Told he will go blind, lose function control, become a vegetable, and die in a couple of months, his divorced parents at first hide the prognosis. Johnny, eager to be back at school preparing for Harvard, accepts harsh tests and treatments with wit and curiosity, corresponds with Einstein, conducts unique experiments, attends the theater, and assists his father on *Inside U.S.A.* The family fuses, indomitable in the face of death. Johnny's mother learns of mustard gas, and his is the first brain on which it is used. A diet treatment they hear of seems to bring remission. After a fourteen-month absence from school, he completes his work and receives an ovation as he walks up the aisle for his diploma. A cerebral hemorrhage brings him a peaceful, fearless, pain-free death—utterly contradicting the specialists' predictions.

March, William. "The Little Wife." In *Fifty Best American Short Stories*, edited by Martha Foley. Boston: Houghton, 1965.

Joe has arranged his itinerary to be home when Bess gives birth. But a month early, a telegram comes from her mother: the doctor does not expect his wife to live through the day and a second telegram will follow if necessary. On the train, Joe is paged three times before accepting the second telegram. Tempted to jump off and escape, he decides instead that the unread message is from his company; therefore, he tears it up and throws it away. Denial revives him. He returns to his seat and maniacally plies the riders with talk of his great wife. Smiling, he greets his mother-in-law, ignoring her dark veil and swollen eyes. Finally, he sobs and admits not reading the second telegram, saying he wanted to keep Bessie alive a bit longer. In fact, it was to keep himself from disintegrating.

O'Connor, Flannery. "Everything That Rises Must Converge." In *Everything That Rises Must Converge*. New York: Farrar, 1956.

High blood pressure requires Julian's mother to attend a weight-reducing class. Accompanying her on the bus, Julian bristles with hate for her archaic manners, her struggle to put him through college, her readiness to keep supporting him, and her memories of a governor grandfather, a landowner father, and a grand house she has not held on to for him. Thinking himself free of her prejudices and of any attachment to her, he rockets her blood pressure with lessons on race relations. In vain, he warns her not to offer a coin to a black boy, whose mother then floors her with a fist. Still he slashes: her world is dead, her graciousness bankrupt. But a lifetime of tenderness withheld and brutality unleashed suddenly reverses itself as he realizes she has suffered a stroke. His love explodes and he wildly seeks help; but it is too late. A future of sorrow and guilt awaits Julian, who has failed to let himself or his ailing mother know the depth of his affection.

Olsen, Tillie. *Tell Me a Riddle*. Philadelphia: Lippincott, 1960.

When Eva takes to her bed, her daughter-in-law, used to years of marital warfare, labels it hostility. Time is lost before metastasis is discovered. Not being told the truth, Eva painfully misuses her remaining time. Ignoring her pleas for home, her husband drags her to visit a far-off daughter, whose children bewilder her, and from there to Los Angeles' sunny coast, which fails to comfort her. From her husband's pitying look, Eva learns she is dying. A granddaughter's tenderness soothes her somewhat, but her children arrive too late for real communication. Neither is there any communication with her husband, aside from Eva's attacking as treason his plan to hospitalize her. At last, torn by terror and love, he drops his old habit of hurling vicious nicknames and calls her Eva, but she is beyond his attempt to reach her.

Porter, Katherine Anne. "Old Mortality." In *Pale Horse, Pale Rider*. New York: Harcourt, 1939.

This is the story of a family that atrophies at the sudden and mysterious death of daughter Amy. Two other girls brought up in this atmosphere are dwarfed by the legend of Amy's supreme qualities. But they are not the only victims. Years later, they meet their mythic cousin, Gabriel, Amy's husband for six weeks, and find him to be a shabby drunkard still mourning for Amy. He compares them unfavorably to her, as he has done to his second wife every hour of their life together. He even chooses burial beside Amy, and it is to that interment one of the girls is riding when she meets Cousin Eva, whose whole life—from childhood on—has been poisoned by Amy's superior looks and ways. The girl rejects as ruinous the romanticizing of Amy and her death; she resolves to live in the present and face events with unvarnished honesty.

Saroyan, William. *The Human Comedy*. New York: Harcourt, 1943.

Since Mr. Macauley's death, his wife has kept their family together and his memory strong. Now their eldest son, Marcus, is shipped overseas. Before going into battle, he sends a long letter expressing his love and hopes for each member of the family and giving instructions for the disposition of his property in case of death. He also tells of an orphaned buddy with whom he has shared them in conversation. Kid brother Homer works in the telegraph office and is present when the telegram comes announcing Marcus' death. Fury and grief overwhelm him. But Marcus' buddy arrives and convinces the distraught boy to withhold the telegram from the family; he is welcomed into the household as a new brother and son. Saroyan offers deception and replacement as viable ways to confront the reality of death.

Steinbeck, John. "The Harness." In *The Long Valley*. New York: Viking, 1938.

Each year, Emma takes sick after Peter's "business week" in town. This year, she fails to recover. Still, she refuses nursing care; Peter does everything. After two months, during which time he hardly eats, she dies. Wild with loss at first, Peter soon admits feeling free. He will discard the harness and belt that hold his shoulders out and stomach in. He will drink, date big-breasted women, track dirt into the house, and plant all 45 of their acres with the fragrant, colorful sweet peas Emma always vetoed. His harvest is a success, but her disapproving voice spoils it. Dying has not loosened her grip. His life and home remain as before, but even dead, memory of her still controls his life. He still must break loose for a business week in town.

Williams, Tennessee. *Cat on a Hot Tin Roof*. New York: New Directions, 1955.

On his sixty-fifth birthday, Big Daddy's sons—Gooper and Brick—know he is dying of cancer; but he, told that he has a spastic colon, feels no need to make a will. Instead, he plans a fling—after 45 years—with a despised wife. What should be a day of tenderness and unity turns into a hate-filled jockeying for position. Gooper, disliked by his father though he has given him grandchildren, already has papers drawn to guarantee his inheritance. Brick, favored though childless, would rather get drunk than satisfy his father's need for a talk. The unwelcome talk so enrages Brick that he blurts out the truth of the prognosis, breaking his parent's spirit. But into this household of greed, subterfuge, and deceit, Brick's wife now introduces the ultimate lie. To sweeten the dying and perhaps win the estate, she announces what Big Daddy has longed to hear: that she is expecting a child.

Film

Beaches. Touchstone Home Video. 1989. 123 min. Bette Midler, Barbara Hershey, John Heard; Garry Marshall, Director.

This is the story of two women friends; CC is a rock star, and Hilary is the mother of a young child and is dying of cancer. During a summer spent together, CC helps Hilary overcome her resentment about dying and gains the affection of Hilary's child. When Hilary nears her end, CC sacrifices her career priorities and rescues Hilary from an impersonal hospital death, for a reunion with her child. After Hilary's death, the child accepts CC as her mother, and CC and the child begin their future with a mutually sustaining love. Key issues here are the care for the needs of the dying and the support survivors must give each other.

An Early Frost. TVM/RCA Columbia. 1985. 100 min. Aidan Quinn, Gena Rowlands, Ben Gazzara; John Erman, Director.

When Michael's pneumonia uncovers AIDS, his lover remains loyal, but Michael expresses his rage by blaming him and throwing him out. His mother and grandmother are supportive, but when he most needs solidarity, his father shuns him and his sister shuts him out to protect her children. During a violent seizure, when the ambulance drivers refuse to touch him, Michael's father rushes him to the hospital, then keeps away. With only a year or two left, his one weapon is hope; however, witnessing the death of others breaks his spirit. Only then do his loved ones come together, as they must (but seldom do) in AIDS cases. His father thwarts his suicide and convinces him to fight hard. His sister apologizes for her behavior. Bolstered by the indispensable embrace of his family, Michael returns to his lover and his work.

Garbo Talks. CBS/Fox Video. 1984. Anne Bancroft, Ron Silver; Sidney Lumet, Director.

Stricken by cancer, a mother clings to her dignity and independence as long as possible, and wistfully tells her son of her one desire to meet Greta Garbo, a lifelong idol. As his mother dies, the son deals with his grief not by expressing it, but in a passionate quest for the elusive star that devours all his time and ingenuity, costing both his wife and his career. Eventually, he finds and persuades Garbo to visit the hospital, where the two women chat about Garbo's glorious past and her admirer's supreme moments at the movie theater. The mother's ecstasy briefly transcends her pain, and the son has the satisfaction of proving his devotion; however, neither confronts his or her feelings any more than does her ex-husband in a silent visit—a failed opportunity to arrive at some understanding of their life together. Garbo, in fact, serves as a *deus ex machina*, granting mother and son a celluloid farewell.

Going in Style. Warner Home Video. 1979. 96 min. George Burns, Art Carney, Lee Strasberg; Martin Brest, Director.

Refusing to "go silent into that good night," three septuagenarians execute a spectacular, rejuvenating bank heist. When one dies, the others are at first frightened of their own mortality, but they dedicate to his memory a wildly defiant Las Vegas spree. When the second dies, the third remains calm; he arranges the funeral, informs the family of its loss, and leaves the money from the bank heist with them. His zest for life increases with each loss, and imprisonment for the robbery makes him even more saucily rebellious. What the trio did was, of course, immoral, and death will, of course, come soon enough to Joe. But they rejected society's perception of the old as already dead and chose to die of exhilaration.

Harry and Son. Orion-Vestron Video. 1985. 117 min. Paul Newman, Joanne Woodward, Robby Benson; Paul Newman, Director.

Ignoring a sight loss that finally endangers others and gets him fired, a widowed demolition worker rejects medical attention. After two years, he still mourns the death of his wife. Refusing her friend's overtures, he wars with his uncaring daughter and devoted son. Eventually, he realizes that dying emotionally with his wife was a loss of precious time. At this hopeful moment, he is struck down by his untreated ailment. The daughter absolves herself of the situation. The son, however, has learned much: he will not repeat Harry's pattern; he will pay his respects to the dead by living and loving.

Mask. MCA Home Video. 1985. 120 min. Cher, Sam Elliott, Eric Stoltz; Peter Bogdanovich, Director.

For twelve years, Rocky and his mother have dealt with both his abnormal head growth (lionitis) and the prognosis of an early death. Thanks to their courage, he has had a good boyhood. Now, undaunted by a prediction of death in three months, he triumphs at a new school, graduates with honors, and finds love at a camp for the blind. When his friend backs out of their planned European lark and his girl's parents keep her from him, his spirit breaks. Sensing the next onslaught of the disease to be fatal, he removes the markers on his map of Europe, draws the shades, and lies down to a private, unwhining death. But the beauty of his life and of his written credo is a legacy that enriches those who knew him and inspires his mother to go on.

Movers and Shakers. MGM/VA Home Video. 1985. 79 min. Walter Matthau, Charles Grodin, Tyne Daly; William Asher, Director.

Joe reveres his dying mentor Saul, whose dream film is an expensive flop. Summoning his disciple, Saul extracts a deathbed vow that Joe will film another doomed project, which bogs down after a huge outlay. Joe remains true to his hero, who died fighting for his dream. A heart attack fells Joe, and death is a distinct possibility; but this experience bestows on him a hitherto elusive story line. Saul's legacy affects others too: the director weds his long-time mistress, and the writer, whose marriage has all but ended, achieves a rapprochement with his wife—this will be the soul of the script he is finally able to complete. A good man's force has proven more powerful in death than in life.

Nothing in Common. HBO Cannon Video. 1986. 118 min. Jackie Gleason, Tom Hanks, Eva Marie Saint; Garry Marshall, Director.

Max loses his wife after 36 years of noncommunication; then his job fails, then his health. His alienated son becomes increasingly concerned and, at the sight of Max's gangrenous feet, drags him to be examined. Immediate surgery is required. When Max's estranged wife visits, they are finally able to discuss the failure of their marriage and to recall the good times. With Max's prognosis uncertain, his son interrupts his career to care for him, unlike his employer, who ruefully recalls being too busy to visit *his* father until the dying man no longer recognized him. Their profession—glib words to sell products—fades; each now has a beloved friend.

Promises in the Dark. Warner Home Video. 1979. 115 min. Marsha Mason, Kathleen Beller, Susan Clark, Ned Beatty; Jerome Hellman, Director.

This is the story of parents paralyzed by shock who love their stricken teenage daughter, Elizabeth, but respect neither her wishes nor her capacity to deal with the truth. They try to keep from her the nature of her ailment, but she insists on knowing and researching it. After a leg is amputated, she feistily returns to school and her friends. The parents, however, are unable to give each other and their child emotional support. The mother, desperately hunting for new treatments, accuses her husband of passivity; yet it is she, not he, who stands motionless when they hear Elizabeth choking. Only with a totally honest, committed doctor can Elizabeth communicate; the doctor pledges not to keep her alive artificially. When she enters an irreversible coma, the parents ignore that wish; but the doctor, her cherished friend, risks career and imprisonment by disconnecting the life-support system.

Six Weeks. RCA/Columbia Pictures Home Video. 1982. 117 min. Dudley Moore, Mary Tyler Moore, Katherine Healey; Tony Bill, Director.

Nicky, a preteen dancer in her third leukemia relapse, refuses further treatment. All her distraught mother can do is cater to the child's every whim. A political candidate is drawn so completely into the situation that he leaves his family and campaign to help realize Nicky's dream: a New York adventure, including a successful *Nutcracker* audition at Lincoln Center. The adults even yield to a "wedding" imposed by the girl. Their contrived fairy tale ends abruptly on the subway, when Nicky's collapse is painful and fatal. The grieving mother is consoled by her child's grateful last note urging her not to mourn. Few parents in this predicament can afford such a final fling, but it is not costly to surround a dying child with love and to fulfill at least a few of her yearnings. Those who survive can take some measure of satisfaction.

Steel Magnolias. Tri-Star Pictures. 1989. 118 min. Sally Field, Julia Roberts, Shirley MacLaine, Olympia Dukakis, Daryl Hanna; Herbert Ross, Director.

The severely diabetic Shelby takes a calculated risk in becoming pregnant. Death does not frighten her; she would rather have the brief joy of motherhood than a long, uneventful existence. Her overprotective mother is terrified, but eventually allows herself to enjoy the prospect of having a grandchild. The medical warnings prove accurate. Childbirth leads to kidney failure. Shelby's mother donates one of her own kidneys but the reprieve is brief. The transplant is rejected and she falls into an irreversible coma. The family agrees to disconnect her life-support system. At the cemetery, the distraught mother lashes out against her cronies' trite phrases of consolation, then unleashes a barrage of rage at her daughter's early death and her own survival. This release, as well as the solidarity of family and friends, helps pull her toward acceptance. She can now appreciate the gift of such a daughter and is even able to laugh again. The need to care for her grandson takes precedence over her paralyzing grief. The pregnant woman whose religious comfort she has attacked most violently names her child Shelby.

Terms of Endearment. Paramount Home Video. 1983. Shirley MacLaine, Debra Winger, Jack Nicholson, Jeff Daniels; James L. Brooks, Director.

A young mother discovers both cancer and her husband's cheating. She fails quickly, and the doctor advises her to settle her affairs. This involves choosing a guardian for her children and coming to terms with family members, especially her mother. Begging her pardon and expressing his love, the husband eases his wife more than morphine can. From the resentful older son, she extracts an admission that he loves her; shedding the role of disciplinarian, she declares her love for him and bids both sons to cherish the father she had excoriated. Her death allows her warring husband and mother to embrace. Having the children subdues their grandmother's agony; even her lover, accepting a long-avoided maturity, moves toward commitment.

Unnatural Causes. TVM/New Star. 1986. 100 min. John Ritter, Alfre Woodard; Lamont Johnson, Director.

Told by an unfeeling doctor that he will soon die of a sarcoma, Vietnam veteran Frank sinks into depression until he recalls an intense chemical barrage by U.S. planes that once hit his unit. His remaining time becomes focused, each hour valuable, as he contacts former buddies, discovering one dead, others sick. He teams up with Maude, a VA claims clerk, who is, despite orders, investigating Agent Orange. They galvanize many vets who are dying bewildered and alone. With his last strength, Frank pressures the media to air a powerful exposé. At the end, he transmits his spirit to a young son and to Maude. Stirred by his example, she intensifies their campaign for his stricken brothers. Purposefulness and a warm partnership have allowed his life to end richly.

5 Sudden and Untimely Death:

James Agee's *A Death in the Family*

By Charles Ansell

It is inherent in the nature of human beings to demand, perhaps unconsciously, that all things new seem familiar before they take hold in our memory. The strange and the sudden disarm us, and thus we either deny their existence or we struggle against their claims. Whether forecasting pleasure or pain, the news of a sudden or strange incident is barely credible. But when a new event enters our lives to become a cause of grief, the familiar proves to have great appeal. Sudden changes paint the past in glowing colors.

The Paradigm

The sudden death of a beloved family member is devastating. It crashes down on the mourners with the force of a shock that quickly disintegrates all normal defenses against sudden disaster. It puts to trial all of our inner resources we need in moments of sudden crisis.

A Death in the Family is a searing narrative of the sudden death of a beloved family man that forces those closest to him—a young widow, two young children, and several adult relatives—to look into themselves for strength and an understanding of the enigma of order in the universe. Each of the principal characters struggles through the early hours of their grief in curiously different ways. Even the children's struggle to encompass the sudden tragedy is painfully portrayed.

Summary

Simply put, James Agee's story *A Death in the Family* (Bantam Books, 1971) is a classic tale that vividly traces the hour-by-hour effects of sudden death on a young family. The story, for all of its 339 pages, is simple. Jay Follet, barely 36 years old, is awakened in the middle of the night by a long-distance phone call from his brother, who implores him to rush to his dying father's bedside. Mary, Jay's wife, awakes and joins him in the kitchen to prepare his breakfast for the long car journey ahead. In the simple scene of Jay and Mary in the kitchen, each concerned over the other, Agee builds scenes of surpassing tenderness. They speak of their children fast asleep in their beds; they speak of family; and in their predawn whispers, we are enveloped in the warmth of a husband and his wife whose lives together have forged a bond of the deepest affection between them and their children.

On his return trip home, anxious to keep his promise to be with the children at supper that evening, Jay feels his 1915 tin lizzie careen out of control when the cotter pin that controls the steering wheel drops from the car. Despite his futile effort to regain control, the car springs forward and rolls down an embankment. He is fatally struck by the steering wheel and perishes in an instant from a massive concussion.

The narrative is set in Knoxville, Tennessee, in 1915. It was a time that celebrated the simple virtues of family life, the openness of neighbors to one another. Models of masculine deportment and feminine devotion were available to the young. Engagements and marriages were festive occasions for an entire community. And deaths were solemn. Grief did not dissipate quickly, most certainly for one so young and so promising as Jay Follet.

Jay Follet left a family of three—his wife and two children, six-year-old Rufus and three-year-old Catherine. The author leads us on a journey through the labyrinth of Mary's grief-stricken mind. She is a devout Catholic and kneels in prayer, frantically asking her Lord to explain her husband's death. For brief moments, she falters in her devotion, flooded by doubt and disbelief, only to be later swept up by massive waves of guilt, which then drive her to pray even more fervently.

Agee portrays the confusion and the mystery that Rufus finds in the sudden death of his father. In the opening scene of the narrative, there is a touching account of a summer evening with his father. They had gone to the movies together to see Charlie Chaplin. Later, they walked down familiar streets, but on the way home his father stopped at a saloon to "hoist me a couple." In the saloon, he lifted Rufus up to sit on the bar, then turned proudly to the man next to him: "That's my boy." Later, they sat silently on a knoll in the darkness, father and son, in a scene filled with a child's awe at a father who had earlier boasted of him, his son. The boy sensed a warming joy at his closeness to a protecting father.

How can a six-year-old handle the news of his father's sudden death? He is ordered to stay home from school that first morning, but he ventures out in the streets and walks aimlessly this way and that. He comes upon older boys he recognizes from school. When they ask him why he does not hurry to get to class, he says, "My father's dead"; then he looks at the older boys for signs that might help him to understand its meaning. They disbelieve him until another boy comes on the scene and verifies Rufus' announcement. It was in the papers that morning. For a moment, Rufus is proud because one of the boys says he is now an orphan; now they will not tease him as they always have about his name, Rufus.

The stark meaning of death is slow to come to children. At the news that God has taken his father to heaven, the boy is mystified. God is kind, and he will let his father come back to take up his life with his family. The reality of his father's loss does not come to the child within the few days of the narrative. Even when he is brought to the parlor to see his father in the casket, the reality of his father lying so still strikes Rufus as strange. The talk among the adult members of the family that swirls around him is heard as snatches of disconnected conversation.

Rufus' sister, Catherine, is even less aware of any meaning in her father's death. Her mother has reached out to her children to hold them tightly to her. Little Catherine has seen and heard her mother's sobs, and she is frightened. Relatives fill the house and talk quietly among themselves, but she flees from the adults and hides under a bed; unaware of her fears, she wets herself in daylight. She is cross and impatient with her brother. Most of all, she is frightened by her mother's grief.

The sudden loss of a beloved family member touches all of the adults, each in different ways. For instance, Mary's father and uncle are quietly angry at Mary's God, of whom she now asks forgiveness. The suddenness of the tragedy, the insanity of the accident, leave the men bitter at the thought of God's plan. They voice their anger quietly, out of Mary's hearing. However, their anger finally explodes at the performance of the priest who is called to officiate at the funeral. He cannot and will not perform the Catholic rites of burial because the deceased was not baptized. Mary implores the priest to give her husband the full rites of the Church. He was an honorable man, God fearing, kind, and loving; he deserved a proper burial. But the priest remains adamant. Mary's grief is made even more painful at this denial of grace to a good man.

Each member of Mary's family—father, mother, Uncle Andrew, and Aunt Hannah—is portrayed as a distinct individual in the way each feels, thinks, and talks of Jay's sudden death. Agee presents them with surprising perception. For example, Uncle Andrew, devoted to Mary and deeply involved with her bereavement, will not speak of his religious cynicism to her, but as he observes her crying out to God, even asking for his forgiveness for her doubts, he rages silently.

Each character in this gripping tale of grief appears to stand in the distinctive roles and attitudes toward death that have become familiar to us in the work of Elisabeth Kubler-Ross. Each member of the family responds characteristically. Uncle Andrew's anger is seen in his bitterness toward Mary's God, who could plan Jay's sudden death, yet a lurking need to find mystery in the universe persists. At the grave site, he sees a monarch butterfly come to rest on the lid of the coffin. In the momentary magic of the butterfly's stillness, the sky opens to release a shaft of rare sunlight to shine down on the butterfly atop the casket; in another instant, the butterfly gracefully flies upward into the light on its ascent into heaven.

Mary's father finds strength in his denial of the meaning of death. He moves through the days of bereavement, a pillar of strength. He secretly denies Mary's childlike faith in a senseless God. Mary's mother's deafness removes her from the talk that swirls around her, but one senses that her deafness is somehow worsened in these hours, perhaps in an effort to protect herself from a great sadness.

Aunt Hannah, a spinster, takes over Mary's role as mother and housekeeper. Aunt Hannah's role is etched with radiance. Her strength and her depth of compassion are displayed with the silence and wisdom of a modern saint. Yet we are not privy to her thoughts. We are asked to view her only from her place in the lives of Mary and her children. Aunt Hannah's behavior is carefully drawn by the author, as if to portray the most human of the various responses we turn to at the moment of death. Aunt Hannah reveals her own lifelong familiarity with sadness by linking herself fully and easily to Mary's crushing grief. She becomes eyes and ears, arms and legs for the suddenly helpless widow. She moves quietly and efficiently through the tragedy's early hours with the grief-stricken widow and her children. It is as if she finds comfort in standing at the widow's side to serve her, to protect her from further woes.

Mary's shock has traumatized both children. They move through the early hours of their father's death in a storm of bewilderment. Except for Aunt Hannah, the adults appear to be unmindful of the special grief of children. One is left to wonder whether this strange detachment from the children's fright is an unconscious projection of the adults' own denial, as if in their silence the children will learn to share their denial.

Beneath Agee's vivid character portrayals of family members drawn together to share the burden of grief, he leads us to witness the unique meaning of death each family member reveals in the early hours of the sudden tragedy. Mary's father and Uncle Andrew grow suddenly rational, sensible men who dismiss any talk of God's plan. Yet they are puzzled at the senseless cruelty of man's fate in the universe; their good sense and their skepticism give them no comfort. The alternative of believing, as

Mary does, that striking a man down at the start of his life is part of God's plan seems like dangerous folly. And so we are left to wonder about Mary's father and Uncle Andrew, to wonder with them at the meaning or even the necessity of faith.

Overriding each page of *A Death in the Family* is the saving grace of affection that infuses each encounter among the members of the family. One is tempted to believe that Agee has used the tragedy of death to teach us about human relationships, for in a life glowing with love given and love received, death is softened by the comfort of loving hands and loving hearts.

Even at the depth of our grief, we are sustained by memories of the love we knew and by the love we know will sustain us in the months and years ahead. Agee has spread a large table for us to feast upon. For the believer in God's plan, there is momentary comfort; for the nonbeliever, there is the gnawing need to find order in the universe; for the Aunt Hannahs, there is mainly the here and the now, a void that must be filled with loving deeds, lest the void empty us of all meaning. Aunt Hannah is not moved by either God's wisdom or the fortuitous ways of life for which no explanations exist. The Aunt Hannahs of our world know only the deep pain that the suddenly bereaved suffers, and knowing this they move quietly and directly to the heart of the pain to bring assurance to the sufferer that she is not alone in the universe.

Questions for Discussion

1. How can the death of a father be explained to a six-year-old? To a three-year-old?
2. How well does Mary handle the task of telling the children of the tragedy?
3. Would you comfort a religious widow in bereavement with the thought that her husband's death was in God's plan?
4. What comforts the nonbeliever in this story?
5. How would you assess Aunt Hannah's place in Mary's grief?
6. Each member of the family in this work was carefully chosen by the author to represent or symbolize a special statement. Explain each character in general terms.

Annotated Bibliography

Print

Baldwin, James. *Just above My Head.* New York: Dial, 1980.

Grief over the unexpected death of a beloved brother is here compounded by the wider experience of blacks in American society. The author narrates the story of a young man deeply devoted to a talented older brother who comes to a violent death, largely (one suspects) because of his homosexuality and the color of his skin. The story turns into a protracted dirge of grief at the tragic outcome of life for many talented blacks who die ignobly—murdered, lost to insanity, or, too often, lost to drugs. Black grief, the author implies, is not only the personal suffering the young man felt at the death of his brother; his grief is best understood as a general grief over the harm to black people in American life.

Gardner, John. "Redemption." In *The Best American Short Stories*, edited by Ted Solotaroff. Boston: Houghton, 1978.

This is the grim story of a farm family that turns away from its grief at the death of an eight-year-old son who is killed accidentally by his twelve-year-old brother. The father turns to a deep silence, then leaves his family, saying nothing to his wife and children. The father's leaving leads the remaining family to deny their grief in an imitated silence. The twelve-year-old son is left to run the farm alone. The boy, unable to find a willing ear in his mother or sister, grows obsessed with thoughts of suicide. Months later, the father returns and begs his wife's and children's forgiveness; however, the twelve-year-old is deaf to his father's pleas. He walks away from his father, whispering his hatred at his abandonment and at the cruelty of leaving him to suffer his guilt over the tragic accident. The story's title is a mockery of the father's effort to find redemption by his return to his family.

Gertler, T. "In Case of Survival." In *The Best American Short Stories*, edited by Stanley Elkin. Boston: Houghton, 1980.

That unearned guilt can cause grief among the innocent is here portrayed in an engaging tale that borders on the mystical. A man about to board a plane is seized with a sudden premonition that the plane will crash. Standing on the jetway ready to enter the cabin, he seizes his wife at the elbow and orders her to follow him off the plane. The plane crashes. There are no survivors. The man thereupon falls into agitated guilt that cannot be quieted. It soon numbs him against the crises his grown daughters face daily in their lives. He is deaf to his wife's appeals to talk with her about their daughters' problems. The reader soon senses that his guilt over the death of strangers is actually guilt displaced from his unwillingness to deal with his daughters' problems.

Malinchak, MaryAnn Mishel. "Status." In *The Best American Short Stories*, edited by Ted Solotaroff. Boston: Houghton, 1978.

The sudden death of his wife leaves the protagonist, a simple man, lost to the world; he had grown to depend on her for cues and directions in his relation to people. Childless and alone and only recently retired from the fire department, the widower moves through his days, a lost and lonely child. In the months following the death of his wife, he spends long hours at her grave pursuing the simple fantasy of restoring her to life by cleaning the ground at her grave site. In time, family and friends call on him to do minor repairs in their homes to occupy his time. Though he is invited for occasional meals, he moves through his days heavily, draped in brooding silence, unable even to display outward grief.

McCullers, Carson. *The Heart Is a Lonely Hunter*. Boston: Houghton, 1940.

A lonely deaf-mute befriends a feeble-minded neighbor. They are inseparable in the limited life they make together. Eventually, the feeble-minded man grows troublesome, and he is removed to a mental institution. The deaf-mute rents a room in a home near the institution to visit his only friend. Here, he finds new friends, each in need of the tenderness and understanding that the deaf-mute offers easily. But his visits to his feeble-minded friend are his primary tasks in life. When his feeble-minded friend suddenly dies, the deaf-mute takes his own life. There is a purity in this portrayal of two simple people who have grown so attached to each other that one cannot survive without the other. The felt grief is portrayed starkly; it is the terror of the abandoned infant.

O'Brien, Tim. "The Things They Carried." In *The Things They Carried*. Boston: Houghton, 1990.

The title of this grim account of a group of American soldiers in Vietnam symbolizes the weighty things each soldier carries within himself. The author also methodically describes, pound for pound, what each soldier physically carries into battle. The list is agonizingly long. The 22-year-old protagonist, First Lieutenant Jimmy Cross, carries photographs and letters from his hometown sweetheart, Martha. As Jimmy trudges through the rice paddies of Vietnam, Martha takes on a mystical quality—part fantasy, part real. When one member of this closely knit unit of soldiers is suddenly killed, each soldier in the unit is strangely changed. With one mind, they enter a village and burn everything, shooting chickens and dogs as they trash the village. Alone that night, Jimmy digs a deep hole, where he sits and sobs wildly, then burns Martha's photographs and letters. The following morning, he is changed. He has become a human war machine—correct, distant, and unfeeling.

Price, Reynolds. *The Tongues of Angels*. New York: Atheneum, 1990.

The sudden death of a fourteen-year-old boy at summer camp leads his counselor, a twenty-one-year-old man, to cloak his grief behind a veil of mysticism when he blames himself for the young boy's death. (The boy was fatally bitten by a timber rattler while on a hike to a mountain top, where both the counselor and camper planned to celebrate Indian rites.) The counselor, the narrator of the novel, turns his shock and grief at the boy's quick death into a morbid obsession with the meaning of responsibility for another's life. "This is about a death I may have caused" is the haunting refrain uttered throughout the story.

Price, Reynolds. "The Final Mother. A Short Story." *New Yorker*, May 21, 1990.

A twelve-year-old boy is called home from his classes to learn that his mother died suddenly. The shock strangely quiets the boy into a confusion over how to respond to the loss of a mother who only hours earlier kissed him as he went off to school. When his father rushes home, his anguish increases. He is conflicted between affecting a grown-up stance at his mother's death or yielding to the frightened child who is suddenly abandoned by his mother. The death of his mother is a trauma that forces this twelve-year-old only-child to turn to one of two grim options: act grown up and check his grief or yield to the loss by reverting to an earlier age and suffering the fright of sudden abandonment.

Rossner, Judith. *August*. Boston: Houghton, 1983.

The month of August becomes the symbol of separation for people under psychoanalysis. For some patients, the month-long vacation period is the symbol of death in life. The principal character, a young woman undergoing psychoanalysis, faces the prospect of the month-long separation from her analyst as a replay of the death of her parents during her infancy. The grief that was denied her as an infant haunts her later years. She turns to her analyst as a substitute parent. August, the month of separation, inevitably stirs the repressed grief into life. Grief, like a dormant virus, strikes us at our most vulnerable moments.

Saperstein, Alan. *Mom Kills Kids and Self*. New York: Macmillan, 1979.

In this brief tale, we witness the protagonist's profound state of shock and denial of death. This normal man, a hard-working husband and father to six children, comes home after his day of work to find his wife and six children brutally slain in an act of murder and suicide. The sight of his family strewn about his house numbs him against so grim a reality. He is without apparent feeling. We see here how massive shock mercifully delays grief. The instinct for survival seems to numb us against catastrophe.

Styron, William. *Lie Down in Darkness*. New York: Random, 1979.

A young woman dies suddenly. The father is depicted standing alone on a dock in a port city awaiting the shipment of his daughter's body, to be interred later that day. He waits silently amid the noise of freighters unloading. He hears the shouts of workmen, who are oblivious to his purpose in standing at the center of a world busy at its work. Grief demands the whole world to be quiet for even a moment as a solace to the mourner, if only as a recognition that he once lived among them and will be remembered. The dread of anonymity haunts his grief.

Wolterstorff, Nicholas. *Lament for a Son*. Grand Rapids, Mich.: Eerdmans, 1987.

The death of his 25-year-old son in a mountain-climbing accident leads a father into a soul-searing search for meaning in the tragic death. The result is an outpouring of grief and anguish too difficult to overcome. His search brings him to friends and professional comforters, clergymen, and philosophers, who strike him as hollow and meaningless in the face of his cherished son's death. The father concludes from his long night of meditation on death that death seen naked of all illusion is physical, a final act. In the end, death is the enemy. Thus, he emerges from his thoughts, his grief tamed by the vacuity of well-meaning friends and colleagues. The father's search for meaning seems to be a euphemism for the grief he sought to avoid, lest succumbing to grief would be too disastrous for him. The reader is left to wonder whether his overworked rational struggle against grief can truly circumvent the pain of his loss.

Film

The Accidental Tourist. Warner Bros. 1989. 121 min.

This haunting film tells the story of a man whose only child, a ten-year-old boy, is tragically killed, an innocent victim of a neighborhood robbery. The father denies his grief by becoming emotionally numb, yet the child's death hovers over the two-hour film as an invisible presence. His marriage quietly erodes, but he remains indifferent. He slowly turns inward and moves through life, a zombie. The outside world is kept at a cold distance. He is at last returned to the world through the love of a remarkable woman.

Ordinary People. Paramount Pictures Home Video. 1980. 124 min.

The accidental death of an older brother in a boating accident quietly transforms the remaining family—mother, father, and younger brother—into brooding islands of silence. The mother becomes grim. Her speech is crisp; she moves through her days mirthless and cold to her husband and her son. The younger son, who survived the fatal boating accident, is isolated from his parents. He is helpless against his own guilt and against his mother's distance. His father's feeble efforts to deny grief by faking small talk become painfully transparent to the boy. No one, it appears, is permitted to speak of the tragedy, as if to speak of it would force words of blame and guilt better left unsaid. But it is an impossible state. The inevitable collapse of this charade of denial comes crashing down on mother, father, and son in the final scenes.

Pete 'N Tillie. Universal Pictures. 1972. 100 min.

Pete and Tillie marry after leading carefree lives as singles. They are gentle, loving people for whom marriage and family seem remote from their accustomed lives as independent adults. To their surprise, they have a child who quickly wins their hearts. The child, a bright and talented son, wakens them to the joys of parenting. However, their child falls ill when he is twelve years old and dies. His death stuns Pete and Tillie into crazy bouts of rage and deep mourning. Tillie's grief reaches a dramatic climax in a terrifying scene in which she curses her God for the death of her only child. Her grief has the terror of a Greek chorus in wild lamentations.

Sayonara. Warner Bros. 1957. 147 min.

The suicides of an American soldier and his Japanese betrothed seem incidental to the larger purpose of this film. The central character, played by Marlon Brando, is severely shaken by the tragic suicide of his friend, a victim of racial prejudice against his friend's Japanese wife-to-be. The grief the young officer feels leads to a revulsion of the army's racism. He turns his back on a promising career in the army and breaks his engagement to the general's daughter.

The Scoundrel. Ben Hecht and Charles MacArthur. 1935. 75 min.

This classic film is a parable on the meaning of redemption. The central character is despicable, thoroughly evil. He betrays a lovely young woman into believing he will marry her, but later tells her casually that he is flying to a distant city to marry another woman. The young woman is devastated and cries, "I hope the plane crashes!" The cursed plane does crash and the evildoer perishes, but in the magic of the parable he is ordered to return to earth to find someone who will weep for him. He calls on the young woman whom he betrayed, but she is betrothed to a young man who knows of her betrayal. At the sight of the betrayer, the young man shoots him, then kills himself. Redemption at last comes to the evil man in his prayer that the Lord take his life instead of the innocent young man. His prayer is answered, at which the young woman weeps for her former lover.

6 Suicide:
Willa Cather's "Paul's Case"

By Owen E. Heninger

Human self-destruction or suicide is pervasive through all but the earliest stages of life. It is of great concern because it stops the victim's development and emotionally tarnishes the survivors. Those closely associated with a suicide usually suffer profound and often deleterious effects on their own development. They may be left feeling disgraced or marked. When one thinks of all the causes of death—natural, accidental, suicidal, and homocidal—suicide is the most difficult to understand. Suicide, in real life, usually triggers a strong urge to find the motives behind such a life-confounding act. After suicide, the dominant question is Why? Literature deals with suicide by exploring and illuminating both its motivation and the context in which it occurs.

The Paradigm

"Paul's Case" (in *Youth and the Bright Medusa*, Vintage, 1920), a short story written by Willa Cather in 1904, is an example of literature that details some of the many psychological and interpersonal forces that may lead a person to suicide. It is an apt illustration of how literature can add to the understanding of the otherwise inexplicable act of self-sought death. With its revelations of the human mind, this story makes the motivations of a suicide discernible to the reader. It conveys the state of Paul's mental perturbation and the lethality of his intent in a way that any interested reader can comprehend. This story, through illuminating Paul's life and the causes of his suicide, can be generalized to apply to many cases of suicide.

Through her fealty to human thought and behavior, Cather would have us learn that the motivations for suicide can be understood. By giving us insight into the pressures on the suicidal person and the motivation behind suicide, by extending our experience and adding to our knowledge, the writer enlarges our capacity to empathize with the suicidal person. From this, we can see that there are things we can do for a person at risk that will lessen the threat of suicide. By gaining more understanding of the motivations leading to suicide, we are better prepared to help prevent it.

There are many ways of treating the topic of suicide. The protagonists of literary works on suicide cut across many avenues of endeavor—from sailor to professor, from convict to lawyer. The developmental age groups represented stretch from early adolescence to late middle-age. Though the social and interpersonal stresses as motives for suicide are featured in fiction dealing with suicide, there are many other notable motivating forces mentioned. Some of these deal with the biological forces of heredity: drug or alcohol addiction, epilepsy, mutism, deafness, and anemia; some deal with psychological malfunctioning: paranoid disorder, melancholia, stress reaction, post-traumatic stress disorder, hysteria, and depression. But whatever motivations an author attributes to a suicide, its occurrence has a powerful effect on anyone close to it, and its influence can last through many years.

Summary

"Paul's Case" depicts the terminal events and disruption of interpersonal relationships that lead up to one particular suicide—frail adolescent Paul's. He is misunderstood both by his teachers and by his only parent. He demonstrates his problems more in his behavior than in his speech. When he is expelled from school and shut out from the theater, his only source of happiness, he reacts by stealing a large sum of money. He uses the money to have a brief, glorious spree in New York City. As his revels end, as his funds run out and he is on the verge of being caught, he escapes by self-destruction. This story offers the reader an up-close look at the individual, family, and school dynamics that play such an important part in Paul's strange behavior and suicide. It is a warning story, a cautionary tale especially for parents and teachers.

When we are introduced to Paul, he is in trouble at school because of "misdemeanors." His father does not understand him and is rigid in his discipline. The school blindly uses its powers of coercion and expels Paul, as if that would—in and of itself—bring about the wished for improvement in his ways. As Paul is described, we realize that he is no ordinary lamb of a boy to be chased through the academic pastures by the barking and nipping of faculty sheep dogs. Not all of his teachers agree on the methods of discipline to be used against him, but the majority wins out for its brand of punishment. When we see behind Paul's facade as he sleeps, we can begin to fathom the insecurity behind his world of make-believe. He wears a red carnation as an attention-getting device that represents both his lust for life and the fragility of his *carpe diem* existence.

When Paul works at the music hall as an usher, he enters a fantasy and escapist world. On these occasions, we get a good look at the mainstay of his life, his whole reason for living. He is able to vicariously experience the glitter of fame and greatness through his imagination. His peers have no understanding of the inordinate hunger for attention that motivates Paul's boastful stories as he teases and plagues them. We witness Paul's encounters with the ordinary reality of home and school and see him retreat from it into his fantasy world of enchantment and vicarious celebrity. There is little emotional support or recognition for him at home from his single-parent father, and we find out that he has no memories of his absent mother.

When Paul's father forces him back to reality by taking him out of school, having him shut out of the theater, and barring association with his favorite actor and his juvenile idol, Paul escapes by thinking about death. His main goal is to become important and celebrated like his artist idol, but he uses inadequate methods to achieve that goal. Having experienced only the immediate gratification of magical thinking, he lacks the drive and capacity to work toward an artistic career.

The reader is let in on the root cause of Paul's condition: There was a lack of "good enough" early nurturing from his absent mother (symbolized by his narrow chest and his inability to remember his mother). Subsequently, he has a voracious hunger—for love, for recognition as someone special, for attention—that is not adequately met by his father or teachers. Parental deprivation is painfully obvious from the description of his bedroom. From his mother, he received a stitched motto, "Feed My Lambs," an inscription rather than real nurturing; from his father, pictures of models, George Washington, and John Calvin, rather than support appropriate to his interests and temperament. To feel significant and fill this deficiency left by his early life, Paul allows his imagination to dominate his sense of reality; he feels important when he vicariously experiences the theater and theatrical idols.

Paul's father restricts his access to his "bone," the lustrous places, trappings, and very means that Paul uses to facilitate his vicarious existence, the very things that support and make life worth living for him. Without that medium as a psychological supporting structure, hollow as it is, Paul is threatened with turning to mush.

Stymied by his father's putting him to work, Paul desperately seeks other means to sustain and support his frail self-image and regain his feeling of significance. He strains mightily to make a new world for himself by using his devices of pretense, imagination, and mingling with people and places he deems important. With boastful pretension and stolen money, he enters New York City, purchases admirable attire, and rents prestigious rooms at a grand hotel. This gives the reader yet another look at Paul's *modus operandi*. We see the temporary return of his feelings of aggrandizement with his reentry into his world of make-believe, where he can feel important and insulated from the world of reality.

Paul reaches the end of his temporal resources of money and time. He is about to be apprehended, taken back to Pittsburgh, and forced to face the real world. His usual techniques of fantasy and significance by association fail him, and he desperately resorts to another kind of escape—he commits suicide by throwing himself before an onrushing train.

There are many connotations to the story title's "Case." If we think of it as a physician's clinical case study, it has dimensions that are uncommonly detailed and memorable. If we see it as the report of a school psychologist, it shows an unusually broad view of the forces that influence one student's failure in school. If we look at it as a social worker's report, it gives valuable social information, helping us appreciate more of the factors that motivate Paul's behavior. If we consider it a coroner's case, it bespeaks astute and conscientious investigation, un-earthing and linking up the clues given here to present an accurate picture of why and how Paul's death happened. If we view it as literature, this "Case" allows us to see and follow the story of a peculiar person, Paul. With any or all of these connotations of "Case" in mind, we can view, appreciate, and gain more insight into the real world of a suicide and the real motives behind such an act.

On analysis, we see that Paul's problems stem from his ways of thinking and relating to others. Like a child, he is egocentric in his thinking and overvalues himself as the center of the world. With this handicap, he cannot bridge the gap between the make-believe world of childhood and the real world of adulthood. His interpersonal relations suffer. His relationship with his father is awful, strained and cold. The fear he has of his father, who he thinks might want him dead (note the incident of hiding in the basement), effectively blocks any help he might get from him. The father ignores Paul's mother's admonition to "Feed My Lambs" in his attitude toward Paul. He makes no effort to understand that Paul craves attention and has not been able to progress past an egocentric, puerile way of thinking. This leads to the unresolved conflict between them. Many children get some emotional support from their memories of important people in their lives. We learn that not only is Paul's mother gone, but he does not even remember her. He has sisters, but they just exist to Paul; he has no emotional closeness with them. He is left to his own devices to gain a feeling of significance.

Looking at Paul's connections with his teachers, we again see the stressful, detached relationships that follow their failure to understand his need for attention and his way of thinking. The exasperation and frustration of his teachers over this failure is well indicated. Then, too, Paul's braggadocio alienates him from his peers. Though Paul needs help and understanding, he remains isolated from all those who might otherwise assist him. He is confronted with the tasks of growing up in reality, but unfortunately meets these tasks with inept attention-getting devices, with arrogance, pretense, and simulation that hinder his getting the support he so desperately requires.

Paul is not able to establish a real identity for or of himself. Instead, he loses himself in a pretend world symbolized by pictures of Paris streets and an "airy blue Venetian scene or two," where he obtains all his pleasure. He has no real intimacy with anyone and is dependent on his imagination for all gratification and cheer. His preoccupation with getting attention and his fanciful thinking, as the mainstays of his life, lead to his undoing. When we look to the chimera of the false show, we see he lives in a fool's paradise and is misled by his own self-deception. He has no real way of supporting himself either materially or spiritually. When his fancy wrought bubble bursts and he is faced with reality, he has no effective coping means.

Behind a facade of insolence and defiance, Paul is an insecure, frightened, and defensive adolescent. At a time when Paul falls asleep in class, his drawing master notes the unhappiness and tension behind the "forced animation of his eyes," and sees his "drawn and wrinkled" face in sleep, his lips twitching. We also witness his fear of his father when he spends a terrified night in the basement rather than being accosted by his father upon coming home late. Because of his early deprivation and his present lack of interpersonal support, Paul lags behind his peers in that he still has an uncommonly intense hunger for attention and he still thinks magically, like a younger child. He is bewitched by his own fancy and relies mostly on his imagination for any pleasure in life. He is capable of reveling in a sensational spree by mingling with the trappings of wealth and fame, but is incapable of thinking through to where the spree will lead him. After this brief burst of glory, he cannot face the consequences of his actions and perishes like a hothouse flower (the carnation he wears), exposed to the elements, the snow on the side of the train track.

This short story guides the reader in a cautionary manner. It sheds light on the pitfalls of adolescence, particularly those connected to a lag in the development of the cognitive faculties of awareness and judgment. By implication, it shows that an absence of good early nurturing and compassion by parents, teachers, and peers can further the self-destructive course of a person suffering from a delay of such development. It stimulates the reader to think of what might have been done to prevent such a tragic outcome. This story expands the reader's experience and gives insight into the real world of human relationships. It fosters a better understanding of ourselves and others. It elucidates some of the many motives for suicide and leaves the reader to speculate about the aftermath.

Questions for Discussion

1. What are the defects in Paul's mode of thinking?
2. What clues suggest that Paul is headed for self-destruction?
3. What motivates Paul's suicide?
4. Do you think anything could have been done to prevent Paul's suicide? When? What? By whom?
5. Would anyone in the story feel guilty after Paul's suicide?

Annotated Bibliography

Print

Algren, Nelson. *The Man with the Golden Arm*. Garden City, N.Y.: Doubleday, 1950.

The protagonist has a Purple Heart and an addiction to morphine when he returns from World War II. Because of his rapid reflexes with pool cues, dice, and drumsticks and because he injects drugs into his arm, he is known as the man with the golden arm. On the verge of being arrested for a killing, he hangs himself. By giving the reader a view of a side of life many do not experience, this story shows factors that can motivate suicide, including an unresolved war experience, alcohol use, drug addiction, marital discord, and the threat of loss of freedom. Taken as a cautionary tale, it gives literary guidance to the reader on what to avoid and how to recognize a person at risk.

Barth, John. *The Floating Opera*. New York: Doubleday, 1985.

This novel concerns a 50-year-old man who relives the day, ten years before, when he had seriously contemplated suicide. When he retraces that day, he fills in many of the important events of his life, including events of his childhood, student days, and his professional life as a lawyer. By telling a story from a certain point in time, this novel aptly shows that there are sensible alternatives to suicide. The reader is led to see the many other possibilities, even though one might be at the point where suicide seems the only solution to a problem.

Dreiser, Theodore. *Sister Carrie.* 1901. Reprint. Columbus, Ohio: Merrill, 1969.

Naive Carrie becomes one man's mistress, then falls in love with another man and elopes with him. She develops while her mate declines to poverty. She goes on the stage to support them both, then deserts him to become a star. He sinks to beggarhood and commits suicide. Carrie can be contrasted with the important men in her life. Even though she is not happy, she does not choose self-destruction. The reader is shown how a plethora of life's problems can be met without resorting to suicide.

Hoffman, Alice. *The Drowning Season.* New York: Dutton, 1979.

In this novel, a grandmother rules her clannish family living in a secluded compound on Long Island, New York. Every July and August, her son tries to kill himself by walking into the water. This time of year has become known as the drowning season. His daughter, at age eighteen, is exploring her first chance to flee from her hated and hating grand-mother and the confining world of the compound. The reader can see how the yearly suicide attempts can be compared with the daughter's less drastic means of escape. This story shows other motives for suicide and different methods of coping with oppression.

Humphrey, William. *Hostages to Fortune.* New York: Doubleday, 1984.

When a haggard 50-year-old man reappears after three years' absence from his club, he describes to his friends his and another family's situation. Both were favored by love, friendship, and parenthood, and within months both were ravaged by suicide. He tells of the disgrace and guilt that engulf parents whose child commits suicide. The aftermath of suicide is clearly delineated in this novel. The reader will be able to view two families' methods of coping and consider how he or she might deal with such traumatic events.

Inge, William. *Dark at the Top of the Stairs.* In *Four Plays.* New York: Grove, 1950.

When his business suffers, a man leaves his wife for another woman. As a result, his ten-year-old son becomes afraid of a dark stairwell, which represents the unknown, and sleeps beside his mother. His daughter withdraws from the family. When the daughter's date commits suicide, the father comes back and admits that he too has been afraid of the dark, which represents his fear of not being able to make a living for his family. The family reunites to face the future together. Here, suicide sets off a reaction in a disintegrating family that actually brings it together and strengthens it. The play also demonstrates how the unresolved darkness of the human condition can be met.

London, Jack. *Martin Eden*. 1909. Reprint. New York: Macmillan, 1957.

A sailor educates himself to be part of the wealthy middle class. His girlfriend inspires him to become a writer, then—believing him to be a loser—deserts him. He becomes wealthy, but is shocked when one of his idols commits suicide. When he realizes that he has lost affiliation with his own class and that he is held in contempt by the class he has climbed into, he jumps from a ship and drowns. The impact of distressing interpersonal relationships is highlighted in this novel. The reader becomes aware of how both failed class aspiration and idol imitation can be motives for suicide.

McCullers, Carson. *The Heart Is a Lonely Hunter*. Boston: Houghton, 1950.

An intelligent and sympathetic deaf-mute is saddened when his only friend, another mute, is committed to an institution. He lives only to visit his friend, even though he gets a reputation for understanding people and becomes an important though enigmatic person in the town. People come to tell him their secret thoughts. When his friend dies, he feels alone, detached, and unsupported. He commits suicide, and his admirers sense a loss of the tranquility and understanding that he had bestowed. This novel shows how the loss of a significant other—here, the loss of the one person with whom the protagonist could communicate—plays a significant role in the provocation of suicide.

Madden, David. *The Suicide's Wife*. Indianapolis and New York: Bobbs-Merrill, 1968.

A colorless housewife is shaken out of her complacent and largely unproductive existence by her husband's inexplicable suicide. She is rapidly propelled into a world foreign to her and has to learn to control her own life. People in the town refer to her as "the suicide's wife," and she lives in a state of limbo. In this condition, she remembers some of the mental shocks she suffered at the hands of her abusive father, who was killed by violence. She recalls her brother's criminal life and having submitted herself to gang sex at age twelve. She concentrates on housework to isolate herself from the outside world and feels guilty. After uncovering disturbing facts about her husband, she vents her emotions and emerges from her life-negating existence. She comes out of her husband's shadow to lead her own life in this story of growth after suicide.

Michener, James A. *Sayonara*. New York: Random, 1954.

The setting of this tale is Japan during the United States occupation. When an American major and a Japanese actress live together, it sets off distress among the Americans because the officer is engaged to an American general's daughter. They end up separating. In contrast, a second intercultural couple persist in their relationship despite tremendous obstacles placed in their way by the military. They get married, and when the soldier is ordered to leave his pregnant wife, the couple commit suicide. Racial bigotry is attacked and barriers against intercultural marriage are delineated. Love is opposed by the disciplines of professional life, and the suicidal motive of staying together in death is well depicted.

Miller, Arthur. *All My Sons*. In *Four Plays*. New York: Viking, 1957.

A manufacturer has sold defective airplane parts to the government. As a result, a number of young pilots have lost their lives in plane crashes. When he lets his partner take the larger share of the blame, his son writes that he has learned of what his father has done and is so ashamed that he will never return from his next military mission. When the father realizes that he has not only prompted his own son's death, but has had a hand in killing other pilots as well, he shoots himself. Thus, the audience is shown the roles guilt and shame can play in motivating suicide.

O'Neill, Eugene G. *Mourning Becomes Electra*. In *Nine Plays*. Toronto and New York: Modern Library, Random, 1959.

In a modern equivalent of the Aeschylean Oresteia, this trilogy of plays concerns a general's aberrant family. His unfaithful wife poisons him. His daughter and her brother take revenge by killing their mother's lover. The mother commits suicide. The brother makes an incestuous proposal to his sister, then shoots himself. The sister ends her days alone in a shuttered house. The audience is exposed to some of the "darker," or sexual and incestuous, motives that can propel unfulfilled men and women to self-destruction.

Percy, Walker. *The Second Coming*. New York: Farrar, 1981.

A middle-aged man becomes preoccupied with death and suicide to the point where he suffers a death-in-life disorder: He converses with the memory of his father, who committed suicide. He meets a regressed schizophrenic girl who has lost her memory from electroshock treatments. She nurses him back to health, and they fall in love. This novel shows how, with the help of another person, even a seriously disturbed individual can live through the crisis of suicidal preoccupation and have a second chance at life.

Saperstein, Alan. *Mom Kills Kids and Self.* New York: Macmillan, 1979.

A man comes home to find his wife has murdered their two sons and then committed suicide. In the three days before he reports the deaths, he goes through the madness of discovery and tries to deny the unthinkable. As he gradually accepts reality and takes on some responsibility for the deaths, we learn of the stresses that his wife endured: One son was autistic, she was the victim of a bizarre near-rape, and her husband had withdrawn into his own protective shell. The horrendous impact of both murder and suicide is depicted, and there are clear indications of what may have motivated these inordinate acts.

Sarton, May. *Faithful Are the Wounds.* New York: Holt, 1955.

A professor of English literature at Harvard University commits suicide. The novel's first part explains what led up to his self-destruction. Its last part traces the repercussions of his suicide on others. There is a look behind a refined person's facade to see some of his bottled-up rage, unreasonable anguish, and feelings of alienation. The reader can understand these factors so as to avoid them. The far-reaching reverberations of a suicide are noted for the reader to be aware of.

Stein, Sol. *Living Room.* New York: Arbor, 1974.

The protagonist's father sees her as too smart for her own good because she does not conceal her intelligence from men. Her special combination of brass and brains soon makes her one of the most successful leaders in advertising. She has a complex relationship with a man, and when her father has a stroke and her job threatens to overwhelm her, she attempts suicide. When she is saved, she takes some time away from work to think; she then chooses a new life. The reader can take this as a warning that even successful people can suffer from so many outside pressures that they think of suicide as an option.

Styron, William. *Lie Down in Darkness.* New York: Random, 1979.

A family gathers to bury a daughter who has committed suicide. The father, a drinker, had incestuous strivings for his late daughter; he had a mistress and had long been alienated from his wife. The mother was jealous and abusive of her deceased daughter and had devoted herself to another child. The deceased had left her unhappy home life and separated from her lover to search for other lovers. But coming from such a disintegrating family, she was unable to find satisfying relationships. Plagued by her unhappy life and her family's problems, she sought suicide as a relief. The reader can think as to how family problems, such as these, might be avoided.

Styron, William. *Sophie's Choice*. New York: Random, 1980. (Film: *Sophie's Choice*. CBS Fox Video. 1982. 157 min.)

A novelist, Stingo, meets a Polish Gentile, Sophie, and her volatile lover, Nathan. Sophie has survived a World War II concentration camp and lost both her father and her husband. She has also been forced to decide which one of her two children to save. Sophie feels guilty for surviving her loved ones and suffers from frequent flashbacks of traumatic events. To expiate her guilt, put an end to her misery, and be together with Nathan in death, she joins him in a double suicide. This novel gives an in-depth look at specific antecedents to suicide. These can be taken as warning signs for people in need of professional help to prevent suicide.

Film

The Big Chill. Columbia Pictures Home Video. 1983. 108 min.

The film begins with old college friends meeting at the funeral of a college chum who has committed suicide. They relive the past and show their various methods of coping with adulthood. We see how some of them are parents, how they deal with their sexual appetites, and how they use alcohol and drugs. By spending a weekend with these people, audience members see their reactions to the suicide and can contrast the friends with each other, with themselves, and with what is known about their self-destructive college chum.

Fatal Attraction. Paramount Pictures Home Video. 1987. 120 min.

A married man has what he thinks is a one-night stand, but the woman sets out to ensnare him in her intensely jealous possessiveness. She makes a dramatic suicidal gesture, claims he made her pregnant, kidnaps his daughter, and invades his home. This film aptly demonstrates motives for a suicidal attempt. Whether her actions are deemed manipulative or a cry for help, they have a significant effect on the man involved. The film shows a common way people respond to such a situation.

Interiors. MGM/UA Home Video. 1975. 93 min.

A mother who has had many mental breakdowns has the facade of a perfectionist. After their children are grown, her husband seeks a separation and introduces his lover to the family. Buried family injuries and guilts surface. There are reproofs, accusations, recriminations, and attempts at self-justification among the father, mother, and children. The mother becomes distraught and commits suicide. The audience is exposed to the mother's outer appearance and some of the thinking and feelings that compel her to commit suicide. This film warns of the powerful intrafamilial forces that can play a part in self-destruction.

'Night, Mother. MCA Home Video. 1986. 97 min.

This film, from a 1983 play by Marsha Norman, concerns a widow who lives with her unattractive, epileptic, and unemployable daughter. They seem to lead an ordinary life, but the daughter is a frightened woman. Her husband deserted her, and her son is a criminal and dope addict. One seemingly normal evening, the daughter announces her intention of committing suicide. As her mother gradually recognizes that her daughter is in earnest, she tries to persuade her not to do it but cannot. There is a chilling revelation of the powerful self-depreciating effects of the daughter's nonfulfillment with her husband and her disappointment with her son. The strength of her suicidal resolve, generated by these failures, is too strong to be stemmed by her mother's concern.

Permanent Record. Paramount Pictures Home Video. 1988. 92 min.

Without any warning, one of a group of teenagers in high school commits suicide. There is immediate shock and grief, and feelings of loss and anger are displayed. We see not only individual response to the event, but the reactions of a high school and some of the larger community. The film depicts the immediate fallout effects of suicide. A variety of individual methods of coping is shown, and even the community's way of dealing with the tragedy indicates the beginning of recovery.

Weeds. HBO Video. 1987. 115 min.

This film opens with the protagonist in prison for life for attempting suicide. He begins to read and educate himself; drama enthralls him. He writes a play and puts it on using convicts he recruits. A critic, seeing his work, gets him released. He reassembles his troupe, now ex-convicts, to travel and give performances of his plays. The audience sees the protagonist discovering humanity through his reading. He moves from a hopeless suicidal convict to a successful actor and playwright. This film shows how a person can progress from life-negating self-despair to life-affirming self-development and self-expression.

7 Acts of Man's Inhumanity to Man:

John Steinbeck's *The Grapes of Wrath*

By Ursula R. Mahlendorf
John Brander

Natural disasters like floods and droughts; man-made catastrophes like the Persian Gulf War, the Holocaust, and nuclear accidents; social upheavals like revolutions; and the economic disaster of a Great Depression or change resulting from the industrial and technical revolutions disrupt ordered human intercourse and cause trauma to the development of all humans involved in them. The stress generated by these events exacerbates the tensions between groups, races, and social classes and ferments the social and personal strife that, in normal times, remains largely contained. Intolerable stress makes intergroup violence erupt. It causes some people to break, give up, be annihilated; others meet it well and perform miracles of courage, only to crack after the emergency is over; still others lash out in vicious anger not only against perceived enemies, but against friends.

Catastrophes and great dangers test the mettle of a person and of a society. How a person responds under great stress depends vitally on the basic emotional, interpersonal, physical, and intellectual resources he or she brings to the occasion. And these resources, in turn, depend on a person's favorable or unfavorable development from birth on in the context of a given family and society. But even the strongest person will break if the stress is great enough.

The Paradigm

With grand epic sweep, John Steinbeck's 1939 novel, *The Grapes of Wrath*, depicts the social injustices of the Dust Bowl migration and questions the basic values of American capitalist society. For the purpose of life guidance, the book's particular worth lies in its ability to show how the historic events of both a natural and man-made disaster affect the lives of the members of a seemingly ordinary family. Steinbeck centers on the kind of catastrophe with which we can identify easily—namely that of losing one's home through no fault of one's own—in this case, through the natural catastrophe of drought. The homelessness of the Joad family from the Oklahoma Dust Bowl strikes us as doubly undeserved because it is caused also by social forces, agricultural industrialization, and the Great Depression. In fact, the Depression and its aftermath even makes understandable, if not pardonable, the hostility and cruelty of the Californian tradespeople, farmers, and police to the migrants. Although the Californians have been spared natural catastrophe, they too are affected by the Depression and are either threatened by the immigration wave as competition or use it as a cheap labor supply to compensate themselves for their losses. The quest of the Joad family for work and a home in California illustrates what personal liabilities are exacerbated by the catastrophe and hence are threats to the life of the individual, the family, and the community. It demonstrates which personal qualities and resources of character are life enhancing to oneself and to others. Finally, delineating a program of social reform, the novel shows in a specific series of incidents how supraregional governmental agencies can help resolve social conflict and restore individual and communal well being.

Summary

The Grapes of Wrath begins with the return of Tom Joad, who has served a sentence for manslaughter, to his family's farm just as they are about to leave Oklahoma for California. Having been driven from their home by the tractors of agribusiness and having received handbills advertising farm labor jobs in California, the Joads and their neighbors follow the promise of work in the sun, of green orchards and new homes. Joined by Tom's ex-preacher friend, Jim Casy, the Joads begin their journey as a large clan: Grampa and Granma; Pa and Ma; their children—brothers Noah, Tom, and Al, their pregnant sister Rose of Sharon and her husband Connie, and the preteen Ruthie and Winfield; and unmarried Uncle John.

Torn from his support—the soil—Grampa dies on the first leg of the trip. The further the family progresses toward California, the more human hostility and hardship they encounter, the more they realize that they are part of a great migration. In California, they—together with other migrants—are harassed and chased by posses of angry citizens and state police. They are exploited when they can find temporary work, sheltered in degrading camps, and treated with blows and contempt. Oppressed by hunger and hardship, they are drawn into the maelstrom of hate in which migrant turns against migrant. They gain a brief respite from their suffering in a camp of the federal government, but have to leave again in search of work and food.

In the course of their wanderings, the Joad family disintegrates. The oldest brother, Noah, least bonded with the family, leaves before they cross the desert; Granma dies of exhaustion after they cross it. Brother-in-law Connie deserts them. Jim Casy fights with the police and gives himself up for Tom. Tom must leave the family because he has killed a policeman to revenge Jim's death. Al marries into another family. Rose of Sharon's baby is stillborn. At the story's end, only Pa and Ma, Uncle John, Rose, and the two youngest children are together.

In the course of their disastrous journey, three of the Joad adults—Ma, Tom, and Rose—learn that their salvation lies in forging a community of the disinherited migrants, that the migrants themselves have to stand together and fight for their right to live and to work. When Tom understands that "a fella ain't no good alone," he formulates a future for himself: "Wherever they's a fight so hungry people can eat, I'll be there." And this formulation expresses a hope for the better future of all migrants, even in the midst of the disaster that dominates the last pages of the novel.

Let us now look at the interactions and situations of some of the characters to understand why certain family members are helpful to themselves and others in catastrophic situations and why others are not. Having lost their land, the men of the family most entitled to it by traditional inheritance laws—Grampa, Pa, and the oldest son, Noah—lose their dominant positions, together with their ability to be of help to the family. Grampa collapses and dies right after leaving the land. Pa, well aware of his loss of power, resents his humiliation. Noah, who slaughters the animals for food before the journey, loses his role as provider once he leaves the land and wanders off from the family in despair.

Uncle John, who periodically needs to deaden his guilt and pain for being a burden to his family by getting dead drunk, continues to encumber himself and them. Connie, given to self-centered illusions of bettering his own position, deserts the family after the first hardships of the journey, finding his responsibility for a pregnant wife and her homeless kin too onerous. The ascendant roles are taken over by Ma and the younger sons, Al and Tom, who derive their personal power from sources other than the soil—Al from having learned the mechanical skills needed for survival in the new mechanized world and Tom from having survived prison with his capacity for relating to others intact. Particularly through observing Ma and Tom, however, in their interactions with each other and with family members, fellow migrants, and hostile locals, we can gain insight into those life-sustaining personal resources of character that can counteract the forces of inhumanity.

Though deriving strength from her role as nurturer of her family, Ma is able to take care of her own needs, particularly her need for emotional expression and support from others. She knows herself and is able to do the right thing at the right time. For instance, in a memorable scene at the government camp, where the family experiences a respite from suffering, Ma takes the time to mourn the family's dead and to grieve over the desertions and other losses of family members. It is a testimony to the quality of the Joads' marriage that Pa can join Ma in her grief and support her by expressing his sadness over the loss of their home. Unafraid of emotional intimacy, they console each other by mourning together and recalling the good things of their shared past.

Knowing how and being able to take care of her own emotional needs, Ma also knows how to take care of the emotional needs of her family. When Rose of Sharon is threatened by the religious fanaticism of a fellow migrant, Ma understands the depth of the threat to Rose and her unborn child and drives off the woman with her anger. Ma controls her anger sufficiently not to attack the woman physically, but she warns the camp manager that she would need help in curbing it should the woman renew her tirade. Knowing her own anger, Ma understands Tom's rage at being heckled and humiliated by the American Legion men and holds on to his arm, making him realize that their common survival depends on his responding with restraint. She soothes his bruised self-esteem by praising his patience and emotional resiliency. Repeatedly, anger and violence are Tom's downfall. We meet him at the novel's beginning as a man who has killed another man in self-defense; we leave him as he has killed another in outrage at a friend's murder. The change from self-absorption to concern for and commitment to others that Tom undergoes occurs in Rose as well. Through Ma's love of them, pride in them, and encouragement of their responsible action, her children have become compassionate human beings who can envision the common good.

The reader comes to understand some of the sources of man's inhumanity to man and the origins of man's helpfulness to man most memorably through the migrant children in the story. On their trek, the Joad family comes to their first dilapidated migrant camp, its air heavy with distrust and hostility. With their last portions of meat from home, Ma cooks a stew while the camp's hungry children swarm around her, silently watching her preparations. The Joads realize that they cannot feed the family and all of these children, so they withdraw to their tent to eat, although Ma leaves some of the stew to the children's wolfish hunger. Soon after, she is attacked by a furious woman camper, who berates her and misunderstands Ma's compassion for the children, labeling it boasting. The woman responds to Ma's explanation by sullenly withdrawing to her tent. It is this concern for the well being of their own families that isolates the migrants from each other and sets them against each other. And by isolating themselves, their distrust and hatred of each other grow and poison potentially affiliative actions, like the feeding of the children, turning the actions into additional causes of misery for them all.

Least able to satisfy their own needs, frustrated by having their basic needs for food, shelter, and movement denied, the children suffer the most on the trip. Unwittingly, they act out the stress that all of the migrants experience. Ruthie and Winfield squabble continuously, watching jealously that the one does not get more than the other, resenting it when one of them "gets away" with something. Ma maintains her strict home routine with them, demanding that they help with chores, be respectful, and clean despite the hardships of the trek. Yet she understands that the children are taxed beyond their strength in the midst of uncertainty and violence, and she attempts, again and again, to ameliorate their lot. For instance, when Tom has to hide from the police, his hiding place cannot be withheld from the children without splitting the family apart, and they are sworn to secrecy. Getting into a fight with an older girl over a stolen cracker box and desperate to reclaim her possession against the superior strength of her assailant, Ruthie unwittingly betrays the secret. Rather than punish her angrily, Ma understands that Ruthie is ashamed, frightened, and devastated by her betrayal and comforts her with "You didn't know." The reader understands from this and similar incidents that the Joad children's unusual strength and capacity to grow through hardship derive from just such empathetic and firm handling of their upbringing.

The stress the migrants experience on the journey angers, frustrates, brutalizes, and isolates them. No incident shows the brutalizing effects of continuous deprivation more clearly than that of the children at the government camp playing croquet. And no other incident shows more poignantly the way out of the migrants' isolation, persecution, and helpless hatred of each other. As the camp children, watched over by an elderly woman, take turns at the game, newcomers Ruthie and Winfield join them, eager to play. A girl tells them that they will have to wait until the next game; however, unable to tolerate the frustration of waiting, Ruthie attacks the girl, wresting the mallet from her hands. But the children have been taught how to deal with such disruptions, and the watching adult need only remind them what to do. In a body, the children move off the field and watching silently, let Ruthie play by herself. Winfield, always in opposition to his older sister, joins them in their resistance. Ruthie soon gets bored with showing off how well she can play without them and demands that they play with her. In response, the children silently move back farther. Cowed by their rejection, Ruthie runs off crying, while Winfield is told that he can join in the next game. Lest the children reject Ruthie in the future when she wants to cooperate, the woman reminds them that they were as "mean" as Ruthie had been and that they too had to learn to cooperate.

Similar cooperation between the adult migrants is encouraged in the federal government camp, an oasis in which they can regain their self-respect through decent facilities and their humanity through cooperative responsibility for the conduct of their common affairs. The government manager, by his courtesy and respectfulness, and the camp itself, as a place of safety from persecution, work here as enablers of a process of rehumanizing people traumatized by natural and social catastrophe. The process itself is the people's own. It is democratic, with elective committees in charge of every aspect of daily life together. It is based on each person doing his or her share, on mutual consent and nonviolence. The campers gain self-confidence from the skill and resourcefulness with which they manage disruptions to their common goal—self-help and community. Steinbeck acknowledges the contemporary unreality of this ideal of a cooperative, nonviolent community by showing that the Joads cannot survive in the camp. They have to leave so as not to starve, and a literal flood of misfortune drives them on to the end of the novel.

Today's reader might be even less sanguine than the 1940s reader about the efficacy of ideals of cooperative humanity as antidotes to the traumas of war and other cataclysms. Yet the very concrete situations in which Steinbeck's down-to-earth characters interact provide us with insights into those values, actions, and emotions that are conducive to humanity's survival in dignity and emotional health. Such behavior may not stop wars from occurring; it will not prevent natural catastrophes. But its insightful narration does provide life-enhancing models, point out destructive ways of coping, and give us an understanding of humane and inhumane motivations alike.

Questions for Discussion

1. The Joad children are far from ordinary. How is each unusual, and what in his or her upbringing made that individual so?

2. Despite its bad moments and its inequality, the marriage of Ma and Pa Joad is a good one. What factors make it so?
3. What is Steinbeck's social criticism and philosophy, as expressed in the interchapters? Is the philosophy essential to an understanding of the humanity of the main characters? Why or why not?
4. What are the differences in the outlook on life of Tom and Jim Casy? How are Jim's and Tom's transformations of outlook on life related to each other?
5. How and why are the Joad women indestructible? How convincing and satisfying for today's reader is the ending of the novel? Why?

Annotated Bibliography

Print

Didion, Joan. *A Book of Common Prayer*. New York: Simon & Schuster, 1977.

Through the protagonist, Charlotte Douglas, the principal motifs are presented: the desperate state of contemporary life; the anxious attempts of those who try to live decently on the edge of a yawning void; the unrestrained growth and subsequent rotting of things and people in uncongenial climates; and the disintegration of a society where evolution does not occur or is not allowed, where there is no design or purpose to the doing of things. The novel, set in a Central American country, is about spiritual collapse, both in individuals and in society. Charlotte, at first seeming a silly and pathetic woman, is seen by the end as someone very real and worthwhile. She is shown to be a confused mixture of vulnerabilities and strengths, both passionate and detached, deluded and yet rooted in reality.

Didion, Joan. *Democracy*. New York: Simon & Schuster, 1985.

This novel presents a scathing critique of contemporary American society. In this story of flashbacks and fitful glimpses of the present, the history of the last 30 years can be viewed. Hypocrisy, corruption, and naiveté color both the individual and the national consciousness. What distinguishes this book is the interplay of America as an all-consuming entity and the private struggle of individuals of integrity to survive. The protagonists, Inez Victor and Jack Lovett, share a view of reality that is not fettered by illusion and ambition.

Dos Passos, John. *U.S.A.* New York: Houghton, 1930.

This all-embracing documentary of American life from the turn of the century to the Great Depression presents a host of characters at different social levels. The novel reads like a fictional history of the first third of America's twentieth century. Quoting from newspapers, newsreels, speeches, and popular songs, interwoven with brief autobiographical sketches and the biographies of public figures typical of their time, *U.S.A.* displays the disorderly and chaotic nature of American society as our great grandparents and grandparents lived it. The imagery of the scene in which the various protagonists play their roles offers motifs behind which the American character, its human as well as its inhuman aspects, can be displayed.

Dreiser, Theodore. *An American Tragedy*. Cleveland, Ohio: World, 1925.

The theme that the economic system is unjust and inhuman is individualized in the life of Clyde Griffiths, who—like a victim in a Greek tragedy—faces a moral choice and makes an unwise decision that eventually leads to his ruin. Clyde probably does not repent of his crime. His desires, though unfulfilled, remain. The underlying message is that freedom without opportunity is not freedom. Millions of Americans today, in what we call the underclass, might attest to this assertion. Clyde is portrayed as a victim of economic forces, social inequality, poverty, and lack of privilege. But, in this story, he is a victim who ineffectively fights back in order to gain a future for himself. To achieve this, he succumbs to temptation, one of which he ultimately pays for with his life.

Ellison, Ralph. *Invisible Man*. New York: Random, 1952.

This novel, in contrast to Faulkner's novels of outrage, expresses acceptance. The protagonist, nameless in the story, is literally running for his life. He is like a puppet or a clown. His survival depends on being invisible. The protagonist plays many roles, while remaining the personification of the negative man. It is this ability not to be seen or remembered that allows him to survive. It is a kind of affirmation. The significance of the book lies in its satire of discrimination and prejudice. A chaotic world is revealed where there is no real order, thus allowing infinite possibilities for improvisation.

Faulkner, William. *Intruder in the Dust*. New York: Random, 1948.

Faulkner juxtaposes the problem of African-Americans against motifs such as murder, grave robbing, and lynching. He presents racial attitudes through the harangues and rhetoric of the protagonist's uncle, the unhumble pride of the black, and the sense of obligation the teenage white protagonist (Chick Mallison) feels toward an inferior. Written in the context of prevailing poor-white prejudices, the novel presents the problem of the South, as it existed prior to the civil-rights period, as one the South alone had to solve. The proud spirits of protagonist Chick and old, black Lucas Beauchamp, standing in sharp contrast to one another, are believable. Chick, as he grows in his thinking and understanding, is seen as offering the best hope the South has to come to terms with its own discriminatory past.

Fitzgerald, F. Scott. *The Great Gatsby*. New York: Scribner, 1925.

Set against a backdrop of the roaring twenties, the various motifs of this novel blend the best and worst aspects of the American scene. Prohibition, speakeasies, ambition, crime, fads, irresponsible wealth, reckless pursuit of pleasure, and class attitudes are recurrent themes. Jay Gatsby, the protagonist, is a racketeer in love. Although his love turns out to be an illusion, it is an illusion that motivates him and preserves in him a kind of innocence. Human actions have results that, in this story, follow a logical and ultimately tragic course. Gatsby, immersed in the sordidness of bootlegging and other criminal activities, remains relatively uncorrupted by the life around him. He is redeemed by a purpose, unselfish in its nature, even though in reality it proves to be an illusion. The energy of his life is directed beyond himself, and his accumulation of wealth is not simply for power and self-gratification.

Hemingway, Ernest. *A Farewell to Arms*. New York: Scribner, 1929.

In this love story, Frederic Henry and the woman he loves face the meaning of war, destruction and death, and what war does to human relationships. Despite the idealism Hemingway expresses, disillusionment and the utter waste of war are graphically displayed. In the interplay of the characters, the confusing and shifting nature of events—events that are outside the control of the lovers—is made clear. Concepts such as commitment, duty, obedience, and courage are given human dimensions. Frederic ultimately takes responsibility for his life by deserting the army. Despite the novel's tragic ending, the lovers are seen not as mere victims of events over which they have no control, but as active participants in the world in which they live.

Hemingway, Ernest. *For Whom the Bell Tolls*. New York: Scribner, 1940.

The motifs of this masterpiece, set during the Spanish Civil War, offer insights into the inhumanity associated with civil conflict and show how individuals cope with the daily stress of wartime conditions. Recurrent themes show the brutality of war, ideological disputes among participants, and the emotions of ordinary people caught up in disasters over which they have no control. Acts of compassion, bravery, and love permeate the lives of combatants, peasants, and townspeople. The characters remain themselves in the heightened drama of battle, displaying stoic fortitude and grim resolve. Protagonist Robert Jordan, an American volunteer on the side of the Loyalists, ultimately pays the price of his devotion and ideals. The story provides a human dimension to the destructiveness of war by posing positive attributes of fidelity, duty, and love.

Hersey, John. *A Bell for Adano*. New York: Knopf, 1944.

This war novel explores the various relationships and problems that arise between an occupying army and the occupied people. Unlike other war novels, this one presents the characters sympathetically. The arbitrariness of war, with its senseless cruelties and destruction, is alleviated to some extent by protagonist Major Joppolo's humane and responsible exercise of command. Joppolo, the American military governor, carefully balances the requirements of his command with the civilian needs of the governed. His choices, though detrimental for his own career, create trust between the occupiers and the occupied and exemplify true leadership.

Kennedy, William. *Ironweed*. New York: Viking, 1983.

In this grim story about drifter Francis Phelan, Kennedy shows the starkness of the Depression and the harshness of the underside of Albany, New York, society. It is a story of violence. Phantoms, as it were, stalk Francis until there is no place for him in organized society. Showing the seamier side of urban life, the various motifs of the book present a tapestry of working-class life. Francis, though in the conventional sense a loser, shows considerable courage in handling both his own nature and the circumstances of his life. Though at the end he still drifts, there is also the possibility of his redemption and his eventual coming home. Only his own violence remains unsubdued.

Kesey, Ken. *One Flew over the Cuckoo's Nest*. New York: Viking, 1963.

This book is an indictment of the kind of world that pressures people to retreat from reality. The story can be read as an allegory in which two forces fight for the mastery of mankind. One is social conformity. The other is individualism. As a protest against repressiveness in society, it demonstrates that inhumanity is deeply ingrained in people. Where human energies and enthusiasms are deadened (as in the asylum described in the novel), in the name of the general good, people slowly die in themselves or are forced by others to die as sacrifices. One of the positive aspects of the book is the redemption of Chief Bromden from his self-induced passivity.

Mailer, Norman. *The Naked and the Dead*. New York: Holt, 1948.

Judged to be the best novel to have come out of World War II, this story also presents one of the bleakest pictures of that war ever written. The action of the novel takes place in the South Pacific. What emerges is a sense of total hopelessness about life. The soldiers find in themselves futility, bestiality, no humanity, a pointlessness of any action they perform, no vestige of pride in anything, and nothing to look forward to after the war. There are no heroes.

Mason, Bobbie Ann. "In Country." In *In Country*. New York: Harper, 1985.

"In Country," is the story of a seventeen-year-old Kentucky woman, Sam Hughes, who attempts to deal with her father's death in Viet Nam, her uncle Emmett's evasiveness concerning the war, and her own understanding of what the war means in her life and the life of her community. Through the story of this young woman and her friends and peers, Mason graphically illustrates the futility of the war. Through her uncle, her friends Dawn and Tom, and the diary her father kept in Viet Nam, Sam confronts the war the United States lost, not only in the jungles of Viet Nam, but in the homes of Hopewell and thousands of other communities throughout the country. What comes through is the sense that America did not honor its young men who fought for their country a war they did not realize was not meant to be won. In Viet Nam, the enemy turned out to be ourselves.

Porter, Katherine Anne. *Ship of Fools*. Boston: Atlantic-Little, 1952.

The motifs of this book offer many insights into the dislocation of society and its effects on individuals. Here, this dislocation is capsulized in terms of an ocean crossing, where the intensity of the relationships that are formed inevitably is revealed to be transitory and shallow once the voyage ends. This book, within the limits of a sea voyage, gives a larger image of the human community in ethnic and racial strife. The story, set aboard a German ship prior to the Nazi regime coming to power, allegorizes human relationships under Naziism and explores man's need for a moral order while it reveals his shortcomings and dark nature.

Pynchon, Thomas. *The Crying of Lot 49*. Philadelphia and New York: Lippincott, 1965.

Oedipa Maas lives in a random, chaotic world where there is no sense of political, psychological, or even metaphysical direction. No one knows whether his or her final goal is tyranny or liberty. Time becomes

circular. Coincidences recur. In such madness, the title's key word—
"crying"—takes on significance. Oedipa, as well as the author, cries for the
human condition in a society lacking coherent connection and meaning.
Such a world threatens what is human because, in human terms, the
world is irresponsible.

Sinclair, Upton. *The Jungle*. New York: Viking, 1905.

The Jungle is the story of how a Lithuanian immigrant family fares in
Chicago at the turn of the century. It is an indignant book, hitting hard
at the social injustices and unfair labor practices of the stockyards. Most
of the miseries endured by the family arise not out of their own
shortcomings, but out of economic circumstances wholly outside their
control. Man's inhumanity is portrayed in graphic detail, illustrating how
immigrants were exploited in an age when the social fabric of American
industrial society offered no protection to its workers. The characters
have to deal with a corrupt social order, and live in conditions of abject
poverty, often having to suffer personal degradation in order to survive,
and rewarded with indifference by a social order that does not care. Great
strains are placed on family life when raw economic forces and a rigid
capitalist necessity grind one family member after another into the
ground. Jurgis Rudkus, the protagonist, ultimately discovers a way to live
his life anew. Going outside of himself, he finds self-respect in the socialist
philosophy of the time, which offers him hope and dignity.

Styron, William. *The Long March*. New York: Random, 1955.

The brutality, stupidity, and human waste inherent in war are presented with clarity in this book. The story, set in a Marine training camp,
illustrates the grotesque mentality of the military mind in all its delusional
splendor. Reservists are made to go on a march for no rational reason. On
this march, the physical and psychological stress of the participants are
painfully felt. In such environments, with simulated combat situations to
be endured, young men learn to shed their humanity if they are to survive.

Styron, William. *Sophie's Choice*. New York: Random, 1980. (Film:
Sophie's Choice. CBS Fox Video. 1982. 157 min.)

This novel deals with motifs such as betrayal, guilt, seduction, and
cowardice in a situation as inhuman as any known this century. The
protagonist, Sophie, has spent twenty months at Auschwitz. Her guilt
arises at her having chosen her youngest daughter's death sentence. After
the war, her lover in America is unable to cope with the evil in the world.
The narrator, Stingo, is unprepared to learn that Sophie needs his support. This story tells, in simple terms, how personal is man's inhumanity

and how anyone, given an extreme situation, can witness and even perpetuate evil as if it were an everyday occurrence.

Vonnegut, Kurt, Jr. *Slaughterhouse Five*. New York: Delacorte, 1969.

Billy Pilgrim, an incongruous character, was in Dresden, Germany, when it was firebombed in early 1945. The story, an indictment against war, is a Pilgrim's progress of comic absurdity. The message is that there are no answers to why things are as they are—for example, why Dresden had to be fire-bombed; why evil has to exist; why some live and others die. Though there is no answer, man—as long as he is alive—must endure the question. Life, even under the worst of conditions, is the only meaning there is. Vonnegut's treatment of horror and man's inhumanity is unusual in describing in surreal terms mass killings and destruction.

Warren, Robert Penn. *All the King's Men*. New York: Harcourt, 1946.

All the King's Men tells the story of politics during the Depression—in particular, of Willy Stark's rise to power. This tale of political corruption runs the gamut of motifs, from blackmail to murder, lust, and adultery. There are many insights into how power and greed in political life can change people's characters for the worse. Protagonist Jack Burden, a political lackey to the governor, ultimately comes to grips with his own ambition and self-destruction. He demonstrates that it is possible to change his view of himself from a self-centered, selfish, and egotistical one to a more responsible one that harmonizes his true altruistic and selfless idealism.

Wiesel, Elie. *Night*. New York: Bantam, 1982.

The most influential and memorable memoir of a holocaust survivor, Nobel Peace Prize–winner Wiesel's volume recounts his concentration camp experiences at Auschwitz and Buchenwald. A student of the cabbala at age fifteen at Sighet, Hungary, young Elie experiences the German occupation during the Fascist Horthy regime and later, together with his family, is deported to Auschwitz. Separated from his mother and sister who are sent to the ovens on arrival, he and his father survive the winter of 1944–45 by working in the Buna camp's electrical equipment warehouse. As the Russians approach, the camp is force-marched to Buchenwald. His father dies from exhaustion shortly after arrival, and Elie blames himself for not having been good enough a son to keep him alive. Yet it is the strong bond to his father which allows him to survive terror, beatings, and the whole gamut of acts of inhumanity. When liberated by American troops, the sixteen-year-old feels he is a man who is emotionally dead.

Wolfe, Tom. *The Bonfire of the Vanities*. New York: Farrar, 1987.

This book captures the manners, morals, sights, sounds, and soul of New York City in the mid-1980s. Corruption, crime, sleeze, lack of values and inner resources, greed, and conspicuous consumption are some of the motifs at work. No character presented is wholly admirable, and protagonist Sherman McCoy is a man who exists on the surface of life and may be thought of as the ultimate yuppie. The book's value is as a commentary on contemporary American culture, shaped by wealth unrelated to productivity or social utility. Its message: When everyone behaves self-indulgently, values such as justice and fairness are lost. Man's humanity ceases to be the norm and is seen as something old-fashioned and comic.

Wouk, Herman. *War and Remembrance*. Boston: Little, 1979.

In this fictional epic of World War II, many motifs are woven together. On a societal level, the perspectives of Americans are mixed with those of Jews, Italians, and Germans. On an individual level, the highly educated Jewish-American protagonists refused to believe what is happening would ever happen to them. The novel shows us that evil, though it exists, always seems to exist for other people and never ourselves. Other people are interned. Other people are killed. Never us. The exposing of this blindness in people is just one of the things that distinguishes this book. As the author states, "The beginning of the end of war lies in remembrance." War is shown to be disruptive, and what people think at the start about how it will turn out is never how it does.

Wright, Richard. *Native Son*. New York: Harper, 1940.

The motifs of this story entwine African-American and white attitudes. The protagonist, Bigger Thomas, is the symbol of his people. Distorted in his upbringing by the prejudices of white society, he has to come to terms with himself and find the meaning of life. The themes of racial killing and racial fear are explored in the context of bigotry and fear through means of a criminal trial. The whole spectrum of human emotion is presented in an attempt to bridge the gap in each race's understanding of the other. Ultimately, facing death, Bigger Thomas learns to forgive his enemies and come to terms with himself and with death.

8   Facing Sudden Success:

Philip Roth's *Zuckerman Unbound*

By Norman J. Fedder

Whether or not we like to admit it, nothing delights most Americans more than the attainment of *success* and all that we associate with it—recognition, wealth, and power—the proverbial American dream. It is nurtured in our families, encouraged in our schools, promoted in our media, and pursued in our careers. It is endemic to any free society with seemingly unlimited opportunity, such as ours, and it is the source of much of our misery. Too often, we pay a terrible price in our struggle for success, in the hardships and anxieties attending our frustrated ambitions. One way or another, we must learn how to cope not only with the failure of our hopes, but with their fulfillment. Because the success we crave may provoke reactions quite different from our expectations—especially as some of them will be unanticipated.

The Paradigm

Such is the situation Philip Roth explores in *Zuckerman Unbound* (Farrar, 1981), his satiric portrayal of the plight of Nathan Zuckerman, who suddenly attains his dreams with the publication of his notorious bestseller, *Carnovsky*. But Nathan is far from delighted by this unexpected good fortune. He is misjudged as a pornographer, labeled a hatemonger, and alienated from the environment that nurtured him. He can go nowhere without being recognized and confronted. There are women out to seduce him and men to kill him. His mother is threatened with being kidnapped, and his brother is convinced that the book caused their father's fatal stroke. Roth's graphic and comic account of Nathan's "American nightmare" may serve as a warning to all of us not to take our need for success so seriously as to become too distressed should we fail to achieve it or should success prove to be the reverse of our expectations. An examination of Nathan's aspirations in contrast with his misfortunes provides insight into both the nature of his problems and his means of coping with them.

Summary

For a number of years, Nathan has published stories and novels that are well known and highly regarded by the critics, but not the general public; he craves renown commensurate with his literary standing. This he soon achieves when *Carnovsky* is published and his picture appears on the cover of *Life* magazine; now there are few places he can go without being spotted. But the notoriety gives him little pleasure.

It takes not much more than a ride on a bus to have some loudmouth deplore the celebrity for using so cheap a mode of transportation, which prompts any number of other passengers to get in their say. And one of them, when Nathan tries to escape fifteen blocks before his destination, gets off the bus after him. From this strange-looking lady, he expects the worst. *Carnovsky*'s erotic subject matter has earned him as many enemies as admirers. For his depiction of Jewish characters in acts of sexual perversion and his presumed exposure of himself and his family to ridicule, he is condemned for self-hatred and anti-Semitism and is even identified with the Nazis. Among his foes are those out to kill him. Therefore, as the lady overtakes him and reaches into her "Luger-sized purse," he prepares for his early demise. But the only weapon she produces is a picture post-card of Jesus, which she presses into his hand with the admonition that Nathan's new status will never bring him happiness: "Only He can do that."

Nathan's renown also has made him a media hero. He is sought after for a TV commercial endorsing appetizer snacks because they know he likes herring. After all, they read it in the book. They have an actress ready to play his mother if his own is unavailable. Another producer would like to film a day in the life of Nathan as part of a series to be called "A Day in the Life of. . . ." A reading of *Carnovsky* has this producer convinced that the novelist's average day will be so stocked with lurid incident that the show will surely enhance both their careers. However, Nathan assures him that a day in his life would not only be a great bore to the viewers, but a great flop for the producer. Yet wherever he goes, he is plagued by reporters in search of an interview. Too often, if he refuses, they take it as a personal insult, threatening to make one up anyway and print it. Gossip columns are continually and falsely linking him with movie stars; and when he finally does have an affair with one of them, she deserts him for Fidel Castro.

Worst is the effect of his renown on his family. Nathan is determined that his mother not be victimized by the media like her friend, Flora Sobol, whose interview is entitled, "I Play Canasta with Carnovsky's Mother." Therefore, he flies down to Miami, where his parents have retired (his father is now in a nursing home, following a stroke), to advise his mother on how to cope with reporters. Playing the role of one of them, he rehearses every strategy—from bullying to begging—that might be used to get her talking about her celebrated son; thus, he enables her to maintain her privacy against the pressure of the press.

Not only is Nathan victimized by his overblown reputation, he is embarrassed by it. The popularity of *Carnovsky*, after all, has more to do with the sexual escapades of its hero than the artistic skill of its author. This is not the kind of recognition he ever sought or wanted. Most galling is the misconception that he himself is the depraved protagonist of his novel. Both the praise and the blame are meted out to Carnovsky, not Nathan—from those who want to sleep with him to those who want to wipe him out. As much as the novelist has succeeded at being read by his public, he has failed to communicate with them. This makes him feel outraged and humiliated because it threatens his identity as a serious writer; he has not written a shocking confessional, but a well-crafted work of fiction.

Even those who admire him for his writing skill misjudge him. One such person is Alvin Pepler, who corners Nathan at a local restaurant. To this fellow Newark Jew, Nathan is none other than "our Marcel Proust." Alvin, it turns out, has been no less victimized by sudden success. He has been a winner for three consecutive weeks on a nationwide TV quiz show, winning fair and square with his encyclopedic knowledge of Americana. However, the show's producers want him to take the fall for a WASP named Hewlett from a distinguished New England family who must be fed the correct answers, as must all the contestants except Alvin. When Alvin refuses to do so, the producers bribe him with the promise of a job as a sportscaster, only to renege on it when he is deposed by Hewlett. Therefore, Alvin blows the whistle on them, succeeding in discrediting the show, but bringing himself down with it. He has become a pariah in the industry, which—he claims—made and destroyed him.

It is not long before Alvin joins the ranks of the Zuckerman-phobes. After placing him among America's literary immortals, Alvin now denounces Nathan as an imposter. When the novelist has reservations about Alvin's review of *Carnovsky*, Alvin accuses his idol of having clay feet, of being a plagiarist who has "stolen" Alvin's life for material for the book. He further charges, as Nathan himself fears, that his success has insulated him from his subject. How can Nathan write about his old neighborhood when his new wealth has bought him out of it?

In truth, Nathan has made more money from this book than from all of his other writing put together. He is informed that with the sale of the film rights to *Carnovsky*, he is now a millionaire. But he does not know how to behave like one. His agent, Andre, has little patience with Nathan's ambivalence about spending his new fortune. Andre claims that Nathan has a public image to maintain; he must now behave in keeping with his new opulence: fit himself with expensive clothes, eat in the best restaurants, and get himself a limousine, chauffeur, housekeeper, and secretary. However, Nathan worries that in doing so he will lose touch with the environment that has been the source and inspiration of his writing.

Soon the wealth becomes an even greater cause of discomfort. Nathan receives a call from a man who demands money of the celebrity or else he will kidnap Nathan's mother. The caller reveals himself as a long-time fan who has been waiting for this opportunity to capitalize on Nathan's success. Not that he regards *Carnovsky* as Nathan's best book—all flash and no depth—however, his admiration for the author does not diminish his demand for cash or prevent a guilt-evoking blow below the belt: that Nathan not give his mother any more misery than he did in publishing that book. His agent dismisses the novelist's fears of the threatening message as paranoia. He tells Nathan not to answer the phone and to notify the police, but Nathan reminds him that, with success such as his, bringing in the police will guarantee newspaper headlines like "Pug Threatens Porn Mom." He does not want to inspire another crackpot to go after his mother.

Nathan suspects Alvin Pepler as the mysterious caller when he finds in his mailbox the handkerchief he had lent Alvin—into which, in the manner of Gilbert Carnovsky, Alvin had ejaculated. Staring at it listlessly, Nathan falls prey to a feeling of powerlessness, intimidated by even this loser. Power, one would think, should be the ultimate measure of success.

The novel concludes with Nathan's helplessness against the accusation that his success has been achieved at the expense of his family and loved ones. He is powerless to control his overwhelming sense of betrayal and guilt. A former neighbor, for example, accuses him of portraying his third wife (whom he has just walked out on) as a slut. And his mother reluctantly informs him that everyone she meets is convinced that the crazy mother in *Carnovsky* is herself, despite her assurances to the contrary. She goes so far as to say that she is pleased Nathan's father is so incapacitated he has not heard the slanders against her.

Or has he? According to Henry, Nathan's brother, their father—on his deathbed—had quite a different opinion of his now famous offspring. The old man's last word, "Bastard," was meant for Nathan, Henry charges, and rightly so. Nathan has no respect for responsibility, self-denial, restraint, conscience, morality, or loyalty; nothing is sacred—only "grist" for Nathan's "fun-machine." Henry blames himself and the family for making Nathan think he is too famous to criticize and for protecting him from knowing what he really is, from admitting the crime he has perpetrated against his father. The old man had been exposed to *Carnovsky* after all. An in-law had brought the novel to the nursing home and read his father excerpts. "You killed him," Henry concludes to Nathan in a fury. "With that book."

So Nathan's success, far from what his ambition had assured him would smell so sweet, has the "stale acrid odor" of the handkerchief in his mailbox. And when he attempts to deny his brother's accusations, he cannot help but admit to himself that they are true. Yet he had written the book anyway; the claims of his art and his ego overrode his moral misgivings. He should not have been surprised at his family's reaction; in fact, he deserved it. Upon his return from his father's funeral in Florida, Nathan has his driver take him from the Newark airport to his old neighborhood. He stares at the completely changed setting from his limousine and acknowledges the price he had to pay for his good fortune, as he bids good-bye to his old self and subject. Five times he repeats to himself that it is over; he has served his time; he has come to terms with his sudden success and his relation to it. When a resident, noting the chauffeur and the elegance of his car, wants to know who he's "supposed to be," Nathan replies in keeping with his new awareness: he is no one.

What has success brought Nathan but loss of privacy, threat to identity, danger to life, and betrayal of love? Perhaps Roth is saying that the only success of substance is the value we derive from doing our work for its own sake.

Questions for Discussion

1. Are the troubles Nathan Zuckerman experiences as a result of his sudden success inevitable?
2. Do the rewards Nathan derives from this success make his troubles worth it? Why or why not?
3. Is Nathan's purpose in writing *Carnovsky* as artistic as he claims it to be? Or is he deliberately pandering to the public's appetite for the lurid and sensational?

4. Why couldn't Nathan be satisfied with doing his work for its own sake?
5. Are Nathan's troubles with sudden success comparable with like experiences in other fields?

Annotated Bibliography

Print

Chayefsky, Paddy. *Gideon*. New York: Random, 1962.

In this dramatization of the biblical story, Gideon, a lowly farmer, is suddenly thrust into power and prominence when he is confronted with the Angel of God, who has chosen him to lead the Israelites to victory against an overwhelmingly larger army of Midianites. Gideon overcomes his difficulty in believing both the divinity of the messenger and the credibility of his message. The small force makes short work of defeating the enemy. But, in the name of humanity, Gideon refuses God's demand that he have the remaining elders slaughtered. He is unwilling to do what his new role requires of him. Tempted as he is by the offer, he refuses to become king, and God releases him from the burden of leadership.

Davis, Ossie. *Purlie Victorious*. New York: French, 1961.

Seeming failure becomes unexpected success when Purlie returns to his old village in Georgia determined to acquire a former church, now a barn, from the segregationist owner, 'Ol Cap'n Cotchipee, and turn the building into an integrated house of worship and freedom. To achieve this, he has to obtain a $500 inheritance bequeathed to a black servant and held in trust by the Cap'n. Purlie's attempt to pass off an imposter as the heir to the money is foiled by the Cap'n, which leaves Purlie with no resort but to fantasize the overthrow of his foe. This turns to truth when Charlie, the son of the Cap'n, reveals that he has obtained the $500 for Purlie and has registered the deed to the church in Purlie's name, causing the Cap'n to "drop dead standing up." Through his personal dynamism and sheer good luck, Purlie is victorious.

Hansberry, Lorraine. *A Raisin in the Sun*. New York: Random, 1959.

The misfortunes of the Youngers, a black family living in a small apartment in a Chicago slum, change abruptly with the arrival of the insurance money willed to Mama by her recently deceased husband. Mama puts a downpayment on a house in a middle-class white neighborhood and gives the rest of the money to her son, Walter, to invest in the liquor store he dreams of owning and to deposit in the bank for his sister Beneatha's medical education. But Walter gives all the money to his business partner, who runs off with it. In a desperate attempt to recoup his losses, Walter agrees to be bought off by a representative of the whites, who do not want the Youngers in their neighborhood. But at the last minute, Walter rejects the money, refusing to disgrace himself, his family, and his people and achieving a success of the spirit that makes his material failure bearable.

Hemingway, Ernest. *The Old Man and the Sea.* New York: Scribner, 1952.

A lifetime of fishing has not gotten old Santiago the catch he succeeds in hooking this day: a gigantic marlin, bigger than his boat, the sale of which will put him on easy street. But the fish will not yield to him without a fight—a fight that lasts a full day and draws him far out into the sea. However, as he tows the fish behind him on his trip back to the shore, ferocious sharks attack the fish and devour it so that all he has left when he returns are the marlin's head and skeleton. His fishing days are over; the sea has defeated him. Yet, through his courageous endurance in the face of indifferent nature, he succeeds in his very failure.

Hemingway, Ernest. "The Short Happy Life of Francis Macomber." In *The Short Stories of Ernest Hemingway.* New York: Scribner, 1954.

Success comes to Francis Macomber in a triumphant instant and then is gone. Up to that point, he has led a miserable existence because of his spineless character. His wife, Margot, despises him, so much so that she sleeps around and does not bother to hide it from him. Francis takes Margot on a safari to Africa in hope that the isolation of the place will revive her respect for him. It only makes things worse. When he runs away from a lion he has wounded, to his disgrace and despair Margot goes off with the professional hunter who accompanies them. The next day, however, Francis fearlessly pursues into the underbrush the buffalo he has wounded. Suddenly and unexpectedly, Francis has succeeded at some-thing; he has become a strong, new person who, Margot realizes, she can no longer control. Therefore, as Francis fires at the charging buffalo, Margot raises her rifle and puts an end to his short, happy life.

Jackson, Shirley, "The Lottery." In *The Magic of Shirley Jackson*, edited by Stanley Edgar Hyman. New York: Farrar, 1966.

As usually conceived, a win at a lottery is a joyous occurrence. The power of Jackson's short story derives from her reversal of this expecta-tion. In her version, the person who selects the winning ticket is stoned to death. And to those young upstarts who suggest that the lottery be abolished, Old Man Warner insists that there will be "nothing but trouble in *that*" because "there's *always* been a lottery." The annual event is a time-honored tradition of the town, with mixed results for the contestants: unexpected good fortune for those who survive it; sudden doom for those, like Tessie Hutchinson, who do not.

Lewis, Sinclair. *Elmer Gantry*. New York: Harcourt, 1927.

Football star and "hell-cat" Elmer Gantry quickly rises to success as a preacher after being converted from his heathen ways to evangelical Christianity at a prayer meeting. However, he cannot repress his hedonistic nature, and his career is continually jeopardized by his habitual drinking and womanizing. Sharon Falconer, a female evangelist, is Elmer's counterpart in sudden good fortune. Her achievements in the pulpit, which she shares with her lover, Elmer, are abruptly concluded when she dies in the fire that engulfs her Waters of Jordan Tabernacle; Elmer survives and moves on to further success and scandal.

Malamud, Bernard. *The Natural*. New York: Farrar, 1952.

At the age of thirty-four, Roy Hobbs suddenly achieves his youthful ambition to be "the best there ever was in the game." With his magical baseball bat, he leads the losing New York Pirates to a series of victories, which puts them at the top of their league. (Roy was denied this opportunity as a young man, when he was shot by a disturbed woman who had lured him to a hotel room.) He experiences a slump in midseason, but is renewed by hitting a home run for the sake of a sick boy who idolizes him. He rejects the wholesome woman who loves him for her opposite, who prevails upon him—with the owner of the team and a gambler—to take a bribe and throw the play-off game for the pennant. Finally, however, he refuses to be bought and plays his best. He succeeds in winning for the Pirates; but at the end, he breaks his bat, strikes out, returns the bribe, and leaves baseball for good.

Odets, Clifford. *Golden Boy*. New York: Random, 1937.

Success means so much to Joe Bonaparte that, contrary to his father's wishes, he gives up a promising career as a violinist to become a professional boxer. With each fight, he gets better and deadlier in the ring and, upon winning an important match, makes it to the top—but at the cost of breaking his hands and killing his opponent. This sudden shift in fortune makes all he has achieved seem worthless. Not even his girlfriend, who has always been able to revive his spirits, can comfort him now. He tries to escape his guilt in a wild car ride with her, which results in a crash and the death of both of them.

O'Neill, Eugene. *The Emperor Jones.* New York: Random, 1920.

A former Pullman porter, Brutus Jones, unexpectedly is made emperor of a small Caribbean island by the superstitious natives. But power corrupts him, his rule becomes greedy and ruthless, and the islanders are now determined to assassinate him. However, having convinced them that he can be killed only by a magic silver bullet, he unknowingly delays their attack because they must spend the night making the bullets. But he fails to prevail over his dread that they are, nevertheless, after him. As he rushes through the jungle to escape them, he becomes terrified and circles back to where he started, pursued by the beating of their increasingly loud drums and his own fears. They take shape all around him, threatening figures upon whom he empties his gun; then the natives move in on Brutus and, as abruptly as they made him their emperor, destroy him.

Potok, Chaim. *My Name Is Asher Lev.* New York: Knopf, 1972.

Asher Lev is brought into immediate national prominence as an artist, but at the cost of totally alienating himself from his Hasidic Jewish heritage. As a child, he displays such considerable artistic talent that he seems destined for a career as a painter. But the community in which he has been raised has little understanding of or use for such a career. However, Asher's superlative gifts and achievements cannot be denied. And, at last, the head of their sect, the Ladover Rebbe, recommends him to a leading sculptor and painter, who guides Asher into becoming a first-rate artist. Asher wants to reconcile his art with his religious background, but his paintings, "The Brooklyn Crucifixion I" and "The Brooklyn Crucifixion II," which feature the suffering form of his mother on the cross, make that quite impossible. Successful as the paintings are with the public and the critics, they are more than his parents and community can tolerate, forcing a final break with them.

Steinbeck, John. *The Pearl.* New York: Viking, 1947.

An impoverished fisherman, Kino, strikes it rich when he discovers a highly valuable pearl. It promises to provide him, his wife, Juana, and their infant son, Coyotito, everything they ever wanted. But the pearl brings them nothing but misfortune. Thieves try to steal it, swindlers try to cheat them out of its true value, and their house and canoe are destroyed as a consequence. When Juana tries to get rid of the pearl, Kino beats her. And when three assailants come after it, Kino kills them; Coyotito dies in the struggle. Having had his fill of such "good fortune," Kino takes the pearl and throws it as far as he can, back into the sea.

Warren, Robert Penn. *All the King's Men*. New York: Harcourt, 1946.

Willie Stark, a poor Louisiana country lawyer (like the man the character was modeled on, Huey Long), quickly becomes a powerful political figure and the state's governor. He does so with the backing of newspaperman Jack Burden, who exploits Willie's natural gifts as the people's spokesman. At first, Willie genuinely wants to improve the lives of the "hicks" and "rednecks" he has grown up with. However, he soon turns into a ruthless demagogue who employs Jack to dig up dirt on political opponents whom Willie wants to slander and blackmail. He becomes so vulgar and arrogant that his wife leaves him. But when he appropriates as his mistress the woman Jack loves, it so enrages her brother that he kills Willie and is, in turn, killed by his bodyguard. Jack tries to come to terms with this tragedy of sudden success and failure.

Yezierska, Anzia. *Red Ribbon on a White Horse*. New York: Persea, 1950.

This semiautobiographical novel depicts the troubled career of an immigrant author and her unhappy experience with unexpected good fortune. It begins with her impoverished upbringing in New York's Jewish ghetto and goes on to depict the sudden success of her novel, which is bought by the movies and brings her to Hollywood as a highly paid screenwriter. But she is soon disillusioned by the commercialism of the film industry. She abhors the artistic compromises it demands of her, its indifference to the plight of the less fortunate, and the fair-weather friendships she makes as a celebrity. This dries up her creative energies and leaves her unable to write. Finally, after a number of chastening encounters with other writers, she comes to recognize that she has been too dependent on the approval of others and renews her commitment to herself and her work.

Film

All about Eve. Twentieth Century-Fox. 1950. 138 min.

Eve, a young actress, uses flattery, deception, and bribery to quickly rise to the top of her profession. Her triumph comes when, having maneuvered herself into the part of understudy for a famous actress in a Broadway play, she arranges to get the star stranded in the country for a few days so she can go on in the leading role. Having already buttered up the leading theater critic, she obtains a rave review from his newspaper and instant stardom. But she must pay the price of being despised by her fellow professionals and subject to manipulation by those like her—

particularly a young actress who arrives on the scene, another Eve on the way up.

La Bamba. Columbia Pictures. 1988. 106 min.

Singer Ritchie Valens becomes an overnight celebrity when he records the Mexican song, "La Bamba," which he has adapted for American audiences. The film dramatizes his struggle to succeed against his family's initial opposition, discrimination against Hispanics, and his own revulsion with the world of commercial music. In fact, the very song that makes him famous is at first rejected by his agent as "too ethnic" to be popular. Finally, he achieves national fame, but in order to sustain it he must conquer his fear of flying. This, ironically, leads to his early death in a plane crash.

Bananas. United Artists. 1971. 82 min.

In his sudden accession to the leadership of a revolution in the Caribbean republic of San Marcos, Fielding Melish, a New York loser, hits the jackpot. At first, he is spurned by his political activist girlfriend, who is absorbed in the revolution. But in his red-bearded guise as the country's new president, he wins her back; and even though he is later unmasked and discredited, she agrees to marry him. Their wedding night is featured on ABC's Wide World of Sports, narrated by Howard Cosell, the ultimate measure of "making it"!

Being There. Lorimar/United Artists. 1979. 130 min.

Soon after his wealthy employer dies without warning, Chance, a simple-minded gardener of few words, finds himself a world-famous figure. Until recently, Chance has never stepped outside of his place of employment, and all he knows about the world is what he has seen watching television. Chance creates a sensation when his disarmingly simple answers to complex political questions appear to be the ultimate in wisdom. He is really talking about gardening, but deep meanings are read into his homely pronouncements. Unexpectedly propelled into national prominence, he becomes a political consultant, television personality, and candidate for the presidency. *Being There* is a telling satire of sudden success in politics and the media.

Big. Twentieth Century-Fox. 1989. 104 min.

Thirteen-year-old Josh Baskin yearns to be "big." Frustrated in his affections for a girl taller than he and refused a carnival ride because of his small stature, he brings his desire to a nearby wish machine, Zoltar Speaks, which magically grants it to him; the next day he is 30 years old. However, despite his attempts to explain, his mother mistakes him for his own kidnapper, and he runs away to nearby New York City. There he meets with more unexpected success. His boyish instincts and ways enable him to rise to the top of a toy company and win the interest of an attractive colleague, Susan. But he is not at all comfortable with the cares of adulthood. He locates the machine that transformed him and returns to boyhood, bidding good-bye to the unhappy but understanding Susan and his sudden good fortune.

A Face in the Crowd. Warner Brothers. 1957. 125 min.

Seemingly doomed to a life of alcoholism and failure, country singer Lonesome Rhodes unexpectedly achieves national renown with the support of a reporter named Marcia who discovers him. She manages to get him a radio show, which becomes very popular, and accompanies him to New York, where he becomes a famous television personality. He has asked Marcia to be his wife, but instead he impulsively marries a young majorette. Even more disturbing to Marcia is his support for a reactionary political group promoting an isolationist senator for the White House. Totally disgusted with his egomania and lust for power, Marcia retaliates by keeping his show on the air when he thinks no one can hear him, letting the public know how he really despises them—and denying him his success as abruptly as she had promoted it.

The Inspector General. Warner Brothers. 1949. 102 min.

A musical version of the Gogol play, the film is a comedy of unexpected success deriving from mistaken identity. In a small town in Russia, an illiterate medicine show helper suddenly finds himself a big-shot when he is thought by town officials to be the Czar's emissary, an inspector general. They treat him like royalty; he is wined and dined and has the whole town at his disposal. Therefore, he takes them for all they are worth until the real inspector arrives; then, not only is the deceiver exposed, but the deceived.

Limelight. United Artists. 1952. 145 min.

In a stunning final performance, Calvero, a drunken comedian who has fallen out of favor with the public, achieves one more moment of greatness. He has renewed a suicidal young dancer's faith in herself, so much so that she goes on to become a star, while he can find work only with a band of street musicians. However, she seeks him out and gets him a spot in a prestigious benefit show. Despite his misgivings and self-doubt, he musters up all his old energy and talent, and his act is an immediate and stunning success. Although he dies at the act's conclusion, it is with the knowledge that he has been once again in the limelight.

Trading Places. Paramount. 1983. 106 min.

Rich man Louis Winthorpe III is suddenly forced to trade places with poor man Billy Roy Valentine. This is done at the whim of Louis's wealthy bosses, the brothers Randolph and Mortimer Duke, to determine whether heredity or environment is more crucial to a person's success. Therefore, they frame Louis for a crime he did not commit and have him thrown out of the firm, while they bring Billy Roy into the fold. The latter is a con man of the streets who fleeces his clients by pretending to be blind and lame. He possesses all the skills needed to thrive in business. Louis gets the worst of the bargain, but he becomes a nicer person through his plight and links up with a woman better suited to him than the one he left behind. Louis and Billy Roy unite in the end to turn the tables on the Dukes.

Viva Zapata. Twentieth Century-Fox. 1952. 113 min.

Peasant leader Emiliano Zapata is elevated to greatness when he overthrows Mexican dictator Porfirio Diaz. He wins the hand of a wealthy landowner's daughter and supports the democratic regime of President Madero, who persuades Emiliano to disarm his followers. When Madero is assassinated, Emiliano, along with Pancho Villa, revenges himself against the perpetrator and is made president. However, when his people come to him and denounce his brother for taxing them unjustly, Emiliano turns against them. But realizing he is becoming as dictatorial as the autocrat he has overthrown, Emiliano resigns from office. This only increases his popularity; but at the height of his success, he is assassinated in an ambush.

Wall Street. Twentieth Century-Fox. 1988. 124 min.

Bud Fox, an ambitious young stockbroker from a working-class background, cheats his way to fortune in short order. He does so by following the philosophy and example of millionaire Wall Street wheeler-dealer Gordon Gecko, who advocates that greed is the only good in the world of high finance; that ruthlessness, deception, and betrayal are prime virtues; and that anything goes as long as you do not get caught. But Fox lacks the moral stomach to persist in such criminality and finally turns the tables on Gordon, getting himself indicted and imprisoned. Just as quickly as they had lauded his achievements, his fans have no use for him now, and Bud comes to realize the true malignity of Gordon's credo.

9 Adolescence: Crisis and Loss:

Alice McDermott's *That Night*

By Nicholas Mazza

Fiction offers pathways to understanding adolescent and young adult life transitions. The period of adolescence is marked by changes of body, emotion, and behavior. The struggle for identity discussed in the next chapter is the gravest challenge adolescents must resolve. Adolescence is also the beginning of establishing intimacy and expressing love, which become central to young adulthood. Initially, the direction along which maturation progresses is unclear to the adolescent and his or her family, and conflict results with the attendant stress on parents and children both. The search for identity and autonomy provokes conflicts. The missteps provoke crises, and as a result young people often must give up what they passionately strive to obtain. The realism about what life will bring gives young people a sense of loss. The discussion of adolescence in this chapter emphasizes crisis and loss.

The Paradigm

Even for the adolescent who proposes to have all the answers to problems in life, the need for guidance remains central. *That Night*, by Alice McDermott (Farrar, 1987), provides a safe glimpse of another time (the 1960s) that is distant enough for objectivity, yet close enough to universalize thoughts and feelings about contemporary life. The novel can be discussed as a "there and then" phenomenon or a "here and now" experience. It has the power to match the ambivalence associated with

The author would like to thank Janice Fisher Mazza and Peggy Troast for their assistance in the preparation of this manuscript.

adolescent and young adult stages. Guidance is provided by identifying key issues and problems for adolescents and their families. Lessons on crisis and loss are particularly noteworthy. The solutions, however, are left to the reader.

Summary

That Night is the story of two teenage lovers in the early 1960s, living in a middle-class Long Island suburb. Sheryl becomes pregnant by Rick and is sent away by her mother to live with her aunt and uncle in Ohio. Her mother's decision to send her away reflects prevailing Catholic and community values. The story begins with a bloody street battle between Rick's friends and the neighborhood fathers. Rick, unaware of the pregnancy and Sheryl's departure and thwarted by Sheryl's mother in his attempts to call her, came that night to "claim her." The battle ends with the arrival of the police and subsequent arrests. As the story unfolds, we find that Rick is never to see Sheryl again. Sheryl, living in Ohio, becomes increasingly depressed and attempts suicide. She is saved, delivers a baby boy, and gives him up for adoption. The reader is given only a glimpse of her plight beyond the birth of the baby.

An examination of the relationship between the two lovers reveals troubled family histories, the illusions of first love, loss (including the death of Sheryl's father), and a difficult passage toward adulthood. The aftermath of the neighborhood battle provides a look at parents struggling to preserve and protect their beliefs and their children. Both the adolescents and their parents are prone to self-deception: Sheryl believes that she can somehow, through the power of love alone, be reunited with Rick and keep her father alive; Rick believes that he can, through a show of strength, fortify his identity and maintain his tie to Sheryl; and the neighborhood fathers believe that they are a community and can defend themselves.

Time is the interlocking element in this novel. We see the narrator, now an adult at the end of her marriage, recounting events, beginning with "that night" when the "ten-year-old her was stopped by the beauty of it all." We are taken backward and forward in time as individual, family, and neighborhood histories are developed. This works both as a literary device and as a means to identify the perceptions and personalized meanings of time for many of the characters. One of Sheryl's favorite rock groups was the Shirelles. It is one of their songs that perhaps best captures the theme of this novel: "Will You Still Love Me Tomorrow?" Excitement, urgency, the need for permanence, and the fear of loss are part of the predicament of adolescents.

For the main characters in *That Night*, life is a series of losses. Sheryl sees her pregnancy as endangering her relationship with Rick. Being sent off to Ohio, she loses her lover, independence, friends, and mother. Sheryl will have to be responsible for the child, by herself, forever. She tries to call Rick, but is unsuccessful. Sheryl, experiencing a great pain, runs away from her aunt's house. Feeling remorseful, alone, without support, and hopeless, she attempts suicide.

Sheryl's mother loses her husband, daughter, and home. Sheryl loses her father, friends, lover, and self-esteem. Later in the story, Sheryl is allowed to briefly see and touch her newborn baby before he is given up for adoption. This provides still another loss, another void. Rick loses his lover and strength at a time when his mother's history of mental illness and his father's failed medical practice and physical illness are also of great impact on him. The narrator loses her innocence and marriage.

The novel closes with Sheryl seeking to fill a void. Her strong desire to love someone else is linked to the preservation of her father's importance; her ability to love and be loved is a kind of legacy to her father. She can still remember happier times and has the capacity to recall an earlier friendship. The narrator, referring to Sheryl holding her small cousin, states that despite Sheryl's losses and disillusionments, hope that her "emptiness be filled again" is present.

The use of *That Night* for life guidance requires caution. Sheryl's developmental needs are portrayed mainly as the need to fill a void through her relationship with Rick. This is consistent with Erikson's formulation of female identity development; however, reformulation for today's teenagers must consider current changes in sex roles. *That Night* offers guidance in that it affords the reader an opportunity to be involved in a process of understanding a part of the adolescent's world. The open-ended conclusion also reflects adolescent and young adult stages. It signals to us (at any adult developmental level and from whatever emotional or intellectual distance) the points of departure to make our own choices. Indeed, not too close, not too far, we move in, we move out.

Questions for Discussion

1. How might the story have been told through the perspective of Rick? Sheryl? Sheryl's mother?
2. How is grief handled in this novel?
3. Discuss Sheryl's personal meaning of "love."
4. What decisions have the most profound effect on Sheryl?

5. How do family and social histories affect the development (including gender identity) of Sheryl? Rick?

Annotated Bibliography

Print

Arrick, Fran. *Steffie Can't Come Out to Play.* New York: Dell, 1978.

Steffie, a fourteen-year-old runaway seeking success in New York, encounters Favor, a pimp who befriends her (providing shelter, clothes, and most importantly his attention) and later uses her on the street. Despite difficulties with other prostitutes and fear of the law, Steffie feels secure with Favor. In the end, the police arrest her, Favor discards her, and she returns to her small home town in Pennsylvania. The theme of a good girl being drawn into a destructive lifestyle, although simplistic, invites an examination of a young person's problems with unmet expectations, interpersonal relationships, intimacy, and sexuality. Although its protagonist is fourteen years old, the book also relates to older adolescents and young adults.

Betancourt, Jeanne. *Sweet Sixteen and Never.* New York: Bantam/Starfire, 1987.

Sex, teenage pregnancy, single-parent families, and intergenerational linkages are all part of this novel. Sixteen-year-old Julie's best friend, Gale, is pregnant and seeking advice. Julie must cope with her own emerging sexuality as she struggles with pressures from her boyfriend to have sex. At the same time, Julie must face the discovery of her mother's teenage pregnancy, her affair with Fred, and her father's political radicalism. Julie's pressures are compounded, and in their distinctiveness they evoke the problems to be solved by maturing teenagers. This is a novel about female maturation, the right to make decisions, and recognizing these decisions' impact.

Blume, Judy. *Forever.* New York: Bradbury, 1975.

The emerging sexuality of adolescents and the promise, as well as the pain, of first love are explicitly but sensitively portrayed in this novel. The development of the sexual relationship between Katherine and Michael, two high school seniors, is traced from first glance to sexual culmination. Later, Katherine goes away for a summer and is attracted to another young man. The conflicts, disappointments, and development of a perspective on time, people, and place allow her to accept her relationship with Michael as special, but not forever. The dialogue between characters (for example, Katherine and Michael; Katherine and Mother; social worker and physician interviews at Planned Parenthood) accentuates the importance of clear communication and accurate information. This novel's attention to head and heart issues and its provision of sex education help readers master the challenge of young adulthood.

Brancato, Robin F. *Blinded by the Light.* New York: Knopf, 1978.

The attraction of cults to young adults is the theme of this novel, the story of Gail, a young woman (sophomore in college) in search of her older brother, who is in a cult called Light of the World. Gail infiltrates the group in order to locate him, and thus is exposed to cult indoctrinations. The techniques of manipulation and mind control, including friendliness, peer pressure, and guilt, are detailed. The right of the individual to make choices also is addressed, as Gail questions her intrusion on her brother's decision. Sexual, family, and academic content are incorporated in this novel, which has a realistic and thought-provoking open-ended conclusion.

Brancato, Robin F. *Winning.* New York: Knopf, 1977.

Gary Madden is a quadriplegic as the result of a football accident. Once a star player, he now faces the loss of physical abilities and self-esteem because his identity is intricately related to his athletic performance. Gary's hospital experiences offer some timely insights into the physically handicapped. His tutor, an English teacher who has also suffered loss (the death of her husband), provides support that is healing for both Gary and herself. The impact of friends, family, Gary's girlfriend, and others is identified. The metaphor of anagrams in this novel, that is "making something new out of the scrambled parts," captures its essence.

Carter, Alden R. *Sheila's Dying.* New York: Putnam, 1987.

Sheila is a teenager with a terminal illness (cancer). The novel holds fairly close to Elisabeth Kubler-Ross's stages of psychological reaction to death—denial and isolation, anger, bargaining, depression, and acceptance. Generally, this novel is about the effects of death on the survivors; particularly, it is about relationships and commitments. Although Sheila's relationship with her boyfriend, Jerry, is ending, when he finds out about her condition he decides to see her through to the end. The fact that a close and ultimately a love relationship develops between Jerry and Sheila's friend Bonnie, who also is caring for her, is not surprising during this time of grief. The personal, familial, and social ramifications of Sheila's illness on many of those touched by her are addressed.

Cormier, Robert. *The Chocolate War.* New York: Pantheon, 1974.

Sinister fund-raising, group contagion, a range of adolescent person-alities, family issues, and the classic fight of good versus evil are the themes captured in this realistic and powerful novel. Brother Leon, acting headmaster for a small Catholic boys' high school, convinces the stu-dents through mass appeal to commit to selling chocolates for their annual fund-raising event. The goal is to double the amount sold from the previous year. He enlists the help of the Vigils, a strong-armed gang, to ensure success. Jerry Renault, a freshman, refuses to be part of the plan and endures intimidations and brutal measures. Ultimately, however, he is goaded into a boxing match with one of the antagonists to settle the matter. Although Jerry is badly beaten, the story points to the impor-tance of character in realizing a worthy identity.

Crutcher, Chris. *Chinese Handcuffs.* New York: Greenwillow, 1989.

The adolescent dealing with overwhelming stress (both internal and external) during the course of his high school years provides a compelling look at family and social problems today. Dillon Hemingway has witnessed the suicide of his brother and is struggling with guilt and anger. His close friend, Jennifer, reveals her personal struggles as an incest victim. She is too frightened to report to the authorities that she has been victimized (fearing her stepfather would harm her mother and younger sister), and although trusting of Dillon, she refrains from a romantic relationship. Achievement in sports provides an emotional safety valve for the main characters. The title's metaphor of Chinese handcuffs is an apt one, as explained by one character: "The only way to get my finger out of that tube was to quit trying to escape and release the pressure." This novel, through the use of time (for example, flashbacks) and skillful characterization, provides a look at the journey from adolescence to young adulthood and reminds us that the crises of earlier childhood years also must be reckoned with if the journey is to be healthy. The novel also includes a number of therapeutic elements. For example, Dillon's writing long letters to his dead brother serves as a release and a method of working through conflicts. The importance of close relationships and support through difficult times also is made clear.

Gallo, Donald R., ed. *Visions: Nineteen Short Stories by Outstanding Writers for Young Adults.* New York: Delacorte, 1987.

This collection of short stories, all dealing with adolescent and young adult material, covers a wide range of themes, including family relation-ships, friendships, loss, identity, abuse, sexuality, and peer pressure. Various moods as well as economic and cultural contexts are presented.

The following are examples of two stories dealing with identity and friendship.

In "Dream Job," by Marjorie Weinman Sharmat, sixteen-year-old Becky is hired for a summer job as receptionist at a publishing company. According to her boss, her primary function is to smile. Becky's encounters with sexism and ageism (for example, "You're too young to know anything") are told in a timely and humorous manner as she struggles for her creative identity.

"Great Moves," by Sandy Asher, is a story about two boys asking the same girl (Annie) to a dance; female friendship, male competition, and self-identity are neatly interwoven. Recognizing that the boys care more about winning than about her and that they tried to use her friend Brenda to exercise influence on their behalf, Annie makes a delayed, self-affirming decision to choose neither boy for the dance.

Gibbs, Angelica. "Father Was a Wit." 1937. Reprint, in *Family: Stories from the Interior*, edited by Geri Giebel Chavis. Saint Paul, Minn.: Graywolf, 1987.

This story deals with the impact of a father on his daughter Helena's self-identity and interpersonal relationships. Told through the voice of the adolescent, the tale gives us a sample of representative concerns of a female teenager about to move into young adulthood. The familiar distance between father and daughter is revealed as Helena is about to graduate from high school and is waiting to see whether her father will show up for the ceremony. She is aware that she will probably receive an award and wants desperately for him to see her. Helena is awed by her father's ability to penetrate people's defenses and expose their frailties, as well as his standards for success. She idealizes him and seeks his approval, so she has been disappointed in the past by his absences. Helena wins an award in English composition for a poem she wrote, and once again her father fails to show. Helena's thoughts reveal her frailty and the need for her father's support.

Holland, Isabelle. *Heads You Win, Tails I Lose*. New York: Ballantine, 1973.

Melissa's parents' marital conflict, middle adulthood developmental crises, and drugs all impact on the fifteen-year-old's personal relationships and self-esteem. The interplay of family and individual developmental crises is evident in this novel. Overweight and facing the challenge of playing a part in her school play, Melissa copes through the use of drugs (her mother's diet pills). Ultimately, she breaks down, and resolution of her struggle is aided by her friend Joel, with whom she develops a close and trusting relationship, and by two teachers. The novel's ending may seem a bit contrived, but offers a sensitive glimpse of a father-daughter exchange that provides hope and acceptance of life changes.

Hurston, Zora Neale. *Their Eyes Were Watching God*. 1937. Reprint, Urbana: Univ. of Illinois, 1978.

This classic novel portrays the struggle and ultimate triumph of protagonist Janie, who achieves self-definition and reassesses her primary relationships. The journey from young adulthood in the 1930s for a black woman in the all-black rural Eatonville, Florida, to middle adulthood is difficult and painful. The transition involves a series of marriages (one forced on her, one to escape, and one by choice that proves to be empowering). The social and cultural context is established early in the story. The power of language (including 1930s southern black speech), imagery, and theme affirm a view of love (self and other) that is not locked in any one developmental stage. Indeed, self-identity development is ongoing. This novel, written more than 50 years ago, offers much to our current concern with ethnic and gender sensitivity.

Jensen, Kathryn. *Pocket Change*. New York: Macmillan, 1989.

Post-traumatic stress syndrome is the subject of this powerful novel, in which the disorder's impact is examined through sixteen-year-old Josie Monroe. She is confused and distressed over her father's irrational behavior (including uncontrollable rages); her stepmother's denial of the problem; and her own social isolation. The novel offers accurate information about the disorder and its effect on others. It also is helpful in providing plausible courses of action taken by Josie, who initially contacts a veterans' counseling center and speaks with the psychologist and later—when pushed to the brink by her father's behavior—contacts the police. The impact of the Vietnam war (when the mean age of the soldiers fighting was nineteen) on an individual's personal, family, and social life surfaces throughout the novel. (In this novel, the metaphor for the surfacing of repressed memories is coins wearing through the cloth of pockets.) *Pocket Change* does not provide all the answers, but helps raise some important questions.

Klein, Norma. *My Life as a Body*. New York: Knopf, 1987.

Augie, a seventeen-year-old senior in high school, is in the midst of questioning her own sexuality and is prone to the myth that everyone else is having gratifying sexual relations. Then she is assigned the role of tutor to physically disabled Sam (the victim of an auto accident). Sam is wheelchair bound and has suffered brain damage. Their relationship from friendship to sexual involvement develops as Sam's brain functions are restored. Augie's insecurities are reduced as she goes on to college and passes into young adulthood. The physical distance between Sam and Augie results in their breakup, and Augie gets involved in a new sexual relationship with her art professor. Sensitivity to the physically handicapped, emerging sexuality, the struggles of first love, alternative lifestyles, self-identity, and alienation are all subject to introspection for readers of this novel.

Miklowitz, Gloria D. *Good-bye Tomorrow.* New York: Delacorte, 1987.

Alex is a senior high school student diagnosed as having ARC (AIDS-related complex). The aftermath of this diagnosis takes on personal, family, and social dimensions. This realistic story is told through three narrators: Alex, the victim of the blood transfusion that made him an AIDS carrier; his sister, Christy, who provides us with a lesson on friendship; and Shannon, his long-standing girlfriend. Alex is victimized in numerous ways, including the loss of his loving and intimate relationship with Shannon; his shunning by friends; his suspension from school; and his exploitation by the media. Adolescent loneliness is an issue that is placed in a current and compelling context. The novel's realistic portrayal of characters, its provision of accurate information, and its different points of view should serve readers well in recognizing the need to identify myths, overcome prejudices, and seek updated facts.

Peck, Richard. *Are You in the House Alone?* New York: Viking, 1976.

This novel will sensitize the reader to the trauma of rape—in this case, the rape of a sixteen-year-old girl. In addition to the violent physical assault and crime against the victim, readers will be exposed to the social and psychological coercion involved. Attitudes toward rape, politics, and ignorance all interplay in further victimizing the protagonist. In brief, high school junior Gail Osburne receives threatening phone calls and a note. She seeks help, but is not successful in obtaining it. While babysitting, she is beaten and raped by her girlfriend's boyfriend. Later, Gail's previous sexual activity with her boyfriend is held against her. The rapist comes from a wealthy and influential family and goes free from the crime. Predictably, he attacks another girl and kills her. We are not told of his plight, except that he leaves town. The positive characterization of Gail and her response to this traumatic experience, as well as the open-ended conclusion, should promote discussion by readers.

Potok, Chaim. *The Chosen.* New York: Simon & Schuster, 1967.

Two teenaged boys' friendship amidst their families' major theological differences within the Jewish faith is the subject of this novel, set in

Brooklyn in the 1940s. Each family's expression of love is very different. Danny's father is a Hasidic rabbi, and tradition dictates that Danny eventually replace his father in that role. Reuven's father, an Orthodox Jew, is an educator in a liberal institution and provides a more open and warm atmosphere for his son, thus enhancing their relationship. The boys maintain their friendship despite a two-year separation. Father-son relationships and the struggle for understanding are elements in this novel that are beyond time, place, and ethnicity; however, the specifics of culture provide valuable lessons and make the story believable.

Rostkowski, Margaret I. *The Best of Friends*. New York: Harper, 1989.

Being a teenager in the 1960s, with the war in Vietnam an ever present strain, makes future planning a difficult emotional endeavor. This novel deals with the strains on two boys' friendship, as Dan and Will chart separate futures. Dan's sister, Sarah, plays a pivotal role as she provides insight to Dan and emotional support to Will and as her own personal strength is revealed. It is a novel that will stimulate readers to examine themselves and perhaps to reassess their personal convictions (for example, their stances on right and wrong). Although the decisions are reminiscent of the 1960s (for instance, the decision to turn in a draft card), the decision process remains timeless.

Sachs, Marilyn. *Class Pictures*. New York: Dutton, 1980.

This brief novel presents reflections on the friendship of two girls, Pat and Lolly, from kindergarten through high school. The essence of developmental change is effectively captured through the use of Pat, who is getting ready to go off to M.I.T., as narrator. The two girls are from very different family and social backgrounds. Lolly changes from an overweight and socially rejected child to an attractive adolescent who draws the attention of her classmates. Pat changes from a popular childhood leader to a brilliant but less popular adolescent. Sensitive attention to female identity development is also indicated in this story. Lolly's goes beyond a sexist female role that only acknowledges physical attractiveness. She chooses to become an environmental activist, involved in the antinuclear movement. Pat, through determination and the encouragement of a male teacher, pursues her interest in science. The author's use of time (through Pat's memories) and the novel's open-ended conclusion allow readers to reflect and draw their own conclusions.

Salinger, J. D. *The Catcher in the Rye*. Boston: Little, 1951.

This classic story of adolescence is narrated by the principal character, sixteen-year-old Holden Caufield, who in the opening chapter is in a mental hospital. Through the use of flashback, the author skillfully uses time to typify Holden's character, thinking processes, and emotional state. Although this novel was written some 40 years ago, it includes such current adolescent issues as alienation, discontent with a superficial and exploitative society, and questions and confusion about family, friends, career, and sexuality. *The Catcher in the Rye* provides another compelling perspective on the journey from adolescence to young adulthood.

Scoppetone, Sandra. *Happy Endings Are All Alike.* New York: Harper, 1979.

Jaret Tyler and Peggy Danziger, two senior high school girls living in a small town, are in love with each other. Jaret's identity, well being, and human spirit are brutally tested when she is raped by a disturbed youth who spied on the girls and threatens to reveal their secret if she reports the rape. Despite the fear of her lesbianism being revealed and of losing her lover, Jaret presses charges. By the end of this novel, Jaret is able to affirm her integrity and continue her relationship with Peggy. The ambivalence and confusion of teenage sexuality, the trauma of rape, the anticipation of social consternation, and the struggle for self-esteem are effectively interwoven in this book.

Shaw, Janet Beeler. "In High Country." 1985. Reprint, in *Family: Stories from the Interior,* edited by Geri Giebel Chavis. Saint Paul, Minn.: Graywolf, 1987.

The nuances of being an adolescent with divorced parents are sensitively introduced in this short story as it moves to a father's and son's experience on their backpacking trip. Male roles and expectations are identified as sixteen-year-old Bill is exposed to his father's vulnerabilities. When Bill's father suffers an accident, Bill takes on the leadership role (although his father, through his expressions and silences, tries to minimize it). Although there is some bonding between father and son, their distance and inability to express feelings are accentuated. Bill's father turns to him, asking for a promise not to tell what happened on the trip. Suddenly, Bill recognizes that his father is struggling not to cry. The reader may be reminded of the recent song by Mike and the Mechanics, "The Living Years," noting similar generational themes and urging the expression of love between father and son.

Shaw, Janet Beeler. "The Trail to the Ledge." 1985. Reprint, in *Family: Stories from the Interior,* edited by Geri Giebel Chavis. Saint Paul, Minn.: Graywolf, 1987.

Issues of intimacy and ambivalence surface in this short story about a young adult couple, married six weeks and working in a summer camp for children. Individual and couple identity is examined, in part through the context of Jim's secret of spying on young girls in their cabin at night. Ultimately, Gail finds out. She is shocked not so much at what could be called voyeuristic behavior, but rather that he kept the secret. Jim has an intense need for privacy. Gail has an intense need for intimacy. Both have rigid expectations about their marital relationship. This story relates to the young adult task of preserving individual identity while developing a couple identity.

Silko, Leslie. *Ceremony*. New York: Viking, 1977.

This novel deals with the post-World War II trauma for Tayo, a young man who is part Navajo and part Caucasian. The conflicts and painful experiences of a native American family are sensitively portrayed. Developmental and social issues emerging from this story include death and grief (Tayo's cousin was killed in the war), biracialism, the erosion of old values, and family and social acceptance and rejection.

10 Adolescence: Identity and Autonomy:

William Inge's *Splendor in the Grass*

By Samuel T. Gladding

Finding an identity is a dilemma for many young adults. Where does one look for it? Knowing who one is involves actively discovering one's bent through both accidental trial and error and planned decision making. The process is further complicated by the emotional world that surrounds this stage of life and the fact that many decisions, especially educational ones, require cognitive skills and experiences that often are overwritten by feelings and passions. The process also is influenced by the family in which the person resides and its degree of health. If parents have not resolved their own personal problems, the young person will find it difficult to explore freely the alternatives for self-realization and may choose behavior that is self-defeating and socially unproductive. What the young learn about themselves, what talents, inclinations, and emotional strengths they possess, and how well they are able to react to the not always beneficial influence of family and friends will prove crucial to maturation. Vocational choice, if freely made, is a manifestation of maturity.

The Paradigm

The play *Splendor in the Grass*, by William Inge (Bantam, 1961), illustrates the importance of emotional relationships and family influences in educational decisions. It is the story of two eighteen-year-olds facing what all young people their age encounter—the challenge of deciding about their futures at a time when they are romantically involved with each other and struggling with the turmoil within their families of origin. The time is the late 1920s, and the place is a small town in eastern Kansas, but

122

the issues involved in this play are as current as the morning news and as widespread as the great plains of the West.

In many ways, Inge touches a classic theme that transcends time and place. He calls our attention to the difficulty of becoming a rational and purposeful person in an irrational and sometimes unpredictable world. The characters, especially the teenagers and their parents, come alive in reading or seeing the production of this work as unique and universal figures. For the adolescents, there is the problem of understanding what they want to do with their lives and how. There is the struggle for independence and the need for healthy, nonclinging interdependence. For the adults, there is the task of giving guidance without becoming overinvolved or overinvested in the decisions of their offspring. Thus, the difficulty is to reestablish an adult life professionally and personally and to allow the children of the marriage to discover their own values and establish their own lives educationally, vocationally, and emotionally. It is a process of letting go and growing, of finding a different way to relate than as parent to child.

Summary

Deanie Loomis, an innocent and dependent young woman, is deeply in love with Bud Stamper, an athletic and sensitive young man who is the only son of a wealthy, overbearing father and a passive mother. Deanie's major dilemmas involve growing up mentally and learning to be less dependent on Bud and her family, especially her doting mother. Bud has family and independence problems too. His father wants to live life through Bud and is determined to give him the best money can buy, including an education at Yale. He expects Bud to live up to expectations, and anything less than perfection is unacceptable. Instead of openly rebelling against his father's demands, Bud acquiesces. He becomes the family hero and just the opposite of his older sister, who has been kicked out of two schools, has flunked out of college, and has had an abortion. In brief, Bud is caught between his own wishes and those of his father. He is stuck in the role of pleasing others while denying himself.

As the play opens, Deanie and Bud are embraced in each other's arms, struggling to maintain the proper physical boundaries in the relationship. It is apparent that they have been warned by their parents—Deanie's mother and Bud's father, Ace—not to go too far sexually. Thus, when they stop kissing and Bud takes Deanie home, they feel a mixture of pleasure and dejection. Their identity as a couple is strong, but individually each is unsure as to how to grow in life.

It is at their respective houses that we gain insight into the real internal personal struggles Bud and Deanie face with external events. Both are confronted with parents who are overinvolved with them. The focus of the parents' attention is often on future situations that otherwise would not be among the uppermost priorities of these two young adults. The parents control their children for their own gain, not for the children's sake.

In Deanie's case, Mrs. Loomis, a woman in her mid-forties whose vocation is housewife, is afraid that if Deanie yields to Bud sexually, Bud will not marry her. As a result of her own failures in married life, Mrs. Loomis is concerned that Deanie marry, especially someone from a wealthy family, such as Bud's. Thus, Mrs. Loomis questions Deanie frequently about what she has done with Bud. In the process, she denies her own sexual urges when she tells Deanie that nice girls do not feel sexual toward boys. She also hints to her daughter that while the Loomis family is not well off, they may have enough money (if their shares of Stamper oil stock keep rising) to send Deanie to college next year. Such an experience, however, would be a sacrifice and merely tangential to what Mrs. Loomis wants for herself and Deanie.

Bud also encounters conflict with his father when he arrives home. The friction centers around his dating Deanie, and Ace warns Bud that if he is not careful he will get her pregnant and have to marry her. Such a scenario would be completely opposite Ace's plans for his high school football captain of a son. It is in Ace's mind that Bud's accomplishments will achieve esteem for the whole family, especially for him as father. Ace wants Bud to get an eastern education as much as he wants his own growing oil company to merge with a big eastern outfit. As Ace puts it, Bud is running for him now because Ace is physically unable to do so due to an injury he received when, at Bud's age, he fell off an oil rig. In short, Ace sees Bud as the manifestation of his own boyhood dreams. He wants Bud to be athletic, academic, and achieving for his sake, not Bud's.

Like Mrs. Loomis, Ace is so full of his plans that he fails to listen to his almost grown child and give proper guidance. For example, Ace denies Bud's request to attend a state agricultural college and become a rancher. He rationalizes that such an activity is not really what Bud desires because Bud is too young to know what he wants. Besides, this goal is not good enough. Furthermore, Ace criticizes Deanie's father, Del, for not having enough ambition to be more than a grocer. In doing so, he gives his son the message that ambition and money are the most important factors in making grown-up decisions about careers. It is obvious that Ace does not want Bud to get too involved with Deanie, although in an effort to pacify Bud he tells his son that when Bud finishes

Yale, if he still wants to marry Deanie, Ace will give them a honeymoon in Europe as a wedding present.

In addition to dealing with their same-gender parents, Deanie and Bud face other problems that interfere with their making good educational and vocational choices. In Deanie's case, her inability to see herself as anyone other than Bud's girlfriend is devastating to her when Bud decides to break off the relationship because of pressure to do so from his father. At first, Deanie copes and hopes that Bud will come back to her, but as time wears on she becomes depressed and is unable to function effectively at school and in interpersonal relationships. She talks about wanting to die, and the only support her parents are able to give her is hot meals and a denial that the situation is as bad as Deanie thinks it is.

We see just how troubled Deanie has become in her encounter with her English teacher, Miss Metcalf, who asks Deanie to explain the passage from Wordsworth's "Ode on Intimations of Immortality," which emphasizes the importance of finding strength from what has been, such as the splendor of the grass or the glory of the flower. Deanie does not perceive that she has strength, and although she initially tries to explain that growth and development may occur through loss and an acceptance and integration of the past into the present, she ends up running out of Miss Metcalf's class in tears. The rest of the school year is downhill from there, and at the end of the year, Deanie is sent to the state mental hospital in Wichita. Mrs. Loomis blames everyone, including Bud, for her "baby's" deterioration and shows little understanding of her daughter's inner core.

It is at that point in the play that educational and vocational fortunes seem to change. Bud has been dating a "more experienced" girl, Juanita, and an acquaintance of Deanie, Kay, and understands more fully his feelings for Deanie. Yet at the request of Mrs. Loomis, he breaks off relations with Deanie even further. Likewise, Bud knuckles under to the demands of his father (denying his inner wishes again) and goes to Yale. Instead of doing well academically and forgetting Deanie and Kansas, Bud purposely tries to fail his subjects and drinks heavily. He is fortunate that in the midst of such failure he meets Angelina, a young Italian woman who listens attentively to his troubles. It is the relationship with Angelina, along with the suicidal death of Bud's father when the stock market crashes, that gives Bud the opportunity to make important decisions about his own education and vocation. Instead of becoming a Yale graduate, he returns home to farm, marries Angelina, and begins a family. His wild sister, Ginny, has died in a car wreck by this time; thus, Bud is free to deal with himself in a way not possible before.

Meanwhile, Deanie, after two and a half years in the state psychiatric hospital, puts her relationship with Bud behind her. She is still pained by it, but she develops as a person through her sessions with Dr. Judd, her psychiatrist at the hospital. She is even able to confront the fact that her parents will not change, so she must. Consequently, she begins to handle her relationship with her parents better and opens herself to new people and ideas. She meets and falls in love with Johnny Masterson, who is in the hospital to resolve his conflicts with his father about being a surgeon. In a parallel way to Bud, Deanie rises above adversity and disappointment in order to take charge of her life.

In the last scene of the play, Deanie returns home in anticipation of her wedding to Johnny in Cincinnati. She wishes to see Bud and deal with her parents and friends in a more mature fashion. After overcoming her mother's attempt to keep her from seeing Bud, she persuades some high school girlfriends to take her out to the Stamper's old ranch, where Bud is staying. There she meets him laboring in one of the fields. He is wearing dirty denim work clothes and cowboy boots and is obviously enjoying his job. He is taken by surprise by Deanie's visit and seems a little unsure of himself. In the encounter that follows, Deanie discovers that Bud has not only found himself vocationally, but is married, has one child, and is expecting another. She meets Angelina briefly and discloses to Bud that she is getting married in a month.

A focus at the closing of the play is on the resolution of the educational and vocational difficulties of these two young adults. Whereas passion and parental authority ruled them in their late teen years, understanding and purpose now govern their lives as they enter their early twenties. Bud has been exposed to a high-powered educational experience and has decided to settle for what society would label "less." While he has not gone to the state agricultural school he had hoped to attend, it is obvious that he is involved in a profession—ranching—that gives him great joy. His relationship with Angelina also has helped him settle down. Deanie, like Bud, has not received a formal education, but she has learned how to handle herself and her emotions in a healthier manner. She appears pleased to be marrying a physician, and it is apparent that she will settle vocationally into the role of housewife by choice, not default. Thus, Bud and Deanie are much more integrated as persons and much more differentiated from their families of origin at the end of the play than they were at the beginning.

Overall, the experiences of these two young adults, while in the end productive, are bittersweet. Both have worked through the barriers in their lives that inhibited their earlier personal decision making. Deanie's struggle has required her to understand more fully herself as a person, her mother, her father, Bud, and the family and environmental dynamics of her development. Bud has come to a more thorough understanding of himself by dealing with external circumstances passively (by failing courses) and aggressively (by drinking). In some ways, he has been more fortunate than Deanie because the main nemesis to his development, Ace, has killed himself. Some of Bud's problems have been resolved by default.

At the end of the play, both Deanie and Bud confess that they do not think of happiness often and that this last parting for them is truly a sweet sorrow. Yet there is hope, as they leave each other, that their lives will be good in the long run because they are now able to make choices from more informed points of view. Though nothing can bring back their hours of splendor, they are ultimately stronger for their experiences together and apart, and they are on the road to healthier educational and vocational choices.

Questions for Discussion

1. In what ways could Bud and Deanie have handled their same-sex parents more effectively and prevented the later turmoil in their lives?
2. Both Deanie and her mother emphasize the importance of intimacy before identity. How does this pattern hurt Deanie's handling of Bud, their broken relationship, and her mother? How would choosing an education or a vocation first have helped her?
3. Bud allows his father to dominate his educational and relational choices. What strategies could he have taken to make his points of view better understood?
4. Once Bud arrives at Yale, he chooses to fail his courses and drink heavily. What educational and vocational decisions could he have made that would have been constructive and allowed him to develop a mature relationship with Deanie and his father?
5. In this play, both Mr. Loomis and Mrs. Stamper are fairly passive in interacting with their children. What difference do you think their active involvement with their children would have made in regard to Deanie's and Bud's choices about the pleasure and business of life?

Annotated Bibliography

Print

Algren, Nelson. *A Walk on the Wild Side*. New York: Farrar, 1956.

This novel, set in the 1930s, traces the episodes of Dove Linkhorn, a representative of wild young men who have fled their native Scotland because of their unwillingness to adjust to societal rules. Dove is somewhat naive in his outlook on life, but is street wise and able to escape potential danger among the lowlives he encounters. Dove initially takes a job at a cafe in Arroyo, Texas, where he works for a motherly figure, Terasina Vidavarri. However, after he rapes her he flees to New Orleans, where he seeks the American dream. His adventures in the city are marked by shadiness, and in the end—after many run-ins with the authorities in his life among prostitutes—Dove, now blinded but enlightened, returns to Arroyo to search for Terasina. The major thrust of this novel is Dove's search for rewards in the pursuit of pleasure. He is ambitious, but disrespectful of society's rules. Thus, he gets caught up in one losing adventure after another. He is clearly the antithesis of how to establish oneself in business.

Anderson, Sherwood. "I'm a Fool." *Dial* 72 (February 1922):119–29.

The protagonist narrator, a nineteen-year-old young man, is a groom at a local racetrack and is highly dissatisfied with his life. He hates the college boys who come to the track because he thinks they are putting on airs. However, he also puts on a front, including misrepresenting himself to a young woman he likes. When he realizes she deeply cares for him, he is mortified because he cannot be truthful with her and she will leave the area soon. Thus, what the young man despises—misrepresentation—he does. His failure to be himself results in his inability to gain what he most desires. Like many other stories of late adolescence, this account focuses on the painful aspects of growing up and reaching maturity. The young man learns truth through lying. He understands what he has to gain through the painful loss of a prized relationship.

Boyle, T. Coraghessan. "Greasy Lake." *Paris Review* 84 (1982):14–24.

This adventure-filled short story is narrated by a nineteen-year-old young man looking back at one significant night in his life when he and two friends decided to become "bad characters" and went out to Greasy Lake in search of "action." What they found was more than they bargained for—a major fight, a corpse, and immersion in a filthy lake. From this harrowing experience, the narrator discovered that he and his friends are not "bad" and did not even want to be so. They even turned down an offer of drugs at the end of the story. In essence, "Greasy Lake" is the tale of young men learning from experience, although they are fortunate that nothing tragic happens to them. They come out of the experience wiser as a result of their suffering. Thus, this rite of passage helps the narrator and his friends face the adult world more realistically. They will seek a positive identity from now on and make something of themselves.

Callaghan, Morley. "All the Years of Her Life." In *Now That April's Here and Other Stories*. New York: Random, 1936.

Alfred Higgins is caught by his employer in petty thievery. It is only through the poise, skill, and calm negotiation of his mother that Alfred avoids being prosecuted by the authorities. At first, Alfred is relieved and exhibits bravado concerning his fate, but he soon discovers the hard reality of his mother's life, and her actions have a dramatic impact on him. The insight he gains changes him forever and marks the beginning of his moral and vocational maturity. What Alfred eventually does is not revealed in this story but the potential for dramatic change is highlighted. The reader gets the sense that small but significant events can help turn lives around and help head people in productive vocational directions.

Cather, Willa. "Coming, Aphrodite." In *Youth and the Bright Medusa*. New York: Knopf, 1920.

"Coming, Aphrodite" is the story of two young artists—Don Hedger, a talented painter, and Eden Bower, a beautiful singer. Don, who usually is absorbed in his painting, is overwhelmed by Eden's beauty and falls passionately in love with her to the point where he can no longer concentrate on his work. While the relationship is exciting initially, it breaks down when Eden attempts to advance Don's career by introducing him to a successful commercial artist. Don is hurt by Eden's misunderstanding of what he aspires to do. They are separated for twenty years, as Eden sings in Europe and Don paints in New York. Upon returning to the United States, Eden finds that Don has built a strong reputation, but has not enjoyed financial success; she, on the other hand, is commercially successful but not a great artistic talent. The story is a remarkable contrast between the pursuit of art for art's sake, as represented by Don, and art for business, as symbolized by Eden. Both young people are true to themselves and their desires, but the goals, rewards, and outcomes of the directions they take in life vary greatly.

Conrad, Joseph. "The Secret Sharer." In *Great Short Works of Joseph Conrad*, edited by Jerry Allen. New York: Harper, 1989.

Unsure of himself and his leadership ability, a young captain in his first command takes responsibility for saving the life of Leggatt, a young man who has killed a sailor for ineptness on a sister ship. The captain realizes through his conversations and experience with Leggatt that he is more like Leggatt than different from him. This insight forces the captain to recognize his own dark side, yet it also frees him to accept himself more fully and become more aware of his capabilities. Thus, he begins to make decisions that are both courageous and risky, including taking his ship into shallow waters at night in order to drop off Leggatt on a nearby island in an effort to prevent his discovery and execution. Conrad's integration of contrasts parallels the holistic growth of the captain in this story. Through self-examination and courage, the captain grows in his career and exemplifies the transformation of his leadership potential into leadership reality.

Faulkner, William. *The Sound and the Fury.* New York: Random, 1929.

A different young member of the Compton family narrates each of this novel's four parts. Basically, the story is about the disintegration of a formerly genteel southern family, but it highlights the death of Quentin Compton, a promising young Harvard student, and the failure of his sister, Candace (Caddy), to develop vocationally. The only Compton who achieves a professional career identity is brother Jason, who succeeds by being mean and dishonest. Overall, the Comptons take pride in what has been, but little in what is. Quentin was the hope of the family, but became obsessed with Caddy and took his own life. Members of the family are not connected well with themselves or others, and they pay a high price personally and professionally for this isolation and lack of direction.

Fitzgerald, F. Scott. *The Beautiful and Damned.* New York: Scribner, 1922.

This novel traces the life of Anthony Patch between his twenty-fifth and thirty-third years. Anthony has great expectations of wealth; he wants to live the life of luxury and is not very ambitious or disciplined. He marries Gloria Gilbert, a beautiful woman who lacks a basic drive to do more than be pretty. Soon alcohol fills the void at the center of their lives, and when Anthony's grandfather disinherits them, leaving them without income, they become desperate. Anthony is drafted into the army during World War I and after the war becomes broken mentally and physically. At the same time, Gloria finds that at age 29 her beauty has faded and she cannot earn a living in the movies. Overall, the lot of this young couple is a tragic one. They avoid making timely vocational and personal choices that would create opportunities for them. Instead, they try to live beyond their means and escape decision making. In the end, they are pathetic figures overrun by life's circumstances.

Harris, Mark. *Bang the Drum Slowly.* New York: Knopf, 1956.

On the surface, this book is about baseball and the tragic early death of Bruce Pearson, a third-string catcher for the New York Mammoths. Below the surface, however, it is a story about what Bruce and his roommate, Henry Wiggen, the narrator of the novel and a pitcher for the

Mammoths, learn about human life. Henry realizes Bruce is dying and knows he wants to play ball until his death. Therefore, he links his contract with Bruce's to be sure his friend will be able to live his dream. Thus, Bruce plays until the end of the season and the playoffs, just before his death. Even though there is a sadness to this story, there is a sense of joy too. Bruce and Henry purposely choose to find meaning in the leisure game of baseball and play it to the fullest. It would be easy for either man to give up on the other, but the fact that they do not is rewarded.

Hemingway, Ernest. "Big Two-Hearted River." In *In Our Time*. New York: Scribner, 1955.

Simply put, this short story describes the events of 24 hours in the fishing trip of Nick Adams in northern Michigan. Below the surface, it is the story of a young man who returns to nature in order to heal the psychic wounds he suffered in war. Restoration takes place through his direct contact with nature and through the ritualistic activity of fishing, where there is a specific set of skills for fishing well. As indicated by his activities, Nick is clearly choosing to get his life back together and to reenter the world he knew before war in a meaningful way. Nick makes basic choices that one can anticipate are the beginnings of more complex decisions in his struggle to find purpose again. The importance of getting one's life together before reaching an educational or a vocational choice is a primary emphasis of this work.

Irving, John. *The Hotel New Hampshire*. New York: Random, 1981.

Although the time frame for this novel spans the 1940s to the 1970s and the characters are numerous, the book's theme relates simply to educational and vocational choices and centers on the passage from childhood to adulthood. The story of the Berry family—told by John, the manager of the second and third Hotels New Hampshire—reveals that life is difficult, but can be rewarding. The characters of John and his sister, Franny, a successful actress, are the ones most fully developed. They have to overcome their desires and illusions to experience life to the fullest and find strength, meaning, and creative vocational outlets. Their siblings and parents are not able to deal as successfully with the serious aspects of life and thus are caught up in tragedy. Basically, the novel shows how the successful characters accept life as it is in order to live it to the fullest and have fun. For example, they convert disaster (such as rape) into triumph (converting the third Hotel New Hampshire into a rape crisis center). The story of the Berrys shows the importance of attitude within a family in regard to successful decision making.

Knowles, John. *A Separate Peace*. New York: Macmillan, 1960.

The events of this story are related by 31-year-old Gene Forrester, as he reflects on his life at age sixteen in 1942 as a student at the Devon School in New England. Here, Gene feels compelled to compete on an academic level with his best friend, Finny, a superb athlete and a carefree spirit. Beneath the surface of this one-way rivalry is Gene's personal insecurity. When he causes Finny to fall from a tree and break his leg, Gene ends not only Finny's athletic ability but, eventually, his life. As Gene reflects on their relationship, he comes to realize a peace within himself. The pain of the incident has killed his darker side and will now allow him to become a more integrated person. Yet at the end of the novel, Gene seems far from happy or fulfilled. It is tragic that Gene must accidentally destroy his friend to find himself, but it appears that even in his peace, Gene will have to work hard to find long-term rewards from this education in life.

Malamud, Bernard. "The Magic Barrel." In *The Magic Barrel*. New York: Farrar, 1958.

Leo Finkle, a rabbinic student at Yeshiva University, is 27 years old and in search of a suitable wife so he can obtain a better congregation. Because his studies have left him with little time to develop a social life and social skills, he hires Pinye Salzman, a marriage broker, to find him a suitable match. Through this process, Leo comes to understand himself more thoroughly and realizes that all the knowledge he needs in life does not come from books. In the end, this self-realization allows him to woo Pinye's daughter and come to a deeper and richer understanding of what it means to be a rabbi. It is interesting that the pursuit of a mate leads to the discovery of what a particular vocational decision means. Thus, Malamud's story is about relationships and love, not only between people, but between people and the professions to which they aspire. Leo finds pleasure and meaning in experiencing his own inadequacies. It is a paradoxical and remarkable event that leads him into a more mature outlook on the long-term rewards of life.

Nichols, John. *The Sterile Cuckoo*. New York: McKay, 1965.

Pookie Adams and Jerry Payne come from very different backgrounds. Pookie is verbose and outspoken; Jerry is naive and reserved. Yet they fall in love. Both are in college: she at an all-female institution, he at an all-male one. On the weekends, they play and discover different aspects about themselves and each other. Eventually, Jerry loses interest in Pookie as she withdraws from the activities and people he considers fun. Desperately, she tries to cling to him, but in the end she loses his love and abandons school. The lives of these young people tend to go in opposite directions after their first attraction to one another. However, gender is not the issue as much as family background. It is obvious that Pookie attends college because she is forced. Jerry attends to broaden his views on people and places. Their differences create tension and finally a breakup.

Oates, Joyce Carol. "How I Contemplated the World from the Detroit House of Corrections and Began My Life Over Again." In *The Wheel of Love*. New York: Vanguard, 1970.

The narrator of this story is an unnamed sixteen-year-old girl from a "good family" who turns to crime—specifically, shoplifting. The girl is alienated from her affluent environment, which she finds suffocating. She escapes to the streets in a poor section of town and becomes a prostitute. Although life is rough, it is affirming; she gets to know some people intimately, an opportunity she did not have with her real family. After a number of bruising incidents, however, the girl returns to her parents, and it is obvious that she will adjust to this environment for the foreseeable future. The main lesson learned in this episode is that identity is not found through suddenly taking on a negative role. Separating from one's family and furthering one's life are established when a person correctly perceives his or her environment and works through it rather than flees the source of discontent.

Percy, Walker. *The Last Gentleman*. New York: Farrar, 1966.

Will Barrett, a 25-year-old humidification engineer at Macy's and a former Princeton student from the South, falls in love with Kitty Vaught. In falling in love with Kitty, he becomes a companion to her dying brother, Jamie, and her suicidal brother, Sutter. He tracks the brothers down in New Mexico in the Vaught Trav-L-Aire, named Ulysses, and befriends Jamie before he dies, refutes Sutter's extreme views on life, and in the process discovers himself. After five fruitless years of psychoanalysis, Will begins to take more initiative in trying to gain control of his life. He finds that he can make choices and determine his life's course through his own direction—not through the directives of others. There is a maturation in Will's process of travel and encounter, and though the reader is left not knowing Will's future, the metamorphosis in his basic character engenders hope.

Phillips, Jayne Anne. "Home." In *Black Tickets*. New York: Dell, 1978.

The 23-year-old protagonist returns to her mother's house in West Virginia "out of money" and "not in love." The mother, a retired school administrator divorced after twenty years of marriage, lives a quiet life, knitting and watching television. The protagonist, a college graduate, takes a tutoring job and tries to sort out the pieces of both her and her mother's life. There is a tragic dimension to each character. The mother, overwhelmed by caring for her own sick mother after World War II, married the protagonist's father for practical reasons and came to regret it. The daughter, also scarred by relationships with men, is no more successful than her mother, but is smug in her more modern view of life. In fact, she shocks her mother by having sex in the mother's house with an old boyfriend. At the end of the story, the daughter has not found any more purpose in life than the mother. It is clear that the daughter is more interested in outside events than in getting on with her own life. In many ways, she seems destined to repeat the mistakes of her mother.

Sillitoe, Alan. "The Loneliness of the Long-Distance Runner." In *Loneliness of the Long-Distance Runner*. New York: New Amer. Lib., 1959.

Smith, a rebellious teenager in Borstal (an English reform school), has an opportunity to change the course of his life by running and winning a long-distance race. Smith agrees to participate, but in his black and white thinking he believes that if he wins the race, he will be selling out to the authorities of society. Thus, even though he is capable of winning, Smith slows down at the end of the race and comes in second. Consequently, he spends the rest of his time in the reform school doing menial tasks. It is ironic that Smith discovers aspects of himself that he has ignored before. He comes to realize that he can retain control over his life even in desolate situations. For example, he runs the race his own way. Unfortunately, Smith's growth is limited because of his concrete thinking, which isolates him from true social contact with others and from a productive lifestyle. Thus, in the end, Smith spends his final months in Borstal planning another defiant act rather than discovering new meaning and the benefits of a career as an outstanding athlete.

Stone, Irving. *The Agony and the Ecstasy*. New York: Doubleday, 1961.

This historical novel examines the life of Michelangelo, especially his apprenticeship and early work. The book begins when Michelangelo is twelve years old (1487), and it focuses on his struggle to become the complete Renaissance person—painter, poet, architect, and more. To fulfill his dream for completeness, Michelangelo must overcome artistic jealousy, family interferences, religious dogma, and a number of major and minor setbacks. Yet he perseveres. Although he lives in poverty, his life is rich in creativity and satisfaction and is inspiring but realistic in its portrayal here. Although the time setting is far removed, the conditions that cause his problems are contemporary, and adults of all ages can identify with this young man.

Updike, John. "Ace in the Hole." In *The Same Door: Short Stories*. New York: Knopf, 1959.

Fred "Ace" Anderson is a former high school basketball player who continues to live in the past. Like Harry "Rabbit" Angstrom in Updike's *Rabbit Run* (1960), Ace is suffering from the former-jock syndrome, which prevents him from coping with life after athletic stardom. Ace is a victim of the emphasis society places on sports; consequently, he is incompetent in the business world, a domain that his wife, Evey, dreams about. The major conflict in the story is between the juvenile mind of Ace and the business mind of Evey. Ace tries to divert attention from the fact that he just lost his job by retreating into the protection of an overinvolved mother, the playfulness of his baby daughter, Bonnie, and the style of his former success. He is able to stave off Evey's anger at him by romancing her, but it is apparent that this tactic will only buy him time and not resolve the fact that he must put the past behind him in order to live appropriately during his young adulthood.

Walker, Alice. *The Color Purple*. New York: Harcourt, 1982.

The Color Purple is written as a series of letters from the protagonist, Celie, to God and to her sister, Nettie. The letters reflect Celie's struggles to find an identity beyond her status as an uneducated, poor, southern, black woman in the 1920s through the 1940s. Eventually, she finds this identity through strong women mentors, self-actualizing anger, and a newly discovered talent—making colorful pants. Thus, Celie overcomes adversities to find beauty and pleasure in life. Her education is self-made, just like the products of her later vocation. It is through Celie's life that the reader discovers that good choices made in the worst of circumstances can lead somewhere. Celie's story is one filled with hope as she develops personally and professionally.

Webb, Charles. *The Graduate*. New York: New Amer. Lib., 1967.

Benjamin Braddock, who has just graduated from a top-flight eastern school, comes back to California with no sense of direction. Benjamin's parents try to interest him in a number of vocations, but finally decide he needs time to figure things out for himself. In the midst of his confusion, Benjamin has an affair with his parents' friend, Mrs. Robinson, and later falls in love with her daughter, Elaine. When Elaine finds out about the affair, she drops Benjamin, but at the close of the story, Benjamin breaks up Elaine's wedding and runs off with her. Although it is unclear where the couple will go from there, it appears they will make it because they have found each other. This book demonstrates both the power of relationships in influencing vocational decisions and the importance of family in affecting one's ambition. It is an adventuresome story that illustrates the difficulty of finding oneself in the midst of pleasure and confusion. Yet it is obvious that Benjamin finally discovers who he is and the importance of real relationships in life.

Woiwode, Larry. *What I'm Going to Do, I Think*. New York: Farrar, 1969.

Chris Van Eenanam, a 23-year-old graduate student in mathematics, and Anne Strohe, a 21-year-old graduate of the University of Wisconsin, fall in love, but Anne's grandparents, who raised her, disapprove of the marriage. Anne becomes pregnant, however, and the couple wed, only to have their son die at birth. In between the disastrous events in their lives, the couple struggle to find their own values and identity. Chris flirts with suicide and drops out of graduate school to take a job as an accountant, while Anne has difficulty resolving the allegedly accidental death of her parents. Both are frustrated in their attempts to find meaning in life. One main focus of this novel is the difficulty of achieving identity and maturity when intimacy is the first pursuit of life. The influence of past family histories (in this case, negative) also is emphasized as both protagonists seem unable to resolve former difficulties with their families of origin.

Wolfe, Thomas. *Of Time and the River*. New York: Scribner, 1935.

Eugene Grant, the protagonist in this semi-autobiographical novel, leaves his southern home for graduate work at Harvard, where he learns more about life than the classroom can offer. He achieves moderate success as a playwright and a college instructor of English in New York City, but his main education comes from his new, sometimes eccentric, friends and his travels in Europe. For example, he is appalled to discover that one of his closest acquaintances is homosexual. At the end of this epic, Eugene returns to the United States from Europe as a financially broke but wise man. Though this novel takes place in the 1920s, its theme—the universal nature of discovery—is timeless. Eugene takes the fast track into life and discovers that much of what he thought was real is illusion.

Wouk, Herman. *The Caine Mutiny*. Garden City, N.Y.: Doubleday, 1951.

This fast-paced adventure novel centers on the life of Willie Keith, a rich young New Yorker who is commissioned as an officer in World War II and is assigned to service aboard the USS *Caine*. Keith's former life of luxury does not prepare him for his new career, and he makes a number of personal and professional mistakes. Yet through his conflicts and encounters, Keith matures as an officer and a man. He is educated through his experiences in the war, maturing from a self-centered and uncertain boy to a confident man, sure of what he wants from life. At the end of the novel, Keith comes to terms with himself and the sea. He heads back to New York and to a relationship with May Wynn, a young woman with whom he was in love before the outbreak of war. Although Keith's future is not spelled out, it is clear that he will make something of himself because he has faced himself and the facts of life.

Wright, Richard. "The Man Who Was Almost a Man." In *Fiction One Hundred: An Anthology of Short Stories*, edited by James H. Pickering. New York: Macmillan, 1974.

David Grover, a seventeen-year-old laborer, struggles with the fact that he is young, poor, and black. He concludes that in his quest for manhood, he should own a gun—the true symbol of being a man. Through childish maneuvers, he persuades his mother to let him buy a gun, but the results are anything but satisfying. He accidentally kills a mule when firing the revolver for the first time, and he finds he does not like the noise and the violence of this new symbol of adulthood. Nevertheless, after David is laughed at for his foolishness, he fires the weapon one more time to demonstrate his manhood. Rather than face the consequences of his action, he hops a train and thinks in the process he will find a place somewhere down the line where he can indeed be a man. David, in his young adult stage, is unable to act maturely in claiming adulthood status. He does not seem able to delay gratification or find meaning in transition. Instead, he uses a symbol to stand for a stage of life, and in the process goes nowhere in his adolescent turmoil, except in his dreams.

11 Adult Responsibilities:
John Irving's *The World According to Garp*

By Kenneth Gorelick
Peggy O. Heller

The most successful launching in this life is to be born healthy to loving parents. But our way is contested at every step, sometimes from the very beginning. We can learn from those who love us; we also can learn from whoever and whatever contests our path. We must act despite imperfect knowledge and insufficient strength; we must overcome loneliness yet stand alone; we must organize meaningful patterns from the welter of events. To achieve adult success, we must know where we came from, learn from our experiences, and discover who we are. We must master the relationship skills demanded by mating and commitment and also the instrumental skills demanded by profession or occupation. We are challenged endlessly in each of these spheres. We bring to each new encounter habit patterns from previous ones and scars from old wounds, along with some capacity for fresh responses. What we bring, what chance brings to us, determines success and failure.

The Paradigm

Novels teach us new things about perennial human struggles. *The World According to Garp* (Dutton, 1978), by John Irving, presents persons and struggles enlarged and distorted beyond the usual range of experience. Written in earthy language and in a highly ironic mode, it casts a light that shows things and their shadows in bold relief. The extraordinary illuminates the ordinary.

Garp describes Jenny, who—against the wishes of her family—chooses nursing school over a prestigious college; makes her own decisions about marriage and childbearing; and rears her son as a working single parent.

Her son, Garp, grows; makes his vocational choice—to be a writer; and chooses his marriage partner, Helen, daughter of his college wrestling coach. The couple raise two sons while marital ennui sets in and shakes the foundations of the marriage. Despite Garp's fierce, overprotective love of his children, one child dies. The family painfully recovers from the trauma, and Garp achieves moderate success as a writer. Jenny writes her life story, which becomes the first feminist autobiography, a love cry of protest against social conventions that bind a woman's status to marriage and childbearing. Her position, she feels, makes her "a sexual suspect," the title of her book. Because her struggles echo those of many women, the book is a smash success and Jenny becomes a feminist icon. Her struggles are over, as Garp's intensify. Jenny, then Garp, dies in the prime of life. The epilogue shows us the fate of friends and the launching of the children into their adult lives.

Summary

Garp begins with Jenny's story, just as our stories begin with our parents'. A peculiarly sensitive little girl, Jenny responds to the remoteness of her wealthy businessman father, a mother preoccupied with a baronial house, and two older brothers being groomed to follow in their father's footsteps. As she grows older, Jenny views the ivied college to which young women of her class are sent as a glorified milk farm for breeders of families like her own. She rebels at this fate and chooses nursing school. The family judges her to be of low ability and easy morals. Later, when Jenny decides to become a mother but not a wife, she chooses a means calculated to keep her at the greatest distance from male consciousness: she begets a child atop a tumescent brain-damaged pilot about to die.

Let us meet Garp, the product of this act, at the threshold of adulthood. Decided on being a writer (he is in love with Helen and she will marry only a writer), he goes not the conventional route—to college—but with his mother to live and write in Vienna. Determined as he is, three bookish experiences help him break through to his creativity. First, he visits a museum exhibit about the writer Franz Grillparzer, reads him, and judges his writing bad; deflating the successful author provides Garp with "his first confidence as a writer." Second, he witnesses Jenny laboring continuously on her autobiography; this sets up a companionable competition. Third, he reads Marcus Aurelius' *Meditations*, with its evocations of vulnerability, uncertainty, and transience; this empowers him. Thus, Garp begins a story.

The first part is successful, but he cannot complete it until he has tasted the fruit of experiential knowledge, which for him takes the odd form (the odd swiftly becomes familiar in this novel) of a relationship—in health and in sickness unto death—with a prostitute, Charlotte. Now he completes his story: the word is made flesh, and the flesh is made word. The firsthand knowledge of love and death helps complete him as a person. Thus grounded in reality, his imagination soars, transforming his experience into an odd expressionistic piece with an unforgettable cast of characters, including a man without use of his legs who walks on his hands and such unemployed circus performers as a teller of dreams and a bear that rides a unicycle. These characters, drawn from Garp's experience, then filtered through his imagination, become powerful symbols of humanity coping against great odds. Because it is honest writing, it is good.

Garp's first writing success is a paradigm of the path to responsible adulthood. Success requires a dream toward which we are impelled; Garp is impelled by his striving for the love of Helen (a face that, over the millennia, has launched a thousand ships of adventure). Success requires originality; Garp eschews the conventional path of college. Encouragement helps; Garp's English teacher says of his plan, "It's a little ec-ec-eccentric, but many good ideas are." Success requires a sense of time and place. It requires models; Jenny provides this to Garp. It requires a sense of competition; Garp measures himself against Grillparzer. It requires community; Garp finds it among Vienna's prostitutes. To succeed we must act; Garp launches the story, choosing Vienna—a place redolent with nostalgia, resignation, and opportunity for adventure and risk taking. He also is wise enough to realize that he does not know enough yet to finish it. He knows he needs to observe and to continue to learn; he finds that knowledge with Charlotte. Success also requires an overall personal vision, "a scheme of things all [one's] own." Jenny has hers; Garp's is born in writing "The Pension Grillparzer." Above all, to succeed, we must act; Garp completes the story.

In writing, Garp also is courting Helen, whose dream is to marry a writer. Later, Garp and Helen settle into married life with two sons, two careers. Garp and Helen adopt a modern, apparently functional, arrangement: Helen teaches at a college while Garp, no slave to male stereotypes, blends the roles of househusband, parent, and writer. They struggle to maintain the marriage, to raise the next generation, and to nurture career identity.

Garp's past casts long shadows. As a fatherless boy and the son of a mother deeply suspicious of lust, he is distressed by sexuality. As the only child and closest companion of a fiercely protective mother, he is tormented with worries about his sons. As a struggling writer, he labors in the shadow of his mother's instant fame.

Marital and job failure come hand in hand. After his second novel, Garp is in the creative doldrums. Meanwhile, Garp and Helen have failed to keep their marriage alive, and Helen begins an affair with a graduate student, Michael. Inevitably, Garp discovers her secret and confronts Helen to demand she break it off. Now begins one of the harrowing climaxes in literature. Garp—who is lovingly, fearfully, protective of his children, who is so solicitously attuned to their colds and labored breathing, who entertains them with didactic fables warning about life's dangers—now meets the greatest catastrophe to befall a parent: he is implicated in the death of his child.

The scene is unforgettable: Garp anxiously driving home, his boys in the back seat; Helen having let herself be convinced to see her lover once more; Garp filled with hurt and hate, doing his usual daredevil maneuver of cutting off his engine for the glide up his driveway. However, this treacherously icy night Garp unsuspectingly collides with the car in which Helen is placating her lover with fellatio. In a tremendous rear-end impact—and we do not know whether to faint, vomit, or run away—Helen's jaws clamp on her lover, mutilating him (the wages of sin, once again); young Duncan loses his eye on the gearshaft; and little Walt dies in the collision.

The survivors must reassemble the pieces of this catastrophe—and they do. In their need—and after their silence, withdrawal, hate, and self-blame—Garp and Helen, fortified by the loving support of family and friends, muster the courage to find one another again. They dare to conceive another child and name her after Grandma Jenny. Garp also tries to redeem himself through successful work. This is a terrific struggle.

Garp pours his fears, rages, and darkest feelings cathartically into *The World According to Bensonhaver*, a story that begins, in repugnant detail, with the rape of a young wife, who proceeds to disembowel her attacker. The husband is so driven to protect his family against future calamity that he hires a live-in detective. The obsession to protect becomes a menace when the husband takes to spying on his family and is killed by the detective.

Garp demands that his publisher make this book a commercial success, whatever the price. The marketing emphasizes lurid aspects of the author, exploiting the fact that he is the son of famed feminist Jenny Garp and that he has recently lost his son in a tragic accident. Thus, Garp has sacrificed two important principles—of keeping his life and his art separate, and of keeping his name and his mother's fame separate. Out of his terrible defeat as a husband and father, he makes a ruthless thrust at fame and fortune.

Throughout *Garp*, success requires surviving the raw emotions of fear, anger, and lust. These motifs come together in the episode of Ellen James and the Ellen Jamesians, an extremist group. Ellen was raped at age eleven by two men who also cut off her tongue. The Jamesians are a society of women who identify with women's abuse by men and who, in a misguided act of solidarity with Ellen, cut off their own tongues. However, Ellen resents these women, who have usurped her name in a self-defeating bid for sympathetic understanding. She aspires to something beyond the victim role. She wants back her voice, and this she finds through developing her talents as a writer.

An angry Garp enters these turbulent waters, championing fellow writer Ellen James over the Jamesians. He cannot contain his fury at the Jamesians, who rudely extruded him from the feminist obsequies after his mother's death. He writes an inflammatory anti-Jamesian essay that provokes an unstable Jamesian into carrying out two assassination attempts against Garp. The first fails; the second succeeds. The assassin is Pooh Percy, a childhood playmate of Garp who bears ancient grudges. Thus, unresolved feelings and attitudes, which are symbolized as the undertow of life, strike out at Garp at a point when he is weakened by his irrational anger.

The novel's epilogue is a roll call of how the characters go on to deal with their challenges. Ellen James becomes a "late-life swimmer"—that is, a writer—and, like Garp, is lost to the undertow. The Ellen Jamesian cult fades away; most of them "worked hard to discover what they could do" and found they were good at helping the disadvantaged "people who feel too sorry for themselves." Pooh Percy receives psychotherapy in jail, is released in her fifties, finds a vocation helping retarded children, and at age 54 becomes a devoted mother. Jenny willed her wealth to the Fields Foundation, which helps women who are trying to find themselves. The failed attempt on Garp's life jolted Garp out of a fallow period in his writing; he started *My Father's Illusions*, the portrait of a father "who plots ambitiously and impossibly for a world where his children will be safe and happy." The book was uncompleted at his untimely death. Helen never marries or falls in love again. Duncan Garp turns aside from self-destructive ways, makes an unusual marriage, and becomes a successful artist. Daughter Jenny becomes a cancer specialist. Just like Garp in his writing, Jenny (as a doctor) struggles to give life to "everyone, forever. Even the ones who must die in the end." Everyone in this roll call has worked hard to survive and succeed.

Our success as adult humans lies in our capacity to rebound after failure, to stand again after we fall, to learn from our errors. Some seem graced with good fortune, good health, nurturing experiences, and abundant gifts used and shared. Some have the capacity to make the best of meager resources; like one of the characters in Garp's first story, they show "the brave optimism of the man who could only walk on his hands." Others lay waste their bounty.

Garp repeatedly warns his son of the ocean's treacherous undertow, which the son picturesquely renders as the "under-toad." And indeed

Garp's world brims with monstrous fears and dangers, ever ready to snatch the swimmer of life. To confront or to avoid one's inner monsters, that is the question. *Garp*'s characters, although handicapped by circumstances of birth and rearing, grapple with their demons, trying doggedly to cope successfully. Jenny sets a fearless life course squarely away from her greatest fear—intimate contact with a man—and makes that tack work for her, though it places a burden on her son. Garp, deprived of a father and gripped hard by his mother, is fated to enact his greatest terror—of being the agent of his child's destruction. He makes a successful novel of the experience.

The only unredeemable failure depicted in this novel is that of raw, uncontained, irrational rage, which kills both Jenny and Garp. However, the survivors eventually heal from this catastrophe too.

Even when love, compassion, forgiveness, and determination fail, the storyteller seems to subtly admonish: "It doesn't have to be this way. Try again."

Questions for Discussion

1. How do the peculiar circumstances of Garp's birth and rearing contribute to his successes? To his failures?
2. What is Garp's most successful work as a professional writer? Why? What is the interplay between the work and Garp's personal life?
3. What is Garp's complicity in the accident that kills his son Walt? Does he successfully repair this trauma, as evidenced in his marriage? In his professional life?
4. What are the origins of Garp's constant struggles with lust, anger, and fear? How successfully is he able to master these?
5. Garp's first successful piece, "The Pension Grillparzer," uses striking images: the man who walks on his hands, the fortune teller who foretells death, the unicycle-riding bear. Where do these originate in Garp's life? What do they symbolize about the quest for success?

Annotated Bibliography

Print

Baldwin, James. "Sonny's Blues." In *American Short Stories since 1945*, edited by John Hollander. New York: Harper, 1968.

An older brother feels responsible for protecting his younger brother from the plagues of Harlem; however, he has failed. He reads in the newspaper that Sonny has been jailed for drugs. They have never been close, the younger resenting the older's paternalistic stance. The older, a teacher, has his own problems, including the recent death of a child. But blood is blood in a time of need, and the older brother offers a haven. He wants Sonny to forswear drugs, but to Sonny drugs are the most reliable source of courage. In response to his new chance, Sonny works hard at mastering the jazz piano. With his mastery comes self-confidence and a constructive way to express his inner pain. He also finds new "family" in his musical colleagues. Sonny eventually is ready to invite big brother into his world. His brother witnesses Sonny struggling to make his music. Baldwin wonderfully conveys in words a profound musical experience in which are expressed suffering, doubt, courage, and finally triumph as Sonny solos. Will Sonny's triumph last? It is precarious and there are never guarantees, but Sonny has made progress in confronting his escapist and self-destructive tendencies. Accepting his brother's help initially, Sonny has employed his talent to free himself from the bondage of dependency.

Carver, Raymond. "Cathedral." In *Where I'm Calling From*. New York: Atlantic Monthly Pr., 1988.

"Cathedral" delivers the great promise that even emotionally closed adults can learn to experience warmth and contact. A quite ordinary man and wife, not life's winners, receive a visitor—a blind man for whom the wife worked years ago. They have remained friends and correspondents. As the wife and blind man share camaraderie, the husband scarcely conceals his discomfort. He acts condescendingly and insultingly to both. It is clear that such warmth and affection are absent in the marriage. When the wife falls asleep, the blind man tries to connect with the husband. Unused to such attempts, the husband flips TV channels. But the visitor wishes to be included in this activity. The chosen show is about the great cathedrals. Trying to describe what he is seeing to the blind man, the host stumbles and wants to give up, but the blind man encourages him and proposes that the seeing man draw what he sees on the blind man's hand. This communication becomes a communion. With eyes closed, it is a moment of epiphany for both, as they give themselves to the experience.

Hemingway, Ernest. *The Old Man and the Sea*. New York: Macmillan, 1952.

The old man has been 85 days without a catch. When the boy reluctantly abandons him for a more successful fisherman, the old man goes out alone, never losing hope, though he knows he has lost much of his physical ability. Just when it seems hopeless that he will catch anything with his cunningly baited hook and skillfully coiled lines, a fish strikes. From the fish's behavior, the old man recognizes its hugeness, against which he pits his patient endurance and determination in an epic struggle. Against the physical odds, he takes the fish. However, on the journey back to port the fruit of his labor is taken by the sharks despite the fact that he uses all his remaining strength and resources to defend his prize. Physically exhausted, knowing he has lost, he maintains his dignity. Although his energies and skills have not failed him, the force of circumstance has overwhelmed the old man. Yet, though defeated in his objective, his spirit of courage survives intact.

O'Connor, Flannery. "Everything That Rises Must Converge." In *The Norton Anthology of Short Fiction,* edited by R. V. Cassill. New York: Norton, 1976.

Julian, a would-be writer, has returned home to live with his mother and work as a typewriter salesman since graduation from a third-rate college. Despite her genteel poverty, the mother feels her sense of place in the social order. After all, her great-grandfather owned a plantation with 200 slaves, and her grandparents were socially prominent. Because the wealth and position have been lost, the mother has made a career of sacrificing so that her son can have the best and rise again. But along with the sacrifice, she has conveyed obligation and ownership. For this, Julian hates everything about her, especially how she lives in the past, blathering about how uppity the Negroes have become. Julian jabs at this prejudice because it is the point of greatest distance between them. When his mother asks Julian to accompany her on a bus ride, he seethes with resentment. He is roiled to fury when she shares her biased views with fellow passengers and when she patronizes a black woman sitting beside her. When the woman strikes at his mother, Julian is glad in his heart. His mother immediately suffers a stroke and dies. Whether she is shocked at her antagonist's aggressiveness or at her son's betrayal, we do not know. Julian is finally left alone. However, to succeed as a writer, or in any other career, Julian must break the ties of dependency and anger binding him to his mother. Was blaming her, as she blamed others, and injuring her a path to freedom? We are left wondering how Julian can effectively free himself from the burdens of his heritage.

Selzer, Richard. "Imelda." In *Letters to a Young Doctor.* New York: Simon & Schuster, 1982.

Dr. Hugh Franciscus, professor of plastic surgery, is a technical virtuoso, but his medical students perceive him as removed from his patients' suffering. He is worshipped, but from afar. Accompanying his professor on a medical mission to Honduras, one student witnesses the proud professor confront a humbling defeat: a fourteen-year-old girl whose cleft palate he is about to repair dies suddenly on the operating table. What he next sees, the student interprets as arrogance. When the body is taken away the next day, the lip of the girl has been expertly repaired. The student concludes that not even death will stay Dr. Franciscus from displaying his skill. But something about this incident stays with the student. Years later, he comprehends the events differently: Dr. Franciscus showed compassion in granting a last wish to the dead girl and to her mother, who took solace in the idea of her child entering heaven whole. The doctor was able to rise above himself to salvage something from a hopeless catastrophe. Sometimes success may be of modest proportions, but of large significance. This story helps us appreciate this aspect of success.

Tally, Ted. *Terra Nova*. New York: Dramatists Play Service, 1981.

This play gives us an imagined ending to the true story of Robert Scott and his crew of four, who did not return from their South Pole expedition of 1911. Flashbacks from the doomed trek show us the strong-willed sculptress who conquered Scott's heart, but lost it to his mistress—adventure. We also see Scott's great rival, Rolf Amundsen, who succeeds where Scott fails. The Norseman has calculatingly taken dogs, to use first as transportation, then as dinner. To Scott, the romantic, this is unworthy and unmanly. To Amundsen, the realist, Scott's priorities are misguided. Thus, Scott and his men have themselves pulled the sleds and consequently are exhausted and starving. In a land that wishes only for men to die, Scott faces two major tests. The first comes when a member of his crew becomes disabled and he must decide whether to abandon the one for the good of all. He does not. The second comes when it appears all hope is lost and he considers whether to make suicide pills available to all. Amundsen's apparition admonishes that now is Scott's real moment of victory: he must not give in to the temptation to end the pain. Scott made two clear value choices: choosing career over family, and considering the moral code of his social class and time in planning his perilous journey. He failed in his mission. Would he have made other, better choices if he were less rigid? Or is full acceptance of responsibility for choice the most we can expect of anyone?

12 Change and Midlife Crises:

Robert Ward's *Red Baker*

By Charles Rossiter

Change is inevitable throughout adult life. It may be forced upon us by circumstances in the world or by the actions of others. It may be created as a result of our own internal desire to make life different and better, a desire that is often caused by a change in the way we perceive ourselves and our life situations. If the changes in circumstance or perception are too great, a crisis often results. One response to crises or problems is avoidance. However, because avoidance solves nothing, we soon learn that it is far better to cope productively with change and crises as a way of responding to our life circumstances and striving to give our lives direction and meaning.

There are two primary means of productive coping. Problem-focused coping is accomplished by changing the environment. An unemployed person who studies to gain new skills in order to improve employment opportunities is using problem-focused coping. He or she is changing something that can be changed, in order to solve a problem. Emotion-focused coping is accomplished by changing the way we look at our situation and the meaning we give to it. Emotion-focused coping involves a change in attitude, an internal change, in order to make a problem or crisis less troublesome. Our resources influence our ability to cope productively. The most important resources are positive beliefs; health and energy; problem-solving skills; social skills; interpersonal support systems; and material resources.

The author acknowledges Alan Crosby, Mary Ellen Munley, the following reference staff of the Bethlehem Public Library—Rosamond Tifft, Michael Farley, and Karen Levi-Lausa—and Diane Thompson of Leeders Video for their assistance in locating appropriate literature for inclusion in this chapter.

The Paradigm

The novel *Red Baker* provides examples of good and poor coping. The main character uses his problem-solving skills, personal energy, and social skills to cope productively. When coping positively, he seeks and finds work and avoids drinking and drug abuse as a response to crisis. At other times, however, he succumbs to despair and faltering self-confidence. When this happens, his drinking and drug taking increase and he lashes out in anger and frustration, causing harm to himself and his family.

Summary

Red Baker, the main character in Robert Ward's *Red Baker* (Dial, 1985), is faced with a major life crisis when he is laid off from his job at a steel mill because it has been closed. Red's first reaction to the news is to escape by going to the Palace Lounge, getting drunk with his best friend, Dog, and fantasizing about running away to Florida with his girlfriend, Crystal, who works as an exotic dancer at the Palace.

When Red arrives home and tells his wife, Wanda, what has happened, she warns him not to respond to the layoff by drinking excessively, taking drugs, and getting into trouble with Dog rather than looking for work. Because Red loves Wanda and their teenage son, Ace, he resolves to go to the unemployment office right away and to conscientiously look for work.

At the unemployment office, Red spends several hours in line, only to undergo the humiliation of being classified as "unskilled." He argues with the job counselor, but it does no good. For the following week or so, he manages to keep his spirits from sinking, but the situation gradually gets him down. One morning, instead of getting up with the family, he stays in bed watching television. Finally, with great effort, he goes out looking for a job.

Throughout this novel, as Red vacillates between positive efforts at dealing with his crisis and his less productive means of avoidance, the influences of resources on positive coping are clearly illustrated. As Red's stressful problem lingers, his determination and ability to seek work decrease. His positive personal resources have begun to wear down. His faith in himself has decreased.

When Red resumes his job search, he meets with further humiliation and frustration when he is subjected to a cruel interview by a personnel manager who had been a nobody back in high school at the same time Red had been a star basketball player. Red leaves the interview to have a drink at one of his hangouts and learns that another worker laid off from the steel mill has just committed suicide. This quick combination of negative experiences lowers Red's resistance to temptation even further, and he visits Dr. Raines for a prescription for speed. For the next couple of weeks, Red looks for work, drinks too much, and stays up late because he cannot sleep. He does all of this high on speed.

In addition to his declining personal resources, Red's major sources of social support also suffer as time passes. One source of support is Wanda. When Red told Wanda he had been laid off, she was encouraging of him and immediately went out and got a job waitressing. Neither she nor Red liked her taking the job, but they accepted it, she better than he, as a necessity. Throughout his difficulties, Wanda shows patience toward Red and encourages him. However, she threatens to leave him when he reverts to heavy drinking and drug taking. Dog is another source of support for Red. Dog has been Red's friend since childhood. He is devoted and loyal; he loves and respects Red. However, Dog has also been laid off and is not coping well with unemployment. Because Dog is unable to cope with his own difficulties, he is not there for Red.

Red's relationships with Wanda, Dog, and Ace are further strained in the next phase of Red's downward spiral, which begins when Red's unemployment benefits are cut off because he failed to file his papers properly. Red goes by the unemployment office to straighten things out; then he starts drinking, takes some speed, and goes out with Dog. In the course of the evening, Dog gets into a fight and must be taken to the hospital with cracked ribs. Red discusses Dog's mood swings with the physician on duty and agrees to try to convince Dog to get help.

Dog's psychological difficulties hit Red hard. Although it is never explicitly stated, the suicide of one fellow worker and the psychological deterioration of his close friend increase the shakiness of Red's own self-confidence for handling his situation.

Frightened by his inability to find work and afraid of losing Wanda, Red renews his resolution to find a job. A man he knew from high school, now the owner of a downtown parking lot, hires Red to park cars. Red considers it awful to have such a low-status job, sometimes parking cars for people he knew in his youth who are now successful executives and lawyers, but Red is determined to make the best of it. For several weeks, he is able to do so. Then he visits Dog.

Dog is in bad shape, obviously drinking too much and depressed. When Red suggests Dog visit a clinic, Dog becomes angry and kicks Red out. This is an additional blow for Red, who must now face the fact that there can be no support for him from his old friend. Dog is no longer the person Red has known and loved since childhood.

After leaving Dog's, Red meets an old high school friend, Choo-Choo. Choo-Choo, a cop on the take, tells Red he can put him onto a sure-thing crime that will net Red $5,000. Red is tempted, but turns down the offer.

To add further difficulty to Red's problems, he is involved in an incident on the basketball court that publicly humiliates Ace in front of his son's friends. Ace is a good athlete and, as his father had been, an excellent musician. (In fact, one of Red's sources of anxiety is that he may not be able to afford college or music school for Ace so that Ace can have opportunities that Red did not have.) One of Red's great pleasures in life is his good relationship with his son. They often play ball together and talk openly with one another. Ace, however, is sometimes embarrassed by his father's behavior.

The incident on the court distances Ace from his father and takes away yet another source of social support for Red. In addition, Wanda is angered by the situation and threatens to leave Red. Red again promises to cope better and manages to do so for the next couple of weeks.

A final blow is dealt to Red's social support system when he calls Crystal and finds out that she wants to end their affair. Crystal represents the embodiment of Red's use of avoidance and fantasy, his primary means of coping at the outset of the novel. Before being laid off, Red had been in a rut and not thinking about his future. Although his marriage had lost some of its excitement, he still loved Wanda and did not plan to leave her. Rather than attempting to improve his marriage, he pursued a relationship with Crystal, who represents freedom for Red. Red's primary fantasy involving Crystal centers around the two of them driving down a sunny, palm-lined highway in Florida in a convertible with the top down, completely free of responsibilities. Crystal, however, is wiser than Red. She can see that Red loves Wanda and that she has no future with him. By taking positive action to better her own life, Crystal takes away another piece of social support from Red.

The next morning, Red takes a pill before breakfast and has one of his worst days. At the parking lot, high on the drug, Red refuses to be talked down to by a complaining customer. As a result, he is fired. Red leaves the parking lot and begins drinking at one of his hangouts. He then goes to the Palace and sees Crystal, who tells him she is planning to go to Miami with another man. From the Palace, Red goes out for a night on the town. He comes home late and has a fight with Wanda and Ace, who move out of the house in the morning.

Red has now hit bottom. Wanda and Ace are gone, Dog is "going crazy," and Crystal is leaving him. He spends the next week in bed, drinking. When he gets himself together enough to get up and out, he goes to the Palace, where Crystal tells him she is leaving for Miami in two days. Red argues with her, but it is no use. Crystal knows Red will not leave Wanda and Ace for her. In some part of himself, Red also knows this is true.

From the Palace, Red goes to the unemployment office and accepts a maintenance job scheduled to start in two weeks. Then, at his weakest and most susceptible, Red calls Choo-Choo. They meet and Choo-Choo lays out the plan for a robbery that calls for two men. Red says he wants Dog for his partner. Knowing of Dog's problems, Choo-Choo is reluctant, but he consents and the deal is struck.

At the heist, there is a complication that Choo-Choo had not anticipated. Dog gets shot, so people learn of his involvement in the crime. A few days later, Red gets a call from Vinnie, the small-time hood they had robbed. Vinnie tells Red he knows that Dog would not have committed the crime without Red and demands his money, "or else."

Red decides he must confess to Wanda, who has returned home to him. Wanda has never doubted Red's involvement in the robbery, though she has not said anything. She is supportive of Red, and believes that regardless of what has happened, he is fundamentally a good man.

Throughout the novel, Wanda has coped with Red's situation. Earlier, she responded to Red's unemployment with a positive action (getting a job) and with a positive attitude (encouraging Red). Here, again, she suggests a positive, though drastic, action. With Wanda's encouragement, Red gets his share of the money and he, Wanda, and Ace leave Baltimore to start a new life.

As the novel closes, a new chapter in Red's life begins. He and his family move to El Paso, where Red stops drinking and, through a friend, finds work at a factory. The job is awful, "work for a robot," but Red enrolls in school to upgrade his skills and broaden his job opportunities. It is difficult, but if Ace—who greatly misses his friends and life back in Baltimore—can make the adjustment, Red reasons, he can too. As the story closes, we have the impression that Red will make it this time. He has faced the worst period of his life and, with the support and love of Wanda and others, has come out the other side of the experience ready to cope with life in a more positive way.

In summary, Red Baker sometimes makes good coping decisions, but due to his anxiety over being unemployed and his personal weakness, he sometimes undermines himself and copes poorly. Red shows good problem-focused coping when he uses his energy and determination to seek work and when he takes a low-paying job in order to get through the hard times. Red's decision to upgrade his job skills is another instance of positive coping.

At other times, Red despairs, feels sorry for himself, and behaves in antisocial ways that alienate those who are close to him and who provide some of the strength that can help him cope. Red's use of drugs and his affair with Crystal, as means of avoiding his problems, are other areas where he shows poor coping. Finally, the morality of Red's participation in the robbery is never addressed, although it is made clear that Vinnie, the robbery victim, is a small-time hood and that the money that Red stole from him was gained by Vinnie through illegal means.

Questions for Discussion

1. Red Baker is a factory worker, but his case is a paradigm. How could people in other kinds of work situations find themselves in circumstances like Red's?
2. If you were in Red Baker's situation, what resources would you call on to try to maintain your dignity and get your life back on track in response to this sudden and frightening life change? How similar to or different from Red's reactions would yours be?
3. Could Red make it without the support he received from Wanda? Why or why not?
4. What are some of Red's attitudes toward himself and others that contributed to making his situation more stressful and harder to cope with?
5. What do you think this novel has to say about the role of loyalty, integrity, love, and friendship in coping with change in adult life?

Annotated Bibliography

Print

Barthelme, Donald. "The King of Jazz." In *Sudden Fiction*, edited by Robert Shepard and James Thomas. Salt Lake City, Utah: Smith, 1986.

When the King of Jazz dies, Hokie Mokie becomes the new King of Jazz. However, at his first gig as king he is challenged by the young Hideo Yamaguchi. Recognizing Hideo's talent, Hokie Mokie agrees to relinquish the crown. Hideo suggests that the older musician stay, but that he move over a little to the side of the bandstand. When the two play together on the following tune, Hokie Mokie's superior ability is apparent to all, including Hideo. With this realization, Hideo packs his trombone and leaves, saying he has much work and study ahead of him. Both musicians cope well with the uncertainty brought about by change—Hokie Mokie by his graceful response to Hideo's challenge, and Hideo by his acceptance of Hokie Mokie's superior skill.

Berry, Wendell. *Remembering.* San Francisco: North Point, 1988.

Andy Catlett is confronted with a major life crisis when he loses his right hand in a farming accident. The loss of wholeness Andy feels because of this is matched by the loss he feels in the face of the disintegration of the family farm as an institution, a way of life Andy believes in and loves. Alone in San Francisco, 2,000 miles from home, Andy spends a night walking the city's streets, trying to come to terms with his personal tragedy and the social changes he feels powerless to stop. In doing so, he remembers the things taught him by his heritage, his ancestors, and his way of life about the importance of belonging and community. Andy's emotional centeredness and belief in his way of life allow him to cope with his loss, return to his home and community, and resume his life with renewed meaning.

Carver, Raymond. "Elephant." In *Where I'm Calling From.* New York: Atlantic Monthly Pr., 1988.

This is the story of a middle-aged man with money problems: he does not have much, and close relatives sponge what he has. They continually promise that each time will be the last, but it never is. The situation is extremely bleak until the protagonist has two dreams: one in which he recalls riding on his father's shoulders, feeling safe and cared for; another involving his past drinking problems. Upon waking from these dreams, he experiences a profound emotional change and begins to feel that things are not so bad, that they will improve, and that there is much to hope for in the future. By changing his perspective on his situation, the protagonist uses emotion-focused coping to help him live more comfortably with a difficult situation that is unlikely to change.

Cheever, John. "The Pot of Gold." In *Great American Love Stories*, edited by Lucy Rosenthal. Boston: Little, 1988.

Ralph is hard working and persistent. He and his wife struggle and save their money in order to "make it." They are forever on the brink of striking it rich, but always at the last moment their plans (or the big job for Ralph) fall through. When the surest opportunity of their lives finally presents itself, their struggling is rewarded, but in an unexpected way. After trying for years to succeed, it is ultimately a change in attitude—emotion-focused coping—that helps Ralph and his wife feel more comfortable with their lives and their success or lack thereof.

Cooper, J. California. "Living." In *Homemade Love*. New York: St. Martin's, 1986.

This straightforward and simple tale might be considered a parable of midlife crisis. A 50-year-old small-town farmer awakens one morning to discover that he feels profoundly dissatisfied with his life. Even his wife of many years has lost her appeal. In response to his dissatisfaction, he packs his bags and goes to the city to "live it up." City prices are high, so he must get a cheap room in a poor section of town, not exactly what he had in mind when leaving the farm. When he ventures from his room into the city, he meets with a series of mishaps that leave him bruised and nearly penniless. These experiences cause him to realize that life on the farm was not so bad, and he returns home. Fortunately, his wife is waiting with open and forgiving arms. The protagonist demonstrates good problem-solving skills when he takes action based on his dissatisfaction, but is quick to recognize the consequences of his actions and reassess his situation based on what he learns.

Davis, Lydia. "The Sock." In *Sudden Fiction*, edited by Robert Shepard and James Thomas. Salt Lake City, Utah: Smith, 1986.

The protagonist must adjust to her recent divorce and her ex-husband's remarriage. In cleaning her house, she comes across one of his socks. When she goes out to dinner with her ex-husband and his new wife, she returns it to him. He forgets to put it away, and it dangles from his back pocket all evening. Seeing this simple object leads the protagonist to a stream of reflections about her ex-husband that suggest the degree to which their lives had been intertwined. As time passes, she becomes less dependent on her ex-husband and better able to cope with her life. Later, when she finds a few other objects he has left behind, they do not affect her as the sock had.

Gess, Denise. *Red Whiskey Blues*. New York: Crown, 1989.

Emily, an author of children's books, stops writing and withdraws from life in response to the recent death of her husband. Gene, a middle-aged playwright who is estranged from his wife, rents the apartment upstairs, and a relationship between the two develops. Emily's grief becomes a focus for his new play, and she becomes increasingly interested in him. Although ultimately their relationship does not last, it brings Emily back to life. The story of Emily's mother, Francine, who has never adequately recovered from her husband's departure two decades earlier and is now traveling the country in hopes of finding him, makes a compelling contrast to Emily's more successful efforts at coping with loss. The difference between the two is Emily's willingness to open herself to a new relationship and future, while Francine remains rooted in the past by denying that her husband has left her for good and will never again be a part of her life.

Kenney, Susan. "Facing Front." In *In Another Country*. New York: Viking, 1984.

Sara, a 37-year-old wife and mother, must contend with her mother's psychological difficulties, which resulted from the death of Sara's father 25 years earlier. A series of flashbacks takes the reader through the years as Sara first takes responsibility for her mother, then relinquishes that responsibility to a sister. The story ends in the present, when the mother's condition has been stabilized with lithium so that she is able to lead a normal life. In the course of the story, Sara experiences a wide range of emotions in her different roles: love and caring as a concerned daughter; anger and frustration as a rescuer whose patient refuses to be rescued; and fear as a mother when she must protect her children from their own grandmother. The most difficult changes for Sara to make are in her attitudes and expectations regarding her relationship with her mother. Sara successfully copes with the situation when she finally accepts the reality of her mother's limitations and weaknesses rather than relying on an outdated and unreal image of her mother.

Kingsolver, Barbara. "Covered Bridges." In *Homeland and Other Stories*. New York: Harper, 1989.

The professional couple in this story have noticed that all of their friends are either getting divorced or having babies; their own biological clock is ticking loudly. They decide it is time to seriously consider the question of having children. They agree to babysit a friend's young daughter for a weekend to get a better idea of what parenthood would be like. During the weekend, Lena, the wife, is bitten by a hornet and nearly dies due to an allergic reaction. The experience has a profound effect on her decision about whether she wishes to become a mother. The story provides insight into how one couple use information and insight into their emotions in deciding whether to have children.

Meinke, Peter. "Even Crazy Old Barmaids Need Love." In *The Piano Tuner*. Athens: Univ. of Georgia, 1986.

Daryl, a down-and-out actor, hangs out at The Grouper, a bar where barmaid Agnes works. Out of their individual loneliness, a friendship between the two develops. Daryl experiences a stage triumph for his part in a new play, but has a serious run-in with the director during a cast party at The Grouper and stalks out angrily. Daryl is then faced with the choice of whether to leave the company or swallow his pride and return. With Agnes' support, Daryl makes a decision that is not only life affirming, but cements his relationship with her. The story provides a fine example of the importance of love and support in coping with decisions that involve self-esteem and that have the potential to drastically change lives.

Parker, Nancy Huddleston. "Homecoming." In *The Women Who Walk*. Baton Rouge: Louisiana State Univ., 1989.

Lenora, a 40-year-old professional woman, returns home from the big city because of her mother's death. There, she and her sister, Joan, with whom she does not have a good relationship, spend the night together in their mother's house. In the course of the evening, the sisters have a confrontation regarding their relationship with each other and their mother. As a result, Lenora reassesses these relationships more positively. The tragedy of losing their mother has prompted the sisters to cope, in part, by being more open to each other and thereby establishing a more positive relationship with each other.

Schwartz, Lynne Sharon. "Mrs. Saunders Writes to the World." In *Acquainted with the Night and Other Stories*. New York: Harper, 1984.

Mrs. Saunders is a wonderful older woman. She is kind. She is generous. She is well liked by the young people in her apartment complex. However, Mrs. Saunders has a problem with self-definition and identity. Now that she is older and her husband is dead, no one calls her by her name—Frances, Fran, Franny. People in her neighborhood call her "Mrs. Saunders," and her children call her "Ma" or "Mom." Shopping at Woolworth's one day, Mrs. Saunders impulsively purchases two boxes of colored chalk and begins a one-woman campaign to let the world know that she has a first name just like everybody else. Before long, the neighborhood is festooned with colorful graffiti by the mysterious "Frannie." The end of this brief story indicates that while not completely solving her problem, Mrs. Saunders' graffiti spree has provided a successful way of coping with it.

Schwartz, Lynne Sharon. *Rough Strife*. New York: Harper, 1980.

This novel follows the twenty-year marriage of Caroline and Ivan. From the outset, it is clear that these two people differ in many important ways, and the strength of the novel is that it does not minimize or trivialize these differences. Instead, it fully acknowledges the complexities of the two main characters as they work their way through the stages of infatuation, disillusionment, having children, coming close together for periods of time, and drifting apart at other times. In the course of this marriage, Caroline and Ivan must cope with numerous changes in situation and emotion, and they use a variety of mechanisms to do so. In the end, through persistence, love, and forgiveness, Ivan and Caroline's marriage is affirmed. Anyone who is mystified by the many difficulties that can arise over the years of a long-term relationship and who wishes to make that relationship work will be intrigued and edified by this book.

Schwartz, Lynne Sharon. "So You're Going to Have a New Body!" In *The Melting Pot and Other Subversive Stories*. New York: Harper, 1987.

Written in the tone of an ironic instruction manual or a confidential bit of advice from someone who knows, "So You're Going to Have a New Body!" explores a woman's reactions to undergoing a hysterectomy. The story is both angry and sensitive, as it probes deeply personal issues surrounding this uniquely female experience. "Should I take the ovaries out while I'm there?" the doctor wants to know. Initially, the protagonist says no, but later, in a Demerol haze, she says, "Take them, they're yours." That powerful line epitomizes the central issue of her relationship with her new body. The new body does not feel real, does not feel like her. The new body feels strange and needs to be lived in before she feels like she is herself again. Eventually, with effort and experience, the new body is accepted and comes to feel real. Strength returns, but part of the anger and apprehension remains. As a problem-solving strategy, the protagonist's active confronting and experiencing of her new body brings about the emotional changes that are necessary to live comfortably with her hysterectomy.

Slade, Bernard. *Same Time Next Year*. In *The Most Popular Plays of the American Theatre*, edited by Stanley Richards. New York: Stein & Day, 1979.

George and Doris meet while traveling and have what might have been a brief fling, but they have deep feelings for each other and decide to meet again the next year. This play follows the course of their lives, through their annual weekends together, over the next 24 years. During that time, they go through numerous personal and professional changes. Despite the guilt they feel over being unfaithful, the play suggests that their arrangement is a way of coping with their feelings for each other and for their spouses. Their relationship provides a source of feedback and support outside of their marriages and serves as an anchor for the pair as they experience changes in their individual lives. Their friendship is an important source of support for coping with these changes.

Stegner, Wallace. *Crossing to Safety*. New York: Random, 1987.

This novel, which examines the 35-year relationship of two couples, illustrates the importance of friendship in coping with life changes. At different times, depending on circumstances, one of the couples provides assistance and support for the other. For example, early in the couples' relationship, Larry Morgan loses his job, and Sid and Charity Lang help him secure a new position. Later, Larry returns the favor when Sid is denied tenure at the university where they had met. The two couples also provide psychological support for each other, as when Sally Morgan contracts polio and the Langs step in to help with her care. The novel's climax centers around a difficult emotional issue and demonstrates, once again, the importance of friends in times of crisis.

Film

Coming Home. CBS/Fox Video. 1978. 128 min.

When her Marine officer husband, Bob, is transferred to Viet Nam, Sally volunteers at the base hospital. There, she meets Luke, a wounded and angry vet. As Sally's consciousness is raised by her experiences at the hospital, Luke's anger is tempered by his rehabilitation and his developing relationship with Sally. When Bob returns, disenchanted by the mismatch between his expectations and the realities he saw and ashamed of the self-inflicted wound that brought him home, Sally and Luke's relationship is revealed and confronted. The film's conclusion contrasts the positive developments that have resulted from Sally's and Luke's abilities to cope with the war with the tragedy of Bob's inability to cope. Whereas Bob's denial of much of the reality around him leads to his crisis, Sally and Luke are more ready to confront reality, however distasteful. A superb soundtrack contributes to this film's evocation of the Viet Nam era.

Cross Creek. HBO Video. 1983. 115 min.

Marjorie Kinnan Rawlins must cope with a midcareer crisis. Although she is successful as a journalist, her goal is to write novels. Realizing she must change her life to accomplish her goal, she quits her job, buys an orange grove in the Florida Everglades town of Cross Creek, and goes there to write a gothic novel. After completing the novel, she is confronted with a second crisis when the book is rejected for publication. A combination of factors—the advice of her wise editor, her deepening affection for the simple people of Cross Creek, and her determination to write honestly and well—leads Marjorie to begin writing stories based on her life and the people of Cross Creek. Marjorie's determination, hard work, and willingness to make changes in her life's direction and in her writing ultimately result in success. Marjorie's story illustrates the use of positive personal resources in coping with crises.

The Fabulous Baker Boys. International Video Entertainment. 1987. 116 min.

Frank and Jack Baker are a duo piano lounge act that has seen better days. Their popularity, which was never great, is on the decline, so they decide to add a vocalist. Enter Suzy Diamond, a sultry, dynamic singer whose only previous experience in the entertainment business has been with an escort service. As a relationship between Jack and Suzy develops, Jack comes to question what he is doing with his life and talent. He is a soulful, serious musician who has followed Frank's lead as a Baker Brother rather than taken the far less commercial route of following his muse. This film presents an interesting example of how purposefully sought change can produce unintended side effects—in this case, good ones—to which people must adapt.

Hannah and Her Sisters. HBO Cannon Video. 1986. 104 min.

Hannah's husband, Eliot, must decide what to do about his infatuation with Hannah's sister Lee. Meanwhile, Lee must decide how to respond to his advances, while Holly, the third sister, shifts from job to job trying to find herself. After a brief affair with Lee, Eliot realizes that the relationship is based on infatuation. The affair ends, and Eliot remains with Hannah. Although Eliot is still attracted to Lee, he chooses Hannah and their marriage as a better route to long-term happiness. Like many Woody Allen movies, this one presents serious issues with a light touch. Unlike many Woody Allen movies, this one ties everything up neatly and happily in the end.

Hoosiers. HBO Video. 1986. 114 min.

Norman Dale comes to coach high school basketball in Hickory, Indiana, after coaching a championship college team ten years earlier, when he was banished from college and professional coaching. Now, an old friend has given him a second chance. Norm is hard driving and committed and has learned that winning is not the most important thing. He consistently makes decisions that put an individual's welfare first. In the face of strong opposition from local residents, who want quick results, he sticks to his principles. This inspirational movie shows the virtues of using one's talents in whatever arena one may be working and of sticking to humane principles and larger goals.

Kramer vs. Kramer. RCA/Columbia Pictures Home Video. 1979. 105 min.

Ted Kramer, a career-minded executive, is forced to change his life when his wife, Joanna, leaves him and their young son in search of something that will provide more fulfillment than her current roles of wife and mother. Ted adapts by becoming more open to the personal side of his life and developing a closer relationship with his son. Then Joanna returns and wants custody. By the end of the story, both of the Kramers have changed. Ted is devoting more time to his personal life, and Joanna has found her own creative niche. Joanna's new life is the result of her having made the hard decision to change her life rather than accept the status quo. Ted's is the result of his successfully using his problem-solving skills to adapt to the changes forced upon him by Joanna's decision to leave.

Norma Rae. Twentieth Century-Fox. 1979. 114 min.

Norma Rae, a woman with an independent spirit, is a factory worker in a textile mill in a small southern town. She has always spoken up to management (even though they do not appreciate it), yet conditions remain oppressive for her and her fellow workers. A combination of factors—including the appearance of Ruben Wyshofsky, a labor organizer—leads to a further heightening of Norma Rae's awareness of conditions in the mill and leads her to become an activist on behalf of the union. Suddenly, in the middle of her working career, Norma Rae realizes she is in the midst of a crisis for herself and her community—an exploitive situation that can no longer be tolerated. This is an example of a crisis brought about by a change in perception and shows how one woman's positive beliefs and determined willingness to work for change lead to success.

Twice in a Lifetime. Vestron Video. 1985. 117 min.

The spark is gone from Harry and Kate's marriage of 30 years. He admits it; she does not. Harry begins seeing another woman, Audrey. When their relationship is discovered, Harry tells Kate their marriage is over and moves in with Audrey. This decision causes great pain to all involved, including Harry and Kate's adult children. As the title implies, despite the pain involved, it is possible to take positive action and make major, difficult changes in life and to create a second chance for happiness. Harry's willingness to confront and act on his disenchantment in his marriage is contrasted with Kate's reluctance to do so. By the end of the movie, Harry is better adjusted to his new life than Kate is to hers, but Kate's increasing acceptance has led her to begin to actively cope with her situation and make a better life for herself.

An Unmarried Woman. Magnetic Video. 1977. 124 min.

One day, to her complete surprise, Erica Benton's husband tells her he is leaving her for another woman. Initially, she is devastated, but with the support of a group of women friends and gentle encouragement from her therapist, Erica gradually recovers her equilibrium and builds her self-esteem to the point where she can live as an unmarried woman, love a man, and still maintain a strong sense of self. Erica's story illustrates the importance of social support and self-esteem as resources for coping. It also illustrates the way good professional help can aid a person in crisis.

13 Men's Experience:
David Leavitt's *The Lost Language of Cranes*

By Ronald W. Pies
Ursula R. Mahlendorf

Imagine for a moment that you are harboring an old and frightening secret. Imagine further that if you reveal this secret, you risk alienating those you love; if you do not reveal it, you risk turning your life into a pitiful fraud. This is the central dilemma in David Leavitt's *The Lost Language of Cranes* (Knopf, 1986), an exploration of homosexuality; and, like most works confronting "tragic" choices, it does not offer easy answers. Indeed, Leavitt deliberately undermines the pat, political nostrum of "coming out of the closet," suggesting that personal integrity also has its personal cost. Although *The Lost Language of Cranes* is obviously interested in gayness, it is more fundamentally concerned with what Heidegger termed "authentic existence" as opposed to alienation.

A person can be forced into an *inauthentic* existence for many reasons. An individual's society may be unable to tolerate deviance from its norms or may put so much stress on him that the nonconformist is pushed to the margin. Some men will resist being or putting themselves in that position and will press for their human rights within society; many will not. Psychological reasons of development and character also may place a person in the outsider's position. All too easily, he may resign himself to an inauthentic life rather than face himself with integrity. Because men in our society, from boyhood, are taught to suppress their feelings and to express themselves through action or even violence, the danger of an inauthentic and a physically and emotionally alienated life is particularly great for them. In *The Lost Language of Cranes*, Leavitt shows us that an authentic existence is constructed on a foundation of uncertainty, pain, and ultimately courage.

The Paradigm

Literature has always had its outcasts. From Nathaniel Hawthorne's Hester Prynne to Hermann Hesse's wolf of the steppes, Harry Haller, these individuals have typically struggled either against society's censure or with their own lofty estrangement from the common man. But in David Leavitt's *The Lost Language of Cranes*, the main character is neither the branded victim of a puritanical society nor the alienated artist among philistines. Rather, Philip Benjamin is an unobtrusive gay man living in New York City who yearns for nothing more lofty than love and acceptance. The same could be said of Philip's father, Owen, whose shame and secrecy are even more profound than his son's. Leavitt shows us that in these mundane lives, there is the germ of heroism.

Although Leavitt's novel is most immediately interested in Philip's homosexuality, it is more centrally concerned with human shame and loneliness. Through the particular struggles of Philip Benjamin, the reader is led to a more general understanding of alienation, courage, and reconciliation. Leavitt shows us that personal autonomy rises from a bed of pain and that honesty is occasionally a self-serving snare. At the same time, the author points us toward the redemptive power of courage and love.

Summary

Broken down into its basic elements of plot, the novel tells the story of Philip Benjamin and his struggle with "coming out." It also presents the parallel tale of Philip's father, Owen, as he confronts his own homosexuality. In counterpoint to these two male histories is the story of Rose Benjamin, Philip's mother, as she struggles with the emerging horror of her predicament (as she puts it, "My life is like the punch line to a stupid joke"). Set off against these plot elements are subplots involving Philip's black female friend, Jerene, and her own traumatic coming out, as well as Philip's painful involvement with Eliot, an older and more settled gay man.

The novel is divided into four sections: "Voyages," "Myths of Origin," "The Crane Child," and "Father and Son." In "Voyages," we are introduced to Rose Benjamin and her life as a copy editor in New York City. The family's apartment is going co-op, and Rose is preoccupied with whether or not she and Owen can afford to buy it. We also meet Owen Benjamin, introduced namelessly as "a man . . . hurrying down Third Avenue" on a cold Sunday afternoon. These separate introductions sound the theme of alienation, which we will see repeatedly throughout the novel: Rose and Owen literally walk their separate ways. Each Sunday, Owen disappears to his hidden life—visiting a gay porno theater—of which Rose knows nothing ("Owen walked on Sundays. That was all she knew.").

In "Voyages," we also meet Philip, who (we learn immediately) is in love with Eliot. Almost as quickly, we learn that the relationship is in trouble: Philip suffers with the consuming fear that Eliot "might get tired of him." Ultimately, this proves to be a self-fulfilling prophecy. Philip's insecurity sounds another of the novel's themes—that of personal inadequacy and dependence on others for one's self-esteem. Played off against this is the roseate theme of romantic love, as symbolized by Philip's identification with Greta Garbo.

"Voyages" also introduces us to Jerene, a tall, black, "unladylike" gay woman who is working on a dissertation entitled "The Phenomenon of Invented Languages." The title is clearly linked with the title of the novel. Through Jerene, we learn of several of these invented languages. There were, for example, the twin girls who invented their own language, but who were separated and forced to learn English. In this parable, we first hear the theme of personal invention and society's attempts to choke off such strange language. The parallel with homophobia is evident. Through Jerene, we confront perhaps the most painful kind of homophobia—the disowning of a gay son or daughter by an outraged family. When Jerene tells her parents that she is gay, her father replies that he would rather she were dying of cancer. Similarly, Jerene's mother experiences the revelation as a death.

Jerene's predicament foreshadows Philip's plan to tell his parents that he is gay. He nonchalantly imagines that they will not be destroyed by such a revelation, despite Eliot's cautionary admonition to Philip: Be sure you are doing this for your parents' sake and not for your own. This introduces what is perhaps the keystone theme in Leavitt's novelistic arch—namely, the potential narcissism of honesty.

"Voyages" concludes with a sketch of Philip's adolescence: going out with girls "in a panic of confusion"; running away from homosexual men in Central Park; and wondering whether there would be "some shifting in the hormones" that might yet stir an interest in the opposite sex. Ironically, Philip winds up—like his father—sitting in a theater watching a gay porno flick.

"Myths of Origin" begins with the story of Owen and Rose Benjamin in the early days of their marriage. We learn of Owen's "steady, kind, attentive" role as husband, despite his nascent feelings of estrangement from conventional marriage. When Philip is born, Owen and Rose regard him as a minor deity, an angel sent down to save their marriage. But as Philip grows, his parents seem to know less and less about him. Rose has a fleeting affair with a male friend, which proves to have ramifications later in the novel.

The story then shifts to Eliot and Philip and the peculiar power structures in their relationship. Eliot—the supreme sensualist—has an overweening need to be in control, even when making love. For his part, Philip feels he is less than he was before meeting Eliot, as if he has been drained of some vital fluid. In this, we see the corrosive power of dependent love and its potential to destroy real intimacy between men. We also hear the contrapuntal theme of contaminating love, as voiced by Owen. He is afraid that if he gets too close to Philip, his affection might be misinterpreted by the boy "as something sick, something perverse."

The remainder of this section follows Owen's furtive and clumsy attempts to meet a man and Philip's ill-conceived coming out speech to his parents. Rose and Owen are understandably stunned by Philip's revelation, but Rose is viscerally angered by her son's self-serving honesty. When Philip protests that it is better to be honest, Rose replies bitterly, "For whom?" Philip cannot grasp his parents' grief and says of it—half in hope, half in self-comfort—"I do think it will pass."

The very brief section "The Crane Child" brings us back to Jerene and the theme of invented language. The reader is surprised to learn that the cranes of the novel's lyrical title are not the graceful birds of our imagining, but the machines of our construction sites—"lifting girders and beams, stretching out wrecker balls on their single arms." Jerene describes a boy, Michel, who learns no language except the screeching of these giant machines outside his tenement. Only cranes can make the boy happy. Jerene muses that "each, in his own way . . . finds what it is he must love," even if it seems monstrous to others. The lost language of the boy is implicitly linked with the discovery of what it is that one must love. Sometimes, this love pits the individual against his or her family or society. Sometimes he or she becomes an outcast, a crane child whose language seems to others nothing but screeching. This is no less true of the artist or social reformer than of the homosexual. Leavitt suggests that reconciliation between such individuals and society is sometimes fleeting or incomplete, but possible.

The final section, "Father and Son," puts us in mind of Ivan Turgenev's *Fathers and Sons*, in which the central character, Bazarov, is a youthful rebel. In Leavitt's novel, however, real revolution is an abstract concept, and political power, a pale force against personal turmoil. (The Gay and Lesbian Campus Coalition mentioned earlier in the book seems almost irrelevant in the lives of the novel's characters.) If revolution occurs, it does so at the level of the heart and in the pain of face-to-face encounter. Thus, in this section, we witness the break-up of Philip and Eliot; Owen's attempt to fix up Philip with a young male teacher; Owen's own sexual encounter with Frank; the painful confrontation between Rose and Owen over the ruins of their marriage; and—most important-ly—the poignant confession of father to son. We also discover something about Philip that diminishes him as a revolutionary figure. After Eliot abandons him, Philip wanders the streets in a frozen stupor. He has "no plans for the rest of his life." While, on one level, this empty numbness is an understandable reaction to loss, it also is a sort of implosion of the spirit. Philip's emotional life is so bound to Eliot that he has no creative energy left for anything else. In "a voice that belong[s] to Greta Garbo," Philip says to Eliot, "I am yours." He cedes his inner life wholly to his lover, thereby losing himself.

Characteristically for Leavitt, the last scene of the novel is tinged with a sort of etherized distraction: As Owen reveals his homosexuality to his son, Philip counts the garbage cans outside his window. He cannot "summon the courage to embrace his father" and offers only the bland reassurance that "everything will be fine." And yet there is born a kind of rebellion in both father and son. It is not the rough political rebellion of Turgenev's Bazarov, to be sure. (The closest Owen comes to this is his approving description of the gay porno flicks: "The way those men made love . . . there was rebellion in their eyes.") Rather, rebellion for Owen and Philip lies in their slow, painful slouching toward honesty and self-fulfillment. In the novel's final scene, when Owen sleeps over at Philip's apartment, we find Owen looking "forlorn in his big white boxer shorts, lost." Nevertheless, father and son have been united in their mutual honesty. We do not have the sense that "everything will be fine"—after all, a marriage has come apart and a family has been sundered—but we do have the feeling that everything will be different.

What, then, does *The Lost Language of Cranes* tell us about men and their sexuality? What does it tell us about marriage and family? And more broadly, what are we given to understand about alienation, shame, and reconciliation as basic human issues?

On the most rudimentary level, the novel suggests that homosexu-ality in our society has become a paradox. On the one hand, gays have managed not only to come out of the closet, but to organize as a political force of enduring influence (witness the gay rights bill recently passed by the Massachusetts legislature). On the other hand, Leavitt suggests, homosexuality as a personal choice remains fettered by guilt, loneliness, and a furtive groping for fulfillment. For many gay men, their deepest desires are still satisfied in the sticky darkness of a movie theater.

Leavitt also suggests that men in our culture—of whatever sexual orientation—forge their own emotional fetters. Instead of permitting themselves real intimacy with one another, men are caught up in "locker room laughter . . . validating affection with violence." This is nowhere more evident than in Owen's relationship with Philip, which remains distant even in the intimacy of self-disclosure.

The Lost Language of Cranes does not present us with a sanguine view of marriage or family, at least insofar as homosexuality is concerned. That Rose Benjamin could have gone so many years without suspecting her husband's sexual preference—and without confronting him over his Sunday walks—attests to our powers of self-delusion and avoidance. Even Philip is surprised by his father's confession, though he has the awareness to say, "I guess I never let myself see it before." While these failings are not in themselves an indictment of the American family, Leavitt homes in on this theme in his account of Jerene's horrific experience; in effect, her family transforms her into a nonentity. Conversely, the peculiar family in which Eliot is raised (he is brought up by two intelligent and sensitive gay men) seems benign in comparison. If Leavitt is exhibiting his own bias in this differing portrayal, he also is alerting us to deep-seated problems within the traditional family structure.

Toward the end of the novel, and after much hesitation, Philip becomes lovers with a young man named Brad. Though a minor and relatively undeveloped character, Brad seems a stable and reassuring presence in Philip's life. Thus, we are left with the sense that this relationship will endure. To this extent, Leavitt offers us a scintilla of optimism in his otherwise dusky account of coming out. In more general and existential terms, Leavitt also suggests that the outcast's shame and doubt may be partially overcome, if not entirely surmounted. While Philip and his father are not embraced by society at large, they are, in the final scene, figuratively held by one another. Within this small fold of family, Philip and Owen seem able to shed their guilt and feel the first stirrings of reconciliation. Father and son have reclaimed their lost language and thus have reclaimed integrity for us all.

Questions for Discussion

1. Was Philip wrong to reveal his homosexuality to his parents? Why or why not?
2. Could Philip have come out to his parents in a more sensitive and caring way? If so, how should he have handled it?
3. Is Rose's failure to suspect her husband's homosexuality realistic? What failures of communication could have accounted for her ignorance?

4. Was Philip's relationship with Eliot emotionally healthy? Why or why not?
5. What role does nonsexual friendship play in this novel? Are these relationships as valuable as the sexual ones?

Annotated Bibliography

Print

Carver, Raymond. "Elephant." In *American Families: 28 Short Stories*, edited by B. H. Solomon. New York: Mentor, 1989.

The narrator, who lives alone, has been sending monthly checks to his mother, his former wife, his daughter, his college-aged son, and—most recently—his ne'er-do-well brother. He feels put upon by these financial burdens, but can never find the words to say so, or the courage to change his situation. "They had me," he says of his family, "and they knew it." None of the family interactions in the story occur face to face; all the giving and taking are done by telephone or mail. The narrator reveals his isolation through a dream, in which, as a child, he rides on his father's shoulders and pretends he is an elephant. Metaphorically, this is the emotional support the narrator cannot find as a man.

Cather, Willa. *The Professor's House*. 1925. Reprint. New York: Vintage, 1990.

This is the story of the growing inner alienation of professor St. Peter from his family after they move into a new house. St. Peter decides to keep his study in the old house for a summer alone as his wife and daughters travel. His fame as a historian established and his family grown wealthy through an inherited patent, St. Peter confronts a crisis of middle age. The crisis is brought on by his disillusionment with his wife's and daughters' materialism and his own inability to mourn a favorite student's death and come to terms with the end of his own young manhood and its idealism. Solitude becomes isolation and suicidal despair as, during this summer, St. Peter moves away from all human bonds, even life itself in an episode in which he thoughtlessly risks his survival. The return of his family finds him apathetically putting up with those human relationships he feels responsible for. The novel is rich in evoking the social ideals of young manhood, the sharing of male friendships in paternal and filial relations and their disappointments and disillusionments. The crisis of middle age and the death of an emotional life are traced to the inability to mourn.

Cather, Willa. "The Sculptor's Funeral." 1920. Reprint, in *Youth and the Bright Medusa*. New York: Vintage, 1975.

A tale concerned with the alienation of the artist, "The Sculptor's Funeral," relates the events surrounding the final return of a Boston sculptor who died in his prime to his native midwest town. The encounters with the sculptor's remains by parents and community members are seen through the eyes of Steavens, the sculptor's pupil. From their responses, the narrative resconstructs the emotional isolation and deprivation the sculptor suffered as a sensitive boy and the vulnerabilities and strengths the growing artist acquired in a materialistic and rejecting environment. While the artist is seen to have escaped his alienation through his art, his boyhood friend, now the town's lawyer, having bought into the town's materialistic values, drowns his feelings in alcohol. His angry and self-pitying tirade at the townsfolk reveals his shame in his alcoholic life. The tale contrasts the artist's authentic existence of risk-taking with the inauthentic existence of the alcoholic.

James, William. "The Beast in the Jungle." 1903. Reprint, in *The Turn of the Screw and Other Stories*. New York: New Amer. Lib., 1962.

With keen psychological insight, James delineates the life story of a man who devotes his existence to the obsession that "the real truth" about him is that something extraordinary will happen to him to make him different from all other men. He spends his life waiting for that moment and occupying himself with empty routines. He finds a woman friend to witness his folly but forms neither professional goals and meaningful personal relationships, nor participates in communal life. His is the story of the isolate too afraid to risk meaningful human involvements lest they bring emotional pain. He cannot but end up alienated from everyone, having spent his life and talents in avoidance and inauthenticity. In a moment of horrified final insight, he realizes his self-delusion and collapses on a friend's tomb.

Malamud, Bernard. "My Son the Murderer." In *American Families: 28 Short Stories*, edited by B. H. Solomon. New York: Mentor, 1989.

Leo contemplates his son Harry, who isolates himself in his room. Leo muses, "I hear him sometimes in his room, but he don't talk to me and I don't know what's what." Leo tries to "reach" Harry by reminding him of the affection they shared when Harry was a boy—but Harry won't hear of it. The two men "live like strangers," while Leo recalls a time "when we weren't afraid to show we loved each other." The story is, on one level, about a very disturbed young man; more fundamentally, it explores the painful alienation of fathers and sons.

McFarland, Dennis. *The Music Room*. New York: Avon, 1990.

The novel traces the adult lives of two children of wealthy alcoholic parents and demonstrates the havoc the parents' continuous drunkenness, neglect, and abuse have wreaked on the lives of their children. The childhood memories of the older brother, whose marriage has failed as the novel begins, make understandable for the reader the two sons' later social isolation, failure in their professions, feelings of alienation, need to rescue others, and difficulties with sustaining emotionally rewarding relationships. The younger brother, a graduate music student, fails in his attempts to help himself and commits suicide. The older brother, after escaping into alcoholism in response to his brother's death and to his failed marriage, decides to put his life in order. Relinquishing his self-pity, self-deception, and stance of having been wronged by life, he begins to make friends with his brother's pregnant girlfriend and to work in a home for abused children to which his brother has left his inheritance. The book is particularly helpful with regard to adult children of alcoholics as they grapple with their feelings of alienation, inauthenticity, and despair.

Miller, Arthur. *Death of a Salesman*. In *Plays of Our Time*, edited by B. Cerf. New York: Random, 1967.

Willy Loman is the epitome of the American dream gone bad—a worn-out, embittered salesman who lives vicariously through his sons. He is, paradoxically, both ashamed of and sustained by Biff, an "idealist" who rejects his father's vaunting ambition "always to . . . get ahead of the next fella." In the course of the drama, Willy is revealed as both a deceiver and a self-deceiver—indeed, Biff calls his father a "phony." The drama insightfully demonstrates the damaging influence such a father has on his sons. Fundamentally, Willy Loman is the quintessentially driven man who can no longer find meaning in life once his power to "sell" fails him. He winds up alienated both from his innermost self and from his family.

Monette, Paul. "Halfway Home." In *Men on Men 3*, edited by George Stambolian. New York: Penguin, 1990.

The story of the attempted reconciliation of two hostile brothers, "Halfway Home" movingly and discerningly portrays the situation of the AIDS victim. Tom, the sole survivor of a group of gay friends, lives on disability in the rent-free southern California beach bungalow of an acquaintance. He spends his days waiting for the next strike of the illness, recalling his boyhood in Connecticut and brooding on the sources of his present bitterness and alienation. His brother, estranged from him as are his father and mother since his coming out, arrives for a surprise visit, having learned that Tom is dying of AIDS. The visit illuminates for the reader the painful feelings of the sufferer from AIDS and the complexity of the problems which led to his estrangement from family and community.

O'Neill, Eugene. *The Iceman Cometh.* 1940. Reprint, in *Selected Plays of Eugene O'Neill.* Garden City, N.Y.: International Collectors Library, 1979.

A despairing drama about the many different kinds of self-deceptions which constitute an inauthentic existence, the play explores the "pipe dreams" of the alcoholic derelicts who live in Harry Hope's rooming house and frequent its saloon. The self-deceptions range from the outright dishonesty of the pimp who claims his pimping to be protection of the women he exploits to Larry the anarchist's belief that his disillusionment with life is indifference to death. The arrival of Hickey, a hardware salesman, for Hope's birthday party brings to a crisis the life of each. Hickey confronts their self-deceptions and exposes every man for the failure he is. In response, each decides to change and to realize his dream. But by evening the next day all have retracted and returned to their pipe dreams and drunkenness. Hickey's self-deception, which he seemed to have overcome as he soberly confronted his friends, turns out to have been greater than that of the others. By the delineation of the characters' interactions, O'Neill gives a profound analysis of the connection between alienation and alcoholism.

Roth, Philip. *Patrimony: A True Story.* New York: Simon & Schuster, 1991.

In this quasi-biographical account, the author explores not only his father's mortality—he is suffering from a brain tumor—but also the barriers that have separated father and son throughout their lives. Roth describes "the poignant abyss between our fathers and us. . . . Encouraging us to be so smart . . . they little knew how they were equipping us to leave them isolated and uncomprehending in the face of all our forceful babble." The narrator struggles against both this intellectual divide and "the divide of physical estrangement that, not so unnaturally, had opened up between us once I'd stopped being a boy." In long transatlantic phone calls, Philip and his father engage in play-by-play dialogues over Mets games; they find it far harder to talk about the father's impending demise. Nonetheless, father and son do surmount some of these barriers in the final sections of the book.

Shaffer, Peter. *Equus.* London: Penguin, 1977.

Both the parents and the treating psychiatrist of the boy Alan, institutionalized because of his blinding the horses of his employer, fail to understand and help the troubled adolescent. Because of their lovelessness and inability to deal with emotions and sexuality, the parents have left Alan without any kind of model or guidance to face the storms of adolescence. The psychiatrist, though he can find out through his techniques what motivated the boy's destructive actions, lacks the humanity to do anything but get the boy to adjust to a meaningless contemporary existence dominated by television and commercialism. He sees the boy's problem as a puzzle to be solved. Envious of the boy's vitality as it appears in his cult of horses, the psychiatrist, himself alienated and emotionally bankrupt, is unable to provide that emotional nurturing and model of adulthood that would help the boy to grow into a feeling human adult. The play is a moving example of the alienation between generations and the incapacity of the alienated to assist the younger generation.

Steinbeck, John. *Of Mice and Men.* 1945. Reprint. New York: Penguin, 1978.

The two friends and migrant field workers George Milton and Lennie Small, from a small California town, travel together, the smarter George looking after the feeble-minded, strong workhorse Lennie. George has taken care of Lennie ever since the latter's only relative died, initially because Lennie's simplicity made him feel smart. Because of his simple-mindedness and need for touch and contact, Lennie constantly gets into trouble. Only George can control Lennie's immense physical strength. Their common dream of buying a small farm together and living an independent life out of harm's way comes to an end when Lennie unwittingly kills a woman. The narrative contains a veritable storehouse of outsider types and forms of alienation from the insoluble dilemmas of the solitary black in a white community to the social isolation experienced by the brutal and hardened son of the boss. As is usual for Steinbeck, the oppressed migrants' solidarity triumphs in spirit even while they themselves are defeated.

Swados, Harvey. "My Coney Island Uncle." In *American Families: 28 Short Stories,* edited by B. H. Solomon. New York: Mentor, 1989.

Twelve-year-old Charlie describes "the greatest week of my life"—the week spent in New York City with his bachelor uncle, a somewhat dilapidated physician. For Charlie, Uncle Dan is everything his father could never be: someone "who enjoys us not for what we may become, or may one day owe to him, but simply because we exist." In his rites-of-passage adventure, Charlie sees lunatics, murderers, fallen women, and all the "sweet subtleties of bluff and deception" inherent in his uncle's urbane bachelorhood. Yet near the end of this tale, we see Uncle Dan not as a free spirit, but as a lonely caricature of the man-about-town. The story thus undermines the myth of the carefree bachelor and the idealized uncle who transcends ordinary fatherhood.

Updike, John. "Still of Some Use." In *American Families: 28 Short Stories*, edited by B. H. Solomon. New York: Mentor, 1989.

The main character, Foster, helps his ex-wife clean the attic of the house in which they once lived. His two sons look over his shoulder "at the sad wealth of abandoned playthings, silently groping with him for the particular happy day" associated with each object. Foster's son Tommy takes the housecleaning "harder than he shows." Father and son try to confront each other's pain, but each is inhibited by some unnamed incapacity. The best they can do is drive out to the dump together, with Foster promising Tommy, "You'll feel great, coming back with a clean truck." The story adumbrates the difficulty men often have articulating painful feelings, particularly when these arise between father and son.

Vallejos, Thomas. "Pinions." In *Shadows of Love: American Gay Fiction*, edited by C. Jurrist. Boston: Alyson, 1988.

A 16-year-old Hispanic boy describes the difficulties of being "different" in the macho culture of his family and community, in which he is regarded as "delicado" (too sensitive). Masculine courage is defined in terms of combat, with no room for "sweetness," and the boy is pressured to conform to this ethos. In contrast are the pinions—the hermit-like trees that bear nuts each year. They serve as the metaphor for natural expression, in contrast to the forced bravado of the boy's male role models.

Wharton, William. *Birdy*. New York: Avon, 1980. (Film: *Birdy*. Tri Star. 1988. Alan Parker, Director.)

A novel of extreme alienation, *Birdy* traces the intertwined stories of two young veterans and casualties of WWII, extrovert, rebellious Al and sensitive, introvert Birdy, unlikely friends since adolescence. At the novel's beginning, Al, whose face was torn away by a grenade, finds his friend in an army psychiatric hospital, shell-shocked, silent, frozen in a grotesque birdlike pose. Through Birdy's interior monologue and Al's account of their friendship, the reader learns the meaning of Birdy's fascination and obsession with birds. They are the symbol of the freedom, the love, and the beauty both their lives lacked as they grew up in a Philadelphia working-class district and as they experienced life as adults at war. In attempting to bring Birdy out of his psychotic withdrawal, Al gradually confronts his own war traumas, fears, and emotional pain and expresses them to his friend. The novel's somewhat hasty and hence unconvincing conclusion shows both friends ready to leave the asylum,

Birdy having relinquished his psychotic withdrawal and helping Al to accept "the rest of our lives." The novel contains excellent descriptions of emotionally deprived and depriving environments, of post-traumatic stress disorder (the film excells in giving convincing flashbacks to traumatic incidents), and of psychotic alienation. The emotional interaction between the friends shows the way out from marginality and isolation.

Wolf, Stephen. "The Legacy of Beau Kremel." In *American Families: 28 Short Stories*, edited by B. H. Solomon. New York: Mentor, 1989.

The "Beau Kremel" of the title is a bottle of hair tonic, which serves as the crucible in which a father's estrangement from his son is compounded. The story focuses on the competitiveness and anger between father and son, which "was only the underside of deep pain and frustration." The narrator recollects how once his father, slamming him into the refrigerator, screamed, "Don't let me ever hear you say no one loves you in this house!" In the end, the father's anger overwhelms him, and it is up to the boy's mother to clean up the spill, literally and metaphorically. The story explores both the inarticulate anger that often sunders father and son and the "mediating" role women are sometimes forced to play in such circumstances.

Zacharia, Don. "My Legacy." In *American Families: 28 Short Stories*, edited by B. H. Solomon. New York: Mentor, 1989.

This recollection is of a Jewish-American boyhood, and of the tension between an "intellectual" father and his baseball-loving son. It is also the account of the boy's oscillations between two inauthentic poles of experience: the left-wing youth group he joins in order to mollify his father, and the Italian baseball team which, had they known of his weekly attendance at a Young Communist League, "would have kicked me off the team." The boy, Noel, knew he displeased his father: "I could see the disappointment etched in his face." Noel never speaks of his problems directly to his father—his sister Sarah is his "go-between." Conversely, his father uses Sarah to convey messages to Noel. Later in the story, Noel is able to make his father proud, and ultimately—through the mediation of his own son—he comes to grips with the "legacy" his father bequeaths him.

Film

Apocalypse Now. Paramount Pictures. 1979. Francis Coppola, Director.

Based on Joseph Conrad's tale exploring human corruption in "The Heart of Darkness" and Michael Herr's Viet Nam novel *Dispatches*, the film deals with humans so alienated from each other and themselves that they bring anarchy and destruction wherever they turn. Capt. Willard, a tough agent and six-time killer, is sent by U.S. High Command to assassinate Col. Kurtz, who has left his command and retreated into the jungle. According to High Command, Kurtz has taken right and wrong into his own hands and kills or lets live whomever he pleases. Willard is fascinated by this formerly eminent military man and by the question of what made him place himself outside the law. On a navy gunboat, assisted by helicopters and B52 bombers, Willard blasts his way through peaceful fishing villages and rice fields to Kurtz' encampment. The military system seen at work in these scenes is indifferent to the destruction inflicted on friend and foe alike. It brings destruction and anarchy in order to "cure" destruction and anarchy. At film's end, after having slaughtered Kurtz, Willard is left a numbed witness of the horror that humans inflict upon each other when they place the achievement of an end over the means of getting it.

Jacknife. A Sandollar/Schaffel Production. 1989. David Jones, Director.

A film about Viet Nam veterans and the difficulties they experience in reintegrating into a peaceful life, *Jacknife* follows the personal lives of Max, a wild-maned rebel nicknamed Jacknife, and Davy, a tough talking truck driver and former high school football hero. The film begins with Max picking up Davy for a fishing trip they planned as buddies in Viet Nam. Max finds Davy living with his sister, a biology teacher who keeps house for him. In attempting to resume their friendship, Max finds that Davy denies their friendship and has become an alcoholic. In flashbacks to war experiences of the two, the viewer finds out that Davy, the football hero, cannot come to terms with his own terror and cowardice in action and his guilt over having left Max for dead. Both men struggle with survivor's guilt because the third friend in their trio, their common hero Bobby, died when he went to Max's rescue. Max has dealt with his guilt and grief in speaking and seeking support in veterans' encounter groups and hence he is able to establish a friendship and a love relationship with Davy's sister. Only after a violent and destructive episode and helped by Max's loyalty can Davy begin to experience his grief and overcome his alienation from friends, family, and community.

The Rain Man. United Artists. 1988. Barry Levinson, Director.

This story of a struggle over a paternal inheritance deals with two different kinds of human alienation, that of Raymond, the older brother, an institutionalized idiot savant, and that of his taciturn, unemotional yuppie brother Charlie, an importer of expensive foreign cars. On the way to a Palm Springs vacation with his girlfriend, Charlie receives news that his father has died. As he visits his father's house in Chicago, we find out that he grew up motherless, left home at sixteen after a quarrel with his father, and never answered either his father's telephone calls or letters. Believing himself the sole heir, he attends the funeral without a sign of emotion and expectantly goes to the reading of the will. He is told that his share of the inheritance will be the car over which they quarreled and his father's prize roses. The remainder of the three-million-dollar estate is placed in trust with the director of an institution. Intent on claiming his inheritance, Charlie seeks out the institution and finds that he has a brother there. Charlie kidnaps him in order to obtain guardianship and money. Initially, he cares neither for the pain his brother experiences at being dislodged from his routines nor for the opinion of his girlfriend. But gradually, on a car trip across the country necessitated by his brother's refusal to fly, his anger at his father and his annoyance with his brother's many handicaps dissipate into compassion and he comes to understand his brother's tragedy. The journey from alienation into compassion and love ends as Charlie, realizing his brother's extremely limited ability to establish human contact, relinquishes control of his brother and his claim to the inheritance.

14 Women's Experience:
Gail Godwin's *A Mother and Two Daughters*

By Geri Giebel Chavis

Today's societal messages regarding feminine behavior have evolved both from the powerful, widespread "cult of true womanhood," which flourished in the nineteenth century, and from more recent social movements focusing on gender equality and on women's self-actualization. According to the ideal of true womanhood, females were expected and taught to be self-sacrificing, nurturing, physically attractive, submissive, and dependent. While later developments emphasized women's independence and intellectual, sexual, and psychological growth, the older ideals highlighting women's relational roles and adherence to external standards continue to profoundly affect women's experience. Thus, today's women are engaged continually in soul searching—shaping their feminine identity and defining personal worth, in opposition to the expectations of others, internalized standards of behavior, and cravings for intimacy.

During adolescence, young women typically are engaged in the business of defining a self in relation to their emerging sexual maturation, their unique skills, and their interactions with male and female peers and mentors. As young adults, women generally experience dilemmas regarding lifestyle, mate selection, and career. In their middle years, women typically grapple with the need to juggle familial and work roles and the ways in which aging affects personal attractiveness. Finally, in their years as senior citizens, women tend to experience the losses and gains associated with retirement, widowhood, grandparenting, the death of friends and relatives, and physical debilitation. In reacting to significant life events, women find themselves choosing among roles, combining several roles, or adapting to external circumstances that necessitate taking on new roles and shedding old ones. As they function in these diverse roles, women tend to seek intimate connection even as they fear submergence of identity in relationships with others. This ambivalence perhaps explains why women's existential crises so often involve conflicts over whether to sacrifice for others or fulfill personal desires.

The Paradigm

A Mother and Two Daughters (Viking, 1982), a novel by Gail Godwin, presents a wide array of issues that characterize women's reality and constitute dilemmas for today's women. In this work, Godwin captures both the breadth and depth of women's experience and combines realistic detail with a sensitive and affirmative tone. While this novel can be seen as a detailed triptych of the lives of three women—a recently widowed mother and her two adult daughters—it also presents a panorama of quite well developed female characters who are young, middle-aged, and elderly; poor and rich; black and white. In this novel, we meet women of varied ages choosing creative or destructive solutions to problems associated with change in marital or job status, parenting, illness, alcohol addiction, poverty, unwanted pregnancy, and interracial marriage. We view women in the roles of mother, daughter, sister, wife, divorcée, widow, lover, spinster, grandmother, godmother, single parent, orphan, homemaker, college professor, lawyer, social activist, day-care worker, and servant. We watch as women in one family relate to each other in emotionally charged situations and discover how polarizations, affiliations, and assignment of family roles color their self-images and present interactions. We also watch women in nonfamilial situations play the roles of friend, adviser, rival, and mentor.

The three major characters who provide the focal points of the novel all grapple with the meaning of marriage, motherhood, and personal identity and with the place of work or career in a woman's life. All three struggle with discrepancies between societal stereotypes, family expectations, and individual tastes, beliefs, and aspirations. Each, in her own way, moves toward reconciling these discrepancies and discovering herself in a new way through painstaking assessment of past and present experiences, interaction with others, and response to life's accidents and opportunities.

Summary

Taking place in the late 1970s, *A Mother and Two Daughters* unfolds an absorbing drama of the Strickland women, members of a middle-class family, well connected to the upper echelon of their North Carolina community's stratified social world. Narrated in three parts spanning six months, with an epilogue providing a denouement six years later, Godwin's work captures the consciousness of its three heroines—the recently widowed mother, Nell, and her two adult daughters, Cate and Lydia. Leonard Strickland's sudden death precipitates in his widow and two daughters memories, reflections, and self-assessments and provides the means of reuniting these three heroines in the "pressure cooker of the nuclear family."

Part 1 of the novel introduces us to the personalities, roles, and present life situations of the novel's three women, as it takes us through Leonard's funeral and the beginning of the grieving process. Part 2 reveals the new set of possibilities available to each of the three women, who return to their individual lives after the funeral. This section concludes with the older sister closing doors on several possibilities, the younger sister opening doors on her life choices, and the mother just beginning to emerge from her widow's solitude to assess the social world to which she has reluctantly conformed throughout her married life. The predominant themes in this part can be summed up by three words: possibilities, choices, conformity.

Part 3 brings the women together once again, this time on a trip to the family's vacation cottage by the beach of Pamlico Sound. The titles of this section's first two chapters, "Ghosts" and "Conflict," epitomize the climactic nature of the reunion that takes place here. In sorting through Leonard's beloved possessions at the cottage, the three women grapple with the past as they encounter each other in the present.

At the cottage, Nell realizes new connections with an old high school friend who coincidentally is renting a neighboring cottage with her husband. Left to interact without their mother present, the two sisters are forced into what seems to be an inevitable confrontation. Old hurts and habits crash headlong into present grief and identity crises as the sisters experience the most bitter fight of their lives, a fight whose passion is symbolically reinforced when the cottage burns to the ground during a day of tempestuous weather. While mother and daughters remain physically unscathed by the fire, an entire set of family mementos is destroyed, and the two sisters are left to lick their wounds. After the fire, all three women depart in separate directions. Nell, redefining her priorities, chooses to nurse her friend, who is dying of cancer. Lydia returns home to continue pursuing her intellectual, psychological, and sexual growth. And Cate, the most demoralized of the three—homeless, jobless, doubting yet defiant—returns to the Strickland family home to begin a healing process.

The epilogue describes a party given six years later by Cate for her newly wedded nephew. It reunites not only the three heroines of the novel, but all of its surviving major characters who have influenced the heroines' lives. The Ralph Waldo Emerson quote introducing this epilogue reflects its affirmative mood and its particular theme: "We are not strong by our power to penetrate, but by our relatedness." The gala picnic celebration is marked by fulfilled opportunities for renewal, connectedness, and forgiveness, yet Godwin never loses sight of a reality that intertwines aspiration with compromise, intimacy with the isolation of individual consciousness.

While Godwin's work is about relationships between sisters, mothers and daughters, friends, and lovers, it is essentially about the individual lives of three different women whose separate points of view and experiences dominate the novel.

Nell becomes a widow in the first chapter and goes through several stages of grieving during the course of the novel. She experiences a sense of isolation and unexpected pangs of grief evoked by memories. She reconciles her feelings of emptiness with a newly discovered enjoyment of solitary pleasures and a surprising awareness of self-sufficiency. In losing her spouse, Nell gains an opportunity to become reacquainted with facets of her personality that have been submerged during her years as a wife. Nell confronts the passionate, critical, rebellious side of herself that she buried in order to accommodate a care-taking, peace-loving husband. As a widow, Nell reflects—in a clear-headed way—on how much conformity to social mores and how much sacrifice of individual comfort are right for her. The turning point comes when Nell decides to nurse her dying friend and lighten the burden on this friend's husband. Having "been trained to put duty before pleasure, or peace, or 'self-realization'," Nell finds that she makes this decision without doubt or discomfort. Through this choice, she moves beyond her isolation and half-hearted participation in social events, at the same time affirming her plan to resume a nursing career and her need to affiliate with others in a personally meaningful way. Her recovery from the despair of widowhood culminates in her eventual decision to marry again.

Cate Galitsky, Nell's elder daughter, occupies center stage in most of the novel's climactic scenes, for she is the impulsive renegade who shakes up the family system and continuously challenges others' values and choices. Family members and acquaintances expect the unexpected from Cate, a woman driven by outrage against social injustice and by a craving for freedom to travel her individual life path.

By the time the novel begins, Cate has survived two divorces, earned a Ph.D., and traveled from one college teaching position to another. With her fortieth birthday a half year away and the future of her present teaching job uncertain, Cate is preoccupied with evaluating where she has been and where she is going as a woman in relation to her career, her father's principles and double messages, her love life, and her potential as a bearer of children. She views life as a pattern that evolves from the workings of her will and the adventures that happen to her.

In the act of uncovering her unique life design during the course of the novel, Cate struggles with three major dilemmas. The first two involve marriage and motherhood. When Cate begins a serious relationship with a wealthy, down-to-earth businessman many years her senior, she becomes pregnant for the first time in her life and faces the difficult decision of whether to have an abortion. She contrasts her own lack of maternal feeling against the conventional attitudes that compel women toward motherhood. She also reflects on her influence as a role model or teacher, thus grappling with her identity as a mature woman in relation to future generations. When her lover proposes, Cate's decision to undergo an abortion becomes even more complicated. While she grows ever more certain about her abortion decision, she is torn between her fierce need for independence and her desire for the comforts of security. She reviews details of a past disastrous marriage, where she played the caretaker and enabler, yet acknowledges what is to her a frightening need to be fathered. She is tempted to take on the conventional life she has been consistently rejecting, but decides instead to remain committed to a future of unanswered questions.

Cate's third dilemma involves interactions with family members—her mother and sister, in particular. Ambivalence is the key word to describe Cate's movement between the poles of intimacy and isolation with the women in her family. Following a well-established behavioral pattern of being the disruptive family member and feeling insecure about her present identity and life situation, Cate acts critical and moody when she reunites with her mother and sister. However, she wants connection with these women and experiences pain when she hurts them or distances herself. While she does not give her mother credit for understanding her, she does recognize similarities between them. And while she belittles her sister for her predictability and fear of risk taking, she is dimly aware of the jealousy and admiration she feels when she contemplates her sister's goal-directed behavior and sense of order.

Of the three heroines, Cate pursues the most dramatic life journey. As she denies her need for affiliation, upholding her principles of free choice and free expression at all costs, she hits rock bottom in her fortunes. She finds herself bereft of love, work, worldly possessions, and a plan for her future. Her state of existence is symbolically reflected in a temporary physical disorder that paralyzes her facial muscles. Yet despite her circumstances, Cate, with an innate sense of wisdom, manages to find the time, the people, and the places conducive to a healing process that will renew her for the ventures ahead.

Cate's younger sister, Lydia Mansfield, is in many ways a foil to Cate. Whereas Cate is wild, outspoken, and tactless, Lydia is reserved, well organized, and conventional, focusing almost constantly on what others think of her. Yet, ironically, by the opening of the novel this so-called timid sister has made the bold decision to leave her successful, devoted husband, has moved into an apartment with their younger son, and has resumed her college education. Given her decisions, Lydia is at a turning point in her life. Like her sister, she is assessing her identity, past choices, and future options.

In Lydia's life and thinking patterns, there are three major strains. The first involves her role and evaluation of self as a wife, lover, and mother. As she experiences sexual awakening with a new lover, she evaluates her past self as the seemingly perfect wife in a well-ordered marriage devoid of deep feeling. She also strives to reconcile her newly found freedom of sexual passion with her need for control. She grapples with the decision of whether to remarry or stay single and tries to decide whether it is possible to stay in a committed, loving relationship without the wedding ceremony. As the mother of two sons, Lydia also reflects on her competency and maternal responsibilities.

The second strain in Lydia's reflections and growth involves her past and present functioning within her family of origin. She recognizes how an adult's self-image and behavior are profoundly affected by one's early position in the family system. She gains insight into how her good girl and perfectionist roles have kept her out of the limelight, deprived of parental attention. She also becomes aware of how her position as the younger sibling of an outspoken, critical sister powerfully influences her actions and identity. As a mature woman, she confronts her ghosts, mounting a fight against her own susceptibility to others' real or imagined judgments.

As Lydia strives to make significant changes in herself, she develops her intellectual, achieving side. Her college experiences supply new role models and friends, who enhance her confidence and fuel her ambitions. Her friendship with a black woman professor who is teaching a course called "History of Female Consciousness" provides a lasting positive influence and indirectly leads to a meaningful talk show career.

The psychological issues explored in *A Mother and Two Daughters* are closely intertwined with the social issues that characterize women's experience. The fact that the novel begins and ends with a party suggests the importance of social conventions, role playing, and human relationships in women's lives. Yet the most powerful, memorable portions of the work involve the dynamic inner lives of the three major female characters as they undergo soul-searching self-assessments, confront change, and grow in awareness. A quote from D. H. Lawrence at the beginning of the novel—"We are ghosts, we are seed"—highlights not only the profound effect of the past on the three heroines, but the renewal each woman experiences.

Questions for Discussion

1. What factors facilitate Nell's progress in her grieving process?
2. What effect does birth order have on the adult lives of Cate and Lydia?
3. How do Nell, Cate, and Lydia each manifest their protest against others' expectations of them?
4. How does the story of Wickie Lee, the teenaged, unwed mother, complement or run counter to the struggles of Cate and Lydia?
5. What attitudes do the women in this novel convey about marriage?

Annotated Bibliography

Print

Adams, Alice. "A Wonderful Woman." 1981. Reprint, in *American Wives: Thirty Short Stories by Women*, edited by Barbara H. Solomon. New York: New Amer. Lib., 1986.

The attractive, recently widowed 60-year-old protagonist awaits a romantic rendezvous with a new lover in a San Francisco hotel. His delayed arrival gives her time to review her past—in particular, her love life, her marriage, and her mothering of six children. On the surface a supremely self-possessed woman, the protagonist actually suffers inner doubts as she wonders whether she has the resources to survive without a man and whether she is getting too old to be attractive. A woman who defines herself largely in relation to men, she is nevertheless able to enjoy moments of self-sufficiency in the time she awaits her lover. When he explains that emergency dental work is the reason for his delay, she (along with the reader) recognizes that men, too, are subject to the realities of aging and suffer doubts about their attractiveness.

Beattie, Ann. "Tuesday Night." In *Solo: Women on Woman Alone*, edited by Linda Hamalian and Leo Hamalian. New York: Dell, 1977.

The protagonist-narrator of this story is a divorced woman surrounded by her ex-husband, lover, brother, woman friend, and ten-year-old daughter. All of these people are perplexed at the protagonist's desire to have one night a week to herself. As she explores different ways to spend this time alone, she begins what will be a gradual and lengthy process of discovering her needs and identity as an individual separate from the claims and opinions of the significant others in her life. In a vivid way, this story focuses on the ways women consume and relate to time.

Cantor, Aviva. "The Phantom Child." In *The Woman Who Lost Her Names: Selected Writings of American Jewish Women*, edited by Julia Wolf Mazow. San Francisco: Harper, 1980.

"The Phantom Child" explores the abortion issue in an intensely personal way that relates to the mother-daughter connection. Seven years following her abortion, the narrator shares the agonizing reflections that preceded her decision. Because she was healthy, married, childless, and financially secure, the narrator feels she lacked the usual legitimate reasons for abortion. Guilt and anxiety predominate as she attempts to make sense of her decision. She focuses on the ways in which her bitter relationship with her mother has influenced her decision to remain childless, recalls her mother's struggle to conceive a child after a miscarriage, and recognizes society's pressure on women to bear children. Her guilt over rejecting the mother role is inseparable from her regrets at not being a better daughter. As a woman with a strong sense of Jewish identity, she also explores her decision to abort in relation to Jewish law, ethics, and history.

Cather, Willa. "Old Mrs. Harris." 1932. Reprint, in *Obscure Destinies*. New York: Random, 1974.

Mrs. Rosen describes the lives of her neighbors, a Tennessee family that has settled in Colorado. Like many of her western neighbors, Mrs. Rosen cannot understand Grandma Harris' quiet resignation to a servant's role in her own daughter's household. As readers, we are allowed to see that the old woman accepts her second-class status as the norm in her southern culture. She defers to her daughter's wishes, understands her daughter's frustrations as a mother of five, and enjoys her grandparenting role despite her feeble condition. As Mrs. Rosen observes and interacts with her neighbors, we see how she fills the vacuum caused by her childlessness, particularly by connecting with Grandma Harris and helping Vickie, Grandma's eldest granddaughter, pursue her education. This story pinpoints how cultural norms affect women's behavior and how women respond to cultural dislocation, their maternal responsibilities, and their roles as grandmothers. It also opens the door to an exploration of how self-sacrificing women affect family members.

Ferber, Edna. "The Sudden Sixties." 1922. Reprint, in *One Basket*. New York: Simon & Schuster, 1947.

The experiences, thoughts, and feelings of the 60-year-old protagonist explore such themes as adjusting to widowhood, adjusting to senior citizen status, grandparenting, and relating to friends and an adult daughter. The key dilemma for the story's protagonist involves her daughter's demands and expectations regarding child care versus her own needs for peer companionship and well-earned free time. Guilt, rationalizations, and the sorting out of what a woman owes to herself and to others mark the pages of this tale.

Freeman, Mary E. Wilkins. "The Selfishness of Amelia Lamkin." 1909. Reprint, in *Short Fiction of Sarah Orne Jewett and Mary Wilkins Freeman*, edited by Barbara Solomon. New York: Penguin/New Amer. Lib., 1979.

The protagonist lives by what has been called the cult of true womanhood; she is all-sacrificing in meeting the needs of husband and children and always cheerfully performs her domestic duties. Her sister has chosen an opposite lifestyle; she has decided to remain single and fulfill her own needs. Also, she judges her sacrificing sibling to be selfish because she does not give her family the chance to be generous or learn self-sufficiency. When the protagonist suffers severe physical exhaustion, her family learns to contribute to her comfort and take care of themselves, while the single sister recognizes that her lifestyle has its own elements of selfishness. This story highlights the payoffs and pitfalls of self-sacrificing behavior in women as well as the lifestyle choices women make.

Gibbs, Angelica. "Father Was a Wit." 1937. Reprint, in *Family: Stories from the Interior*, edited by Geri G. Chavis. St. Paul, Minn.: Graywolf, 1987.

In this story, the drama of the father-daughter relationship is intensified by the absence of the mother and by the fact that the protagonist, a senior in high school, is about to enter the adult world. The introspective daughter, awaiting her father's arrival at an honors ceremony, recognizes the profound effect the cynical, critical man has had on her sense of self and her behavior with teachers and peers. Predominant in this story is the daughter's struggle between her craving for her father's approval and attention and her growing desire to develop that side of herself lacking in her father. The presence of role models for this motherless protagonist in teachers and girlfriends also is important in our appreciation of her conflict. This story raises the crucial question of how a young woman learns to nurture herself and others when her sole parent is a man who fears intimacy and whose primary response to others is ridicule.

Glasglow, Ellen. *Barren Ground.* 1925. Reprint. New York: Hill & Wang, 1957.

During a 30-year span, Dorinda Oakley grows in strength and determination after a passionate affair that leaves her a fallen woman. Awakened to romantic love, she learns its power to both nourish and blight dreams, yet she also comes to recognize how it is separate from the inner essential self that drives her to construct a productive, comfortable life. This novel is about choices women can make to combat despair, the grieving process that accompanies the loss of innocence, the sublimation of sexual impulses, and the compromise that takes place between cynicism and compassion and between intimacy and isolation. When Dorinda eventually marries for companionship and adopts her husband's children after reclaiming the land of her forefathers, she achieves a special kind of triumph that transcends gender differences. She successfully combines charm and compassion with shrewd business acumen and courage. Her fate represents the celebration of a woman's strength of will, even as it drives home the message that triumph and joy are never unalloyed with their opposites.

Gordon, Mary. *Final Payments.* New York: Ballantine, 1978.

Guilt, self-sacrifice, and reciprocity in relationships are the themes dominating this powerful novel, in which Gordon invites us to answer one basic question: What do we, as women, owe ourselves and others? The novel's 30-year-old protagonist, Isabel Moore, has cared for her father for eleven years, from the time of his first stroke to his death. Basically, the plot involves Isabel's adventures and self-explorations as she emerges from her celibate caretaker's existence to face a new arena of adult opportunities and challenges, related to herself as lover, friend, and worker. This novel explores what it means to be Catholic and female through Isabel's agonizing struggles to reconcile ideals of purity and self-abnegation with individual needs for passionate expression and self-assertion. Also important in this novel are friendships between women and a daughter's grieving over her father's death. Other secondary themes include women's sexual preferences, body image, expression of anger, and submissiveness versus assertiveness in relationships.

Klein, Norma. *Give Me One Good Reason.* 1973. Reprint. New York: Avon, 1974.

Gabrielle Van De Poel is a feisty, determined 32-year-old career woman who has chosen to stay single, yet feels she can be a good mother and combine efficiently the demands of job and parenting. While all does not go exactly as planned, she bears a child and proves that she can both derive fulfillment from a rewarding career as a medical researcher and enjoy mothering her baby son. The premium she places on independence and perfectionism at times interferes with her ability to form intimate, trusting relationships, especially with men, but she gradually softens her angry defensiveness without compromising her values. Auxiliary themes present in this work include bisexuality in men, women's dilemma over marriage and divorce decisions, and women's experiences with childbirth, maternity leave, day-care options, and child rearing. In this novel, we see women functioning not only as mothers, but as sisters, daughters, aunts, lovers, housewives, artists, and scientists.

Marshall, Paule. "Reena." In *Black-Eyed Susans: Classic Stories by and about Black Women*, edited by Mary H. Washington. Garden City, N.Y.: Anchor Pr./Doubleday, 1975.

At her godmother's funeral, the story's narrator reunites with Reenie, a childhood acquaintance whom she has not seen for twenty years. Listening throughout the night to Reenie's life story, the narrator is struck by the ways in which her old friend's experiences parallel her own, for Reenie's tale is, in many ways, a detailed account of what it means to be an educated black woman in America. This experience involves standards of beauty related to lightness of skin color and the need to be strong in order to survive. Paramount in Reenie's story is the black woman's struggle to find employment and status in the profession for which she is educated. Also significant is the black woman's struggle to combine marriage or love relationships and motherhood with career goals and strivings for social justice. When Reenie concludes her tale by describing her upcoming trip to Africa with her three children, we also get a glimpse of the black woman's search for roots and her efforts to transmit ethnic pride to her offspring.

Marshall, Paule. "The Valley Between." In *American Wives: Thirty Short Stories by Women*, edited by Barbara H. Solomon. New York: New Amer. Lib., 1986.

"The Valley Between" recounts a day in the life of a 24-year-old wife and mother who wants to complete her college education, but meets the resistance of her husband. The story highlights the woman's desire to improve herself, her frantic attempts to juggle successfully the roles of wife, mother, homemaker, and student, and her feelings of frustration and isolation in dealing with a powerful husband whose primary weapons are manipulation through guilt and the age-old tradition that says a woman's place is in the home. When her young daughter contracts a fever, the story's protagonist bitterly relinquishes her plans for an education. Although the husband softens his tone somewhat when his wife agrees to a full-time homemaker role, he is still far from understanding his wife's struggles and feelings, and the chasm between the spouses looms wider than ever. This story's vague and disturbing conclusion invites us to supply our own ending.

Mason, Bobbie Ann. "Blue Country." 1985. Reprint, in *The Graywolf Annual Two: Short Stories by Women*, edited by Scott Walker. St. Paul, Minn.: Graywolf, 1986.

A young wife and mother is in New England with her husband to attend an old friend's wedding, when she learns of her grandmother's death in Kentucky. This event precipitates the central conflict of the story, in which the protagonist feels the tug of family obligations and reflects on what she owes herself and others. She agonizes over whether to pursue plans important to her or to attend her grandmother's funeral, thus pleasing her parents, who have devoted themselves to caring for the elderly woman. In spite of an airline strike and bad weather, which make it nearly impossible for her to go to the funeral, she remains divided in her loyalties and consciousness throughout the wedding and reunion with old friends. The subtle resolution occurs when the protagonist and her husband find themselves swept up in the excitement of the moment on a whale-watching expedition. This episode, in a story about life, death, priorities, and sacrifices, confirms the protagonist's decision to treasure life's joyous moments.

Olsen, Tillie. "I Stand Here Ironing." In *Tell Me a Riddle*. New York: Delacorte, 1956. Also in *Between Mothers and Daughters: Stories across a Generation*, edited by Susan Koppelman. New York: Feminist Pr., 1985.

The focus here is on the guilt a mother feels when she recognizes her daughter's pain and difficulty in dealing with life. As she stands ironing, after a call from her daughter's high school guidance counselor, she reviews choices she made when she was a young impoverished mother struggling to raise her first child without a spouse. As she ruminates over her deficiencies as a mother and the limitations caused by external factors, the protagonist alternates between self-castigation and rationalization. Resolution comes when she recognizes that her daughter has developed specific talents and has found a source of strength despite the limitations of her upbringing.

Portnoy, Marsha. "Loving Strangers." 1983. Reprint, in *Family: Stories from the Interior*, edited by Geri G. Chavis. St. Paul, Minn.: Graywolf, 1987.

This heartwarming story describes a new connection forged between a mother and a daughter who has just become a mother herself. It shows how expectations and past assumptions can keep mothers and daughters strangers to one another. Yet it also shows how risk-taking communication can help mothers and daughters recognize their commonality and can increase the strength of their bond. The struggles of the new mother are suggested in this story, as are the themes of perfectionism, compromise in marriage, and legacies that mothers pass on to daughters.

Shockley, Ann Allen. "A Birthday Remembered." 1980. Reprint, in *Between Mothers and Daughters: Stories across a Generation*, edited by Susan Koppelman. New York: Feminist Pr., 1985.

Ellen is a 44-year-old woman mourning her deceased lover, Jackie, whose daughter, Tobie, was raised for eight years by the two women, until her father insisted on gaining custody of the child. During a birthday visit to her Aunt El, Tobie—now a young woman with a boyfriend—clearly asserts her positive regard for the mothering she received and the loving relationship she observed between her mother and Ellen. Ellen's memories also indicate that both she and Jackie were fulfilled women who derived satisfaction from their careers. The anger that Tobie's father expresses in relation to his ex-wife's lesbian lifestyle is the only indication of the prejudices that homosexuals face in our society. Yet his presence as the voice of convention invites us to speculate on other possible external forces that complicate the lives of homosexuals.

Shulman, Alix Kates. *Memoirs of an Ex-Prom Queen*. 1972. Reprint. New York: Bantam, 1973.

This novel is for any woman who has been taught to believe that her worth is based largely on her appearance and her conformity to standards of traditional feminine behavior. Primary themes in this work include sex role stereotyping, sexual harassment, the double standard governing sexual behavior, parenting, intellectual achievement, and career preparation for men and women in our society. While in some ways dated, the provocative gender issues raised by this novel provide a backdrop against which to evaluate how far women and men have come in the post-women's movement era. In a series of flashbacks, the novel's 25-year-old protagonist, Sasha Davis, recounts her struggles between self-realization and social conformity. Attracted to Ralph Waldo Emerson's injunction to "trust the self," Sasha nevertheless repeatedly turns to others, principally males, to validate her worth. We see how parental attitudes, mass media messages, and peer pressure militate against self-reliance and keep Sasha dependent on men and her mirror. When the novel ends, 30-year-old Sasha, now a wife to her second husband and a mother to their child, is still caught in the trap of her upbringing. We are left to surmise that her search for self-fulfillment and an individualized set of standards is far from over.

Slesinger, Tess. "Mother to Dinner." 1935. Reprint, in *Between Mothers and Daughters: Stories across a Generation*, edited by Susan Koppelman. New York: Feminist Pr., 1985.

Told from the viewpoint of a young woman married less than a year, "Mother to Dinner" highlights, in an often exaggerated way, some of the struggles women face in making the transition from daughter to wife. The protagonist's divided loyalties cause her great anguish as she awaits the arrival of her parents for dinner at her new home. In her state of confusion and anxiety, she sees both her husband and her mother as strangers to her and enemies to one another and does not know how to bridge the gulf between them. While she openly acknowledges and appreciates traits she shares with her mother, she feels driven to agree with her husband's contemptuous view of her mother. Her need to protect both mother and husband and to prevent conflict reflects the caretaking, peace-making, and guilt-driven behavior of many women.

Smith, Betty. *Tomorrow Will Be Better*. New York: Harper, 1948.

Although *Tomorrow Will Be Better* takes place in the working-class world of the 1920s and early 1930s, it raises issues relevant to today's women. The focus is on a young woman's emergence into the adult world of work, courtship, and marriage and on the ways a daughter's self-image and choices are affected by the manipulative messages of a critical, possessive mother, unable to show her love and trapped by her own upbringing and socioeconomic milieu. Important subthemes in this work include women's sexuality in marriage, marriage to a gay man, grieving over a miscarriage, relationships with in-laws, and work and career decisions for the married woman whose husband wants to be the sole breadwinner.

Starkman, Elaine Marcus. "Anniversary." 1980. Reprint, in *Family: Stories from the Interior*, edited by Geri G. Chavis. St. Paul, Minn.: Graywolf, 1987.

Through the reflections of a woman married fifteen years, we see how she loses her sense of a separate identity and how her experience in marriage differs profoundly from that of her husband. Through the protagonist's thoughts and dialogue with her physician spouse, we see how she vacillates between yearning for the freedom to realize her potential as a student and poet and desiring renewed commitment to a viable marriage. Themes paramount in this story are the routine and excitement, the freedom and compromise, and the dependency and independence that characterize marriage.

Thayer, Nancy. *Three Women at the Water's Edge*. New York: Bantam, 1981.

As the novel's title suggests, three women—a mother and her two adult daughters—have arrived at crossroads in their lives. This affirming, often humorous work illuminates the resources and flexibility needed by women to cope with changes in their marital status and life plan. Margaret, a mother and doctor's wife for 30 years, chooses divorce and a rejuvenating, independent lifestyle. The elder daughter, Daisy, following what she thought were her mother's footsteps as the devoted wife, mother, and full-time homemaker, finds change thrust upon her when her husband leaves for another woman. She faces the agony of divorce and the hardships of single parenthood as she rebuilds her life and her self-esteem at age 29. At quite a different life stage is the younger sister, Dale, a single woman with a high school teaching career, who is falling in love and considering marriage for the first time, yet is wary of commitment. In adjusting to the struggles and excitement of their life changes, all three women are challenged to revise their old perceptions of one another and discover new ways of relating.

Tyler, Anne. *Breathing Lessons*. New York: Knopf, 1988.

With two grown-up children and a grandchild wrenched from her life by her son's divorce, the middle-aged protagonist of this humorous and heart-warming novel faces what is commonly called the empty nest syndrome. During a day-long trip to the funeral of an old friend's husband, the emotional, impulsive protagonist reviews many aspects of her past and present life. She explores her relationship to a taciturn, rational husband and evaluates her personality, along with her behavior as a single girl, then as a wife, mother, mother-in-law, friend, and nursing home aide. Her thoughts and the interactions between husband and wife provide insight into why women and men choose particular spouses and how spouses contract on an unconscious level to balance one another. This is a particularly valuable study of women's experience because of the protagonist's ability to ultimately integrate self-acceptance with her tendency toward self-criticism that has been reinforced by both her mother and her husband.

Walker, Alice. *The Color Purple*. New York: Washington Square Pr., 1982.

Through narration in letter form, this life-affirming novel captures the experiences of black women in southern rural communities while providing background on women's lives in emerging African nations. In her addresses to God and the beloved sister from whom she has been separated for 30 years, protagonist Celie tells her story and expresses her feelings as her fortunes change. Through the friendship and modeling of

Shug, a sophisticated, tough-minded, yet compassionate woman, the once passive and apathetic Celie grows into a woman who knows her own mind and can celebrate the spirit within herself. This novel illuminates the ways in which a woman's sexuality and spirituality interwine, as it raises the question of how the concept of a masculinized God affects women. In unvarnished fashion, it presents the physical, sexual, and emotional abuses women suffer at the hands of men, and it challenges the stereotypes of masculine and feminine behavior that cripple human behavior and destroy intimacy in relationships. It portrays women as abused and abusing wives, incest victims, lovers in heterosexual and lesbian relationships, mothers, friends, and workers.

Walker, Alice. "A Sudden Trip Home in the Spring." 1971. Reprint, in *Black-Eyed Susans: Classic Stories by and about Black Women*, edited by Mary H. Washington. Garden City, N.Y.: Anchor Pr./Doubleday, 1975.

On a scholarship to pursue an art degree at a women's college in the South, the talented, attractive young protagonist reflects on how it feels to be a black woman in a culture dominated by white images and standards. Sarah is popular at college, but feels she is admired chiefly for her exotic appeal. Learning of her father's death and returning home to attend his funeral set off a series of reflections and interactions with family members that not only help Sarah understand a father she has always resented, but lead to an inspirational recapturing of her roots. Sarah's concluding thoughts effectively epitomize this story's basic themes: "I am a woman in the world. I have buried my father, and shall soon know how to make my grandpa up in stone."

Yamamoto, Hisaye. "Seventeen Syllables." 1949. Reprint, in *Between Mothers and Daughters: Stories across a Generation*, edited by Susan Koppelman. New York: Feminist Pr., 1985.

"Seventeen Syllables" focuses on the mother-daughter relationship in the context of Asian-American culture. We see how women are affected by the expectations of their culture, how they can be caught between two cultures and affected by changing mores, and how they juggle their roles as wife, mother, worker, and intellectual. In this story, the mother's dual identity as a talented poet and as a household drudge and menial farm worker intrigues her teenaged daughter, who is grappling with her own identity issues and sexual awakening. The father's rage at the mother's artistic aspirations motivates the mother to share with her daughter the story of her youth and marriage. Her tale, focusing on themes of arranged marriage, miscarriage, and the shame of unwed mothering, is designed to protect the daughter from the mother's mistakes.

15 Ethnic Minorities:
Ralph Ellison's *Invisible Man*

By Jay Martin

A contemporary rhythm and blues singer described the central life problem (and its solution) for the child who is a member of a racial or ethnic minority: "I've got to use my imagination to make the best of a bad situation to keep on keepin' on" (Gladys Knight, "I've Got to Use My Imagination," *Imagination*, New York: Budda Records, 1973). Growing up as an ethnic minority dramatically—and oftentimes tragically—forces the child and young person to face his or her "difference" constantly. For the growing personality, "different" often means "undesirable," "unwanted," "unvalued." To secure a stable, confident identity is no easy matter under any circumstances. But the vicissitudes of psychological development are immensely complicated by the constant reminders of difference.

The Paradigm

Ralph Ellison's *Invisible Man* (Vintage, 1989), first published in 1952, often has been pointed to as a remarkable portrait of the difficulties and conflicts in identity formation experienced by blacks and, by extension, members of many racial or ethnic minority groups. The psychologist Joseph L. White has written that, like the protagonist in this novel, "the Black young adult may go through a series of major role changes accompanied by defeat, disillusionment, and disappointment before understanding that the only solid answers come through direct experience" (*The Psychology of Blacks: An Afro-American Perspective*, Englewood Cliffs, N.J.: Prentice-Hall, 1984, p.97).

The aptness of this novel lies in the fact that it dramatizes—from inside his consciousness—a young man's responses to direct experience of various bad situations. We are not *told* about his experience of oppression, hardship, and defeat; *we become part of it* through a direct experience of his inner life. In short, we are allowed to identify with the character. For all readers who make this identification, the book vividly exhibits the life process of identity formation, especially difficult for the young adult who belongs to an ethnic minority.

Summary

Invisible Man has been continuously in print for nearly 40 years. It is widely regarded as a classic work dealing with the uneasy relations of ethnic minorities—in this case, blacks—with majority white culture in the United States. In an introduction to the novel written especially for a 1981 edition, Ellison spoke of his aim to create a fictional character who tries to find his place in a "society whose manners, motives and rituals were baffling." The theme of *Invisible Man* is that individual self-awareness and a sense of authentic personhood can be achieved even against the stereotypes of ethnic minorities held by majority culture. This theme is embodied in this narrative of the growth and education of a sensitive young man.

The novel's protagonist is given no name and has very little personal past because he is meant to represent all people of all races and ethnic minorities who struggle through the intricacies of a majority society whose mores are strange to them. Specifically, the novel tells the story of the various crises faced by a male between the midpoint of his adolescence and his entry into adulthood. The book is built around the form of the picaresque romance, a traditional genre in which the innocent hero encounters various rogues. In *Invisible Man*, the innocent hero—who narrates the story in the first person—is a black teenager who has just graduated from high school; ironically, most of the rogues he encounters belong to or represent majority white culture.

In the beginning of *Invisible Man*, the protagonist tells us that at the ceremonies of his recent high school graduation, he delivered an oration with the thesis that humility is the secret of progress for the black race. For obvious reasons, this appealed to the white leaders of his southern town, and they invite him to repeat the oration at a gathering of the town's leading citizens. There, however, he is forced into a battle royal, in which ten young black men fight each other blindfolded for a prize. They are duped into trying to grab money—which turns out to be phony—from a carpet that has been electrified. Then they are forced to watch a woman strip for the crude pleasure of the audience, and they see the conservative town leaders act like barbarians. Yet the hero has been so convinced by his early training in the correctness of conformity that when he finally has a chance to give his speech, he still argues for humility and patience as the black man's road to success. He nearly makes conscious his inner feelings, however, when he makes a Freudian slip and says that blacks should have "social equality," though he had consciously intended to say "social responsibility."

This first episode in the book is fairly representative of the issues that the novel raises with regard to the relations between white majority society and members of ethnic minorities. The hero has been brainwashed into conformity. By focusing on what majority society wants of him and by aiming at success in relation to dominant white society, the hero is invisible to himself. The town's leading citizens humiliate him as well as the other young men, using them all as vehicles for pleasure, much as they use and abuse the stripper. But though the hero feels the humiliation, he does not question the standards or ideology of majority society. The book provides material that obliges us to face the injustice and cruelty of majority society toward its minorities; because we soon understand more than the protagonist does, the tone of the book is consistently ironical. We readers, not the protagonist, can see the psychodynamics and psychology of racism.

Endowed with a basic trust and optimism, the young man has been given a training in which obedience and respect for authority are primary virtues. We see that in a racist society, these virtues may be important for survival; but we also see that they can injure a person's self-esteem and work against him: trust is of little value when society is itself deceptive. The defenses that keep the protagonist's obedience in place include denial (of the cruelty of majority society), intellectualization (the value of education), depersonalization, isolation, and delusion.

After graduation, the young man is given a briefcase and, inside it, a scholarship to the state college for blacks. The briefcase is an important symbol in the book. It represents the container of his experience—his memory—because all through the book, he puts inside it the documents representing the information, or education, that he gathers along the way.

At the entrance to the college is a statue showing the school's founder grasping a veil before the face of a kneeling slave. The protagonist is never certain whether the veil is being lifted or pressed more firmly into place.

Once settled, the young man serves as a guide for a white trustee. He takes the prominent man on a tour that includes a talk with a black farmer who has committed incest with his daughter and a visit to a sporting house on a day when the black male inmates of a hospital for the mentally ill are there to visit the girls. Such things are supposed to be invisible to the trustee, and the college president becomes furious at the protagonist for disturbing the liberal trustee's benign view of the simplicity and innocence of black culture. Finally, the president gives the young man seven letters of recommendation and sends him to New York City to look for a job before he returns to college.

After several attempts at using his recommendations, the trusting young man finally discovers that the letters urge employers not to hire him and indicate that he will never be allowed back in the school. This discovery cements his dawning recognition of the duplicity and hypocrisy of the college's president; the young man is severely disillusioned by these strong doses of reality. He has been exactly the kind of person that the official social code tells him is necessary for success, yet—in contrast to the Horatio Alger promises—he has failed with absolute consistency.

The protagonist's idealism is cracking, and his defenses are severely strained, but neither is entirely shattered. Still, the process of re-education has begun. For instance, on the bus to New York he is told to "look beneath the surface" and "come out of the fog." After this incident, his adventures increasingly oblige him to see more deeply and more clearly into the patterns of society that conventional social doctrine has made invisible to him, even as he continues to be invisible to society, seen only as a stock image of the Negro, not as a man, and never as himself, an individual.

After discovering that he has been tricked by the college president, the protagonist perpetrates his first deception. He gets a job by trickery, seeing this as an appropriate revenge on the people who betrayed him. Psychologically, he experiences the sort of anger toward majority society that Joseph White (*The Psychology of Blacks*, Englewood Cliffs, N.J.: Prentice-Hall, 1984) and other psychologists argue is a necessary stage in the identity formation of ethnic minorities.

All during this time and continuing on in the novel, the young man is given advice from a great number of sources. He listens to speeches by conservative and rebellious citizens; he recalls his grandfather's dying words about the need to be adaptively deceptive when society is dangerous; he remembers songs that impart wisdom in the broadest sense; he notes advertisements that symbolize society; and he collects documents that encourage conformity or subversity. Thereby, Ellison gives an excellent representation of the growth of experience through object-relations as the self encounters the object world, consisting of other persons, things, and institutions. We see how the young man's basic endowment of trust is tested and refined by experience.

The job that the protagonist gets by deception is itself a deception, in symbolic terms. He works in a factory that produces Optic White paint, which is made by mixing ten drops of black paint into each gallon of white (blacks were 10 percent of the population in 1950); in other words, the black must serve to heighten the white.

When the factory tanks explode, the young man is injured and suffers amnesia, during which he fantasizes that he is the Brer Rabbit of traditional slave narratives—that is, he is the weak creature that uses cunning to triumph over the strong, just as the slave hoped to use his wit to defeat the master's power. In short, the young man forgets the conformist models of his childhood and moves toward a new birth and a changed perspective that will lead him toward a stronger manhood.

At this point, the protagonist gets (symbolically) a new mother, a Harlem woman named Mary who takes him in and urges him "to fight and move us all on up a little higher." At Mary's apartment, he reads and begins to consolidate a new identity. The young man observes the delusions of Harlemites—the appeal of religion, the enticements of advertisements, the promise of commerce or love—and he sees through these delusions. By contrast to the fake world, he ravenously eats real yams bought from a street vendor, and these return him to the fundamental realities of his youth—warmth, food, and sweetness. Thereby, he begins to accept, without shame, his own experience, appetites, and personal history.

A long section follows in which the young man comes into contact with the final delusion—that politics will cure society. He associates with the "Brotherhood"—Ellison's name for the Communist party—and enters its inner circles, where he gets a long, disillusioning look at the power seeking, personal corruption, stereotyping of minorities, and duplicity of radical politics.

Just as the protagonist is continually given advice by others, he himself gives speeches over the course of the novel. Some of his most powerful speeches are given during his attempt at achieving a viable identity through politics. But the themes of his speeches—the need for freedom, justice, integrity, and loving relations between people—do not reflect the correct, scientific party line, and the leaders of the Brotherhood castigate him. Finally, he sees that in being a political spokesman, he has really been like a cardboard Sambo doll moved by invisible strings pulled by others.

If the Communist party does not offer the protagonist an opportunity for self-realization, neither does the black nationalist movement similar to that promulgated in the United States by Marcus Garvey and later by Malcolm X. Ras the Destroyer, the character Ellison created to represent the black nationalist movement, is as committed as the Brotherhood is to collective action and communitarian solutions; both are equally narrow and, as Ellison presents it, out of tune with the ordinary American.

The protagonist goes through one final stage of awareness before he can arrive at a new identity. This is portrayed in a vivid, surrealistic manner, conveying the thorough breakdown of a person's sense of reality that may precede the acquisition of a new vision in a more firm identity. The young man dons a pair of disguising sunglasses and becomes truly invisible: he is like a blank screen, the object of others' projections, the neutral object of their desires. A woman mistakes him for her lover. An addict sees him as a dealer. A petty criminal thinks he is a gangster. A zoot-suiter sees him as a hipster. A gambler mistakes him for a numbers runner. A prostitute takes him for her pimp. In short, he is everyone's dream; but his own dream goes unrecognized. Thus, he learns in a dramatic fashion that reality is shifty and shifting, the separate invention and projection of each person's individual needs. Such inventions, parading as reality, are, of course, barriers to the achievement of an authentic personhood.

This leads to his final stage of identity in the novel. In the course of the book, the young man has given up his delusion that majority values, conventional work, the ideals of justice, ideological equality, and radical politics provide satisfactory vehicles for self-betterment and self-realization. He has also left behind his rigid defenses of denial, intellectualization, altruism, shame, guilt, and isolation. He has become engaged with the roots of his culture and has shed corrupt versions of that culture. He remains an invisible man to others, but is no longer invisible to himself. If he does not yet know who he is, at least he has learned that he is not the image that society holds of him.

The novel has been told in retrospect, but when we arrive at the present we learn that the invisible man has finally become an underground man, resembling the narrator of Fyodor Dostoyevsky's *Notes from Underground*. Literally, the protagonist has made a home in the tunnels beneath the streets of New York. He takes all the contents of his briefcase—all the emblems of his education—and burns each document, starting with his high school diploma. Like Henry David Thoreau at Walden Pond, he vows to live alone, without illusion.

In the end, he has achieved a state of tension-free ego adaptation, without memory or desire, and is ready to process experience on its own terms through his own balanced perspective. From this viewpoint, the young man declares that the fate of the relation between ethnic minorities and majority culture is "to become one, and yet many." With confidence, he foresees an America that possesses both unity and diversity, and unity in diversity, a truly harmonized multi-ethnic society.

That descriptive prophecy and final vision of the invisible man accord well with the general movement of American society, as described by many contemporary sociologists. But each individual, especially members of ethnic minorities, must go through a set of experiences similar to those of the invisible man, fusing trust and early illusion with "disorder and early sorrow"; breaking down rigid defenses—once needed to protect against traumatic disillusion—and replacing them with more flexible defenses that allow for ambivalence, ambiguity, and the ability to tolerate doubt; and finally, proceeding from dependence to independence and from idealization of others' power to acceptance of one's individual capacities as, in D. W. Winnicott's terms, "good enough" (*The Maturational Process and the Facilitating Environment*, London: Hogarth Pr., 1965).

Questions for Discussion

1. In what ways have various ethnic minority men and women experienced the issues of assimilation, discrimination, and personal development in identity formation?
2. How would some of the crises experienced by the hero have differed had he been a woman?
3. Why does the novel end with the invisible man still in his underground den?
4. Why do we learn so little about the invisible man's parents? Who are some of the parent figures who appear in the book?
5. What are the functions of songs in the novel and in contemporary experience for adolescents?

Annotated Bibliography

Print

Baldwin, James. "The Discovery of What It Means to Be an American." In *Nobody Knows My Name: More Notes of a Native Son*. New York: Delta, 1961.

In this essay, the distinguished writer James Baldwin provides a personal account of the complex, difficult relations between a writer from an ethnic minority and American culture as a whole. As a young man, Baldwin left the United States for France, and in this essay gives the reasons for his alienation and exile and his return to his native land. He left America because he felt he could not "survive the fury of the color problem here." But in Europe, he discovered that he really was American, and when he realized that he had a role to play in America, he found that he no longer hated his country. Baldwin's is an impressive recounting of the important relations existing between meaningful work and self-acceptance.

Baldwin, James. "Sonny's Blues." In *Going to Meet the Man*. New York: Dial, 1965.

In this short story, Baldwin portrays the conflict between two major styles of life for young black men in Harlem and, by extension, for most ethnic minorities. These lifestyles are represented dramatically by two brothers. The older brother is a high school mathematics teacher. His ethnic origin has prompted him to play it safe, to use education for upward mobility, and to marry and raise a family. His brother, Sonny, takes the opposite route. Drawing upon the strength of black music, he becomes a musician, but pays the penalty for his daring by becoming a drug addict and going to prison. The story ends with the older brother's epiphany—his appreciation of the imaginative accomplishment of Sonny in his fierce devotion to playing—and living—the blues.

Deloria, Vine, Jr. *We Talk, You Listen*. New York: Macmillan, 1970.

A spokesperson for the protest movement of native Americans, Deloria is a member of the Standing Rock Sioux tribe. His works help give strength to native Americans, who have been especially scorned and abused in American society. Deloria speaks not personally, but as a representative of all native Americans, forcefully analyzing white abuse of Indians. Like Ellison's theme in *Invisible Man*, Deloria's theme is that the native American is invisible to the white man, who sees him only through the stereotypes of films and books. American "mythologies . . . have blocked out any idea that there might be real Indians with real problems." Above all, he speaks for the need of native Americans to achieve racial pride.

Douglass, Frederick. *My Bondage and My Freedom*. New York and Auburn: Miller, Orton, and Mulligan, 1855.

This classic autobiographical account of Douglass' life as a slave and finally a freedman is especially notable for its portrayal of the horrors Douglass suffered as a slave and its vivid account of the growth of his intellectual powers. *My Bondage and My Freedom* is a dramatic and impressive account of the powers of the human spirit to endure the most extreme hardships and yet retain the capacity for love and optimism.

Douglass' account of his reading lessons from his mistress are as powerful as his accounts of his work with abolitionism in the North.

Ellison, Ralph. "Hidden Name and Complex Fate." In *Shadow and Act.* New York: Random, 1964.

Ellison's personal essay concerns the role of the writer in the United States and, more particularly, the role of the ethnic writer who stands outside the Anglophile tradition in American literature. This essay is very appropriately read as an indirect comment on Ellison's intentions in *Invisible Man.* In it, he makes the distinction between a writer's art and his ethnic origins. But he also shows how his own experience as a black child growing up in Oklahoma City provided him with a rich source of realistic materials, stories, myths, and life experiences that gave his decision to become a writer meaning. In its own way, this is as poignant an account of the growth of a mind as the autobiographies of Frederick Douglass and Booker T. Washington.

Farrell, James T. "The Oratory Contest." In *The Short Stories of James T. Farrell.* New York: Vanguard, 1964.

Farrell's trilogy of novels about Studs Lonigan is one of the most famous full-length portrayals of the troubled growth into young manhood of an Irish-American in Chicago. Many of Farrell's stories concern particular aspects of the same scene and themes, mostly emphasizing the bleak aspects of life for the urban Irish poor. In "The Oratory Contest," Farrell portrays sixteen-year-old Gerry O'Dell's hope that he will win applause for his oration. Paralleling Gerry's youthful hopes is Farrell's grim, relentless depiction of the effects of grinding poverty on the O'Dell family, especially on Gerry's worn-out mother. Gerry's words at the oratory contest concerning freedom and liberty for all Americans ring ironically in the cold light of the scarcely free conditions of the O'Dell family.

Hagopian, John V. "Well, My Father Was an Armenian, Yes." In *A Nation of Nations: Ethnic Literature in America*, edited by Theodore L. Gross. New York and London: Free Pr., 1971.

Written by a professor of American studies, this autobiographical essay is a wise and witty reflection on the problems of all ethnic minorities who are trapped by hyphenated identities, "two vaguely defined identities neither of which [one] can fully accept." He speaks about his personal experiences growing up in the 1920s and 1930s, along with his experiences as a visiting professor in Germany. Despite his thesis concerning the conflicts between hyphenated identities, Hagopian conveys a calm, balanced sense of ego integration.

Hansberry, Lorraine. *A Raisin in the Sun.* New York: New Amer. Lib., 1966.

Hansberry's play is a remarkable story of the generational conflicts in a black family that are brought about when the father dies and leaves his wife with a substantial insurance policy. Each member of the family has a different dream for the money. The mother, who has lived her life in poverty despite her hard work, wishes to buy a house to keep the family together. Her son hopes to use the money to gain economic independence. His wife hopes to have a second child. Her daughter, strongly influenced by the Pan-African movement, wants to go to medical school. These conflicts threaten to tear the family apart, but are at last resolved by the strength of the mother and her self-sacrificing love for her family.

King, Martin Luther, Jr. "I Have a Dream." 1963. Reprint, in *Black Writers of America*, edited by Richard Barksdale and Keneth Kinnamon. New York: Macmillan, 1972.

One of the great achievements of black oratory, Reverend King's speech is in the great tradition of the dream of ethnic minorities to achieve freedom, political and economic equality, and collaboration between all races of the United States. Deliberately paralleling his speech to Abraham Lincoln's "Gettysburg Address," King emphasized the psychology of the immigrant's or minority member's hope that his or her children will see a better day in a place "where they will not be judged by the color of their skin but by the content of their character." At the conclusion of this inspiring speech, he suggested that the meaning of the American search for freedom can be found equally in the Declaration of Independence and in traditional black spirituals.

Malamud, Bernard. "The Magic Barrel." In *The Magic Barrel and Other Stories.* New York: Farrar, 1958.

Lew Finkle, a rabbinical student in New York City, is about to graduate from Yeshiva University. He decides that he should marry; and having devoted the previous six years entirely to study, he calls in a matchmaker to find a bride for him—an old Jewish custom, one through which his parents had become acquainted and been married. After a time, he decides he wants to marry for love. Finally, by accident, he sees a photo of the matchmaker's daughter and falls in love with her. The story is a beautiful portrayal of the inexperienced young man's emotions in learning to love.

Malcolm X. *The Autobiography of Malcolm X.* New York: Grove, 1964.

Written with the collaboration of Alex Haley, the author of *Roots*, Malcolm X's autobiography is in the main tradition of black—and generally speaking, ethnic—personal narrative. He tells the story of his remarkable transformations from an early life of incredible deprivation. Owing to the fact that his father was killed and his mother was periodically committed to mental institutions, Malcolm turned to a life of crime and at age 21 was imprisoned. In prison, converted to Black Muslimism, he emerged as a brilliant spokesperson for black integrity and separatism. Converted again by a visit to Mecca, he departed from the movement, led by Elijah Mohammed, and at the time of his assassination was committed to a profound humanistic philosophy, which promoted the unity of all races.

Marshall, Paule. *Brown Girl, Brownstones.* 1959. Reprint. Chatham, N.J.: Chatham Pr., 1972.

Paule Marshall's novel, originally published in 1959, is especially noteworthy for its depiction of the personal and cultural issues at stake when a black family moves from the Caribbean—in this case, the island of Barbados—to New York City. The cultural gap is vast: from an island where family is central to a city where anonymity and alienation are the rule; from a predominantly mixed society to a society where race prejudice abounds; from a relatively small, rural town to an urban setting with many cultural opportunities. Selina Boyce, the novel's young protagonist, is caught in these tensions between her Barbadian parents and the life of Brooklyn, where she is born. Marshall's novel offers a remarkable portrait of the influence of race on the psychology of youth and of individual maturation through facing conflicts.

Momaday, N. Scott. *House Made of Dawn.* New York: Harper, 1968.

The tale of a young Indian who returns from Army service following the end of World War II, this novel tells one of the most enduring stories of the literature of ethnic minorities. The sensitive young man who has lived in white civilization is now caught between two worlds. Unable to give up his attachments to the Kiowa culture of his childhood, he cannot accept life in the non-Indian world. His attempt to recapture faith in traditional rituals and to integrate his tribal identity into his recent experience offers dramatic insight into a central psychological problem for the modern native American.

Mori, Toshio. "Slant-Eyed Americans." In *Yokohama, California.* Caldwell, Idaho: Caxton, 1949.

Himself a Nisei (an American-born child of Japanese immigrant parents), Mori writes of the problems of Nisei in California. "Slant-Eyed Americans" takes place on the historic day of December 7, 1941, when a squadron of Japanese planes bombed Pearl Harbor. This is a striking portrait of a Japanese American family whose members suddenly become aliens in their adopted—and in the case of the two sons, native—land. It gives a striking picture of psychological confusion and alienation during a period when a previously firm identity is threatened with disruption.

Morrison, Toni. *The Bluest Eye.* New York: Washington Square, 1972.

This classic novel explores the daily lives of two black families—that of Pecola, incest and child abuse victim, and that of the narrator and her sister. Both families are poverty stricken, and their children suffer the consequences of the racism that has distorted their parents' lives. By tracing the history of Pecola's parents and by means of parallelism and contrast between the two families, the author shows how one set of parents comes to physically act out on their children the pressures of white society, while the other imposes on their children their self-hatred for being black. The pretty, blue-eyed, pink-cheeked, blonde doll and the storybook middle-class family living in a white and green house are the symbols that the adults, brainwashed by white racism, impose on their children; they are ideals and dreams the children cannot possibly realize, ideals that their daily reality painfully contradicts. The novel is an excellent study of the self-rejection imposed on the black female child and the painful feelings engendered by a racist society.

Ortiz, Simon. "Kaiser and the War." In *The Portable North American Indian Reader,* edited by Frederick W. Turner III. New York: Viking, 1973.

Told from the point of view of a native American boy, this is the story of Kaiser, an Indian who resists being drafted into the army by running away and hiding on Black Mesa. The government finally abandons the search for him, and he returns home. When he then volunteers for the army, he is arrested for draft evasion. Kaiser and the boy who tells his story are both equally confused by the strange ways of the white man.

Salas, Floyd. *Tattoo the Wicked Cross.* New York: Grove, 1967.

The literature of ethnic minorities often is marked by the violence that often is a part of minority culture. Salas' novel is the tale of Aaron D'Aragon's experiences in a juvenile facility. In prison, he is beaten, raped, and psychologically humiliated. Eventually, he murders his attackers, but suffers terrible mental torment over the deed. This is an excellent portrayal of the destructive aspects of violence on young lives in minority cultures.

Salinas, Marta. "The Scholarship Jacket." In *Cuentos Chicanos*, edited by Rudolfo A. Anaya and Antonio Marquez. Albuquerque, N. Mex.: New America, 1988.

An extremely poor fourteen-year-old Texas girl hopes to wear the beautiful gold and green jacket that, at each graduation, is given to the student who has maintained the highest grades for the previous eight years. She overhears a conversation between two teachers that suggests the falsification of records so that the daughter of the small town's only storeowner would win. By holding to strict moral principles, she embarrasses the principal into awarding her the jacket after all. Salinas gives a tender portrait of the protagonist's pride and honesty at a critical moment when these are tested.

Santos, Bienvenido. "The Day the Dancers Came." In *Speaking for Ourselves: American Ethnic Writing*, edited by Lillian Faderman and Barbara Bradshaw. Glenview, Ill.: Scott, Foresman, 1969.

Born in the Philippines in 1911, Santos wrote mostly of the Filipino experience in the United States. This story concerns Fil, an old Filipino man who became a U.S. citizen by serving in the army, and Tony, his friend and roommate. As the story opens, snow is falling and Fil is excited that the Filipino dancers who are coming to Chicago for a performance will see snow for the first time. Though poor, he makes elaborate plans to entertain the dancers, who remind him both of his old home and of his own homelessness. Fil's attempts at friendliness go unnoticed by the young dancers, and the story ends with Fil alone, homesick and lonely. This is a bitter portrait of the difficulties of exile and the psychological problems of adjustment for the émigré.

Thomas, Piri. *Down These Mean Streets*. New York: Knopf, 1967.

As a native of Spanish Harlem in New York, Thomas paints a striking picture of life for Puerto Ricans in the nation's largest barrio. In this autobiographical novel, he focuses on conflicts with other minority groups, the violence of the barrio, drugs, moral issues, sexual preoccupations, and worries about survival and the future—all the concerns of childhood and adolescence intensified by poverty. Unlike the hero of Floyd Salas' novel, Piri manages to surmount the difficulties of his life.

Walker, Alice. "Everyday Use." In *In Love and Trouble*. New York: Harcourt, 1973.

Walker, the author of *The Color Purple*, portrays in "Everyday Use" two different maturational lines and two different identities achieved by two sisters in the rural South. One sister stays home, plans to marry, and abides by the traditional life of her rural culture, in which life is lived for everyday use. The other sister leaves home, goes to college, is influenced by Pan-African and Muslim movements, dresses in stylish African clothes, and regards traditional black culture and its implements as curiosities, suitable only for a museum. The conflict between the two sisters comes to a head over the question of which one should own a traditional family quilt and whether it should be used everyday or as a decorative wall hanging. The conflict represents that experienced by many youths in trying to form identities that will retain the influence of parental models while reflecting changing societal values.

Washington, Booker T. *Up from Slavery*. New York: Doubleday, 1901.

Like Frederick Douglass, Washington was born a slave, but unlike Douglass he was born less than a decade before the Emancipation Proclamation; therefore, he stresses the movement away from slavery, rather than the slave experience, in his autobiography. Washington recounts his experiences working as a manual laborer while he struggled to gain an education. His ability to triumph over hardship, his determination to succeed, his incorporation of the Protestant work ethic, and his development of all of these into an educational philosophy and a theory of peaceful black-white coexistence result in a remarkable triumph of perseverance over adversity.

Wong, Jade Snow. *Fifth Chinese Daughter*. New York: Harper, 1950.

Told by an omniscient narrator as if it were a novel, this book is actually an autobiographical account. Wong writes with warmth and compassion about her girlhood in a Chinatown family. Her gentle tone, attitude of wonder, and patient and caring observation of small details allow insight into the values of the traditional Chinese family attempting to adjust to American conditions.

Wright, Richard. "The Man Who Was Almost a Man." 1940. Reprint, in *Fiction One Hundred: An Anthology of Short Stories*, edited by James H. Pickening. New York: Macmillan, 1974.

Wright's story, originally published in 1940, sensitively portrays a brief period in the life of a black adolescent who feels the weakness, vulnerability, wishes for omnipotence, and narcissistic struggles of youth all the more forcefully because he lives in a society dominated by whites. Controlled by his family, by his rural existence, by his poverty, and by racism, Dave purchases a gun in order to feel powerful. However, the first time he shoots it, he accidentally kills a mule owned by a white farmer. Rather than face humiliation and a hard punishment, he runs away to the city. Bitter and resentful, he feels the stress of never having been able to grow into manhood in a conflict-free environment.

Yamamoto, Hisaye. "The Legend of Miss Sasagawara." 1950. Reprint, in *Speaking for Ourselves: American Ethnic Writing*, edited by Lillian Faderman and Barbara Bradshaw. Glenview, Ill.: Scott, Foresman, 1969.

This story takes place in an American relocation camp for Japanese during the Second World War. Told by a young female narrator, Kiku, it dramatizes the everyday concerns of Kiku and her friend, Elsie, in the camp. Miss Sasagawara, a beautiful, elegant former ballet dancer, arrives in the Arizona camp and at once becomes the object of the girls' attention. From their fragmentary knowledge, gossip, and a long poem by the woman discovered by chance in a small poetry magazine, Kiku pieces together a psychological portrait of Miss Sasagawara's spiritual loneliness and isolation following the death of her mother. Miss Sasagawara comes forth as a sensitive, passionate person, crushed by her experience in the camp and the perfectionist ideals of her father.

Yutang, Lin. *Chinatown Family.* New York: Day, 1948.

Chinatown Family is about a family of first generation Chinese immigrants to San Francisco. Tom, the protagonist, is brought to the United States as a child and educated in American ways. In particular, he develops intellectually skeptical, scientific attitudes, which threaten to bring him into conflict and collision with his elders and Chinese tradition—a story of generational conflict, common in ethnic writing. However, Tom eventually learns to accept and appreciate the wisdom of Taoism and the teachings of Laotse and Chuangtse. His story nicely illustrates his difficulty in accepting diversity and his achievement of a satisfactory identity.

16 Retirement and the Last Years of Life:

Edna Ferber's "Sudden Sixties"

By Sherry Reiter

The greatest challenge of aging is sustaining one's efforts to self-actualize and grow despite the physical limitations and losses that are inevitable in the aging process. The older person continues to confront the life task of remaining true to his or her individuality despite multiple stresses, which may include pressure from family, peers, and society. After retirement, when choices are generally no longer dictated by work or family responsibilities, the older person has greater freedom to follow his or her desires. Retirement may bring with it a narrowing or broadening of one's life experiences, depending on the individual's choices. Those choices are affected by one's self-image, as well as others' images and expectations of the aging person. Psychologist Erik Erikson has aptly described the challenge of this phase of life as one of integrity versus despair. Meeting this challenge requires the aging person to accept the demands on personality that go with being active.

The Paradigm

"Sudden Sixties," by Edna Ferber (Simon & Schuster, 1947), first published in 1922, encapsulates one individual's struggle for self-realization in her later years. Hannah Winter finds that retirement has given her the opportunity to make choices about her lifestyle. However, Hannah is torn between her responsibilities to herself and others. This is further complicated by a distorted image of aging and a negative set of expectations by Hannah's family. In a society that idolizes the young and espouses achievement through work, the retired person may be perceived as neither attractive nor useful. No wonder most persons in American society deny the reality of aging. Hannah is no exception. She is an aging person who must contend with the way society sees her, as well as with her self-image.

Part of the challenge the older person must confront is knowing what he or she can and cannot do and understanding why. The individual cannot allow his or her life to be defined by others. In order to remain true to one's individuality, one must be able to define one's own challenges. Because the older person's environment rarely provides social, economic, or emotional support, the older person must exert continuous effort to create an environment that is nourishing and sustaining.

Ferber hints subtly at those lessons that make aging easier. Self-esteem and understanding one's own needs are essential to making satisfying life decisions. An acceptance of aging is not synonymous with giving up or giving in. Those who believe that life is over at age 60 are certain to find that it is. Aging requires a healthy attitude and a strong desire to enjoy life. Unfortunately, Hannah seems to lack the independence that would enable her to follow her desires.

Summary

It is difficult for Hannah Winter to accept that she has reached the last season of her life. Ferber's use of "Winter" as the protagonist's last name associates the harsh coldness of the winter season with the hard life Hannah has lived. Winter is the season in which seeds lie dormant beneath the earth, waiting for the right moment to flower and come into their own. Hannah's personal desires also are hidden, waiting to surface at a time that is acceptable. However, the ticking clock and the reflection in the mirror warn that time is running out.

The story opens with the heroine rushing down Peacock Alley to meet her daughter, when she sees a familiar woman hurrying toward her. This well-dressed, tense-looking older person will not get out of Hannah's way. When Hannah swerves to avoid a collision, so does the other woman. In the next moment, Hannah crashes into her own image, reflected in the long, full-length mirror of the Chicago Hotel.

At that moment, as she stares into the eyes of the older woman, Hannah comes face to face with the startling truth. The reflected woman is a stranger, a murderer who has permanently annihilated the image of the high-spirited young girl Hannah. The girl of twenty who stood so grandly at the altar in her wine-colored silk wedding gown 40 years before is gone forever. Suddenly, Hannah is 60.

Hannah is a woman who cannot see herself clearly, which Ferber illustrates beautifully in the mirror incident. She has been rushing down

Peacock Alley, never having taken the time to deal with herself; in fact, she does not even recognize her own image in the mirror. It is as though, when she last took the time to look, she was a young, hopeful girl. The 40 years since then she has spent in a whirlwind of obligations and responsibilities to others, whose well-being came first.

Ferber's choice of "Hannah" for the protagonist's first name brings to mind two other Hannahs from the Bible and the Apocryphal literature. Both of these women are strong, courageous, and self-sacrificing. Hannah Winter's sacrifices have been many throughout her life, but they have been made willingly and without qualms, until this last season of Hannah's life.

At this point, Hannah is jolted into realizing that there are limitations to her mortality. Her lack of ability to recognize herself—her needs and wants as an individual—has resulted in a collision. The mirror forces Hannah to confront her self-image, as well as the face she shows the world. Thus, Ferber encapsulates one of the story's major themes in this opening incident.

It is difficult enough for Hannah to come to terms with her image of an aging self. However, it is almost impossible to escape the narrow, stereotyped perceptions of others, who see her as elderly. To Hannah's grandchildren, whom she loves dearly, she is "Grandma," giver of treats and special attention. To Clint Darrow, her aging suitor, she is the available widow, who, if "caught," will take care of him in his last few years. To her daughter, Marcia, she is the all-giving advice giver and baby-sitter, the mother who is always there when needed. The social roles that Hannah feels compelled to play are narrow and constricting, creating dilemmas that are universal in nature and proving that stereotypic attitudes toward aging are suffocating.

In actuality, the protagonist is far from a stereotype of the older person. She is fortunate in face and financial status and still has considerable physical stamina to enjoy her remaining years. She has arrived at a season in her life that, with her considerable savings, she can enjoy. At this point in time, she has the freedom to do as she pleases, provided that she permits herself to do so.

Unfortunately, if a person's will is weak or absent, the individual will be unable to do things for the pure satisfaction of self. In other words, the will may be viewed as a component of one's self-image. Thus, Hannah's ability to enjoy herself is limited. She has never developed a strong sense of self, although she has played numerous roles well enough to satisfy the wills of others.

As the story unfolds, we learn that circumstances have dictated how Hannah has lived. Ferber suggests that life has tricked Hannah. When she is twenty years old, she turns down a marriage proposal from the handsome rascal Clint Darrow, who is considered a poor prospect. Instead, she chooses steady, solid Hermie Slocum, who ironically turns out to be rigid and stingy. The bit of wealth Hermie flaunts before marriage was made for him by a former business partner and quickly dissipates. Despite her husband's lack of business skill, Hannah's quick and shrewd mind manipulates whatever money is theirs. Hannah gives birth to two children and encourages her husband to better himself. When Hermie dies at the age of 45, Hannah, now 36, is left to raise their two children.

Moving back to Chicago, where she grew up, Hannah works as an insurance agent. To the shock of her friends, she sells coal in addition to her full-time job in order to make ends meet. She is determined to see that her children have the very best. The next two decades fly past quickly, as Hannah works day and night. Finally, after seeing her children grown and married, Hannah rents a room in a comfortable hotel on the lakefront to enjoy her leisure.

It is here that Hannah expects to spend her golden years. She has the opportunity to be married once more—to none other than the suitor of her youth, Clint Darrow. Ironically, he is now a wealthy widower who offers to share his riches with Hannah. However, Hannah is not interested in taking on further responsibilities. At the age of 60, she strives to capture the freedom that has eluded her all her life.

Yet Hannah is more of a slave now than ever before. Every morning at 8:00 A.M., her daughter phones with a formula that almost never fails. After several questions about her mother's health, she says, "You're not doing anything special today, are you?" Scenes of the day as she hopes it will be flash before Hannah's eyes. Nothing special, Hannah answers; perhaps she will attend a lecture or a concert. These simple desires, which are of no consequence to her daughter, and which she never indulged in before, could now be hers. When Hannah gives in to the demands others make on her, she gives up something of herself. Ironically, despite all the hardships she has faced, Hannah has less control over her life now than ever before. She seems unable to say no; the needs and wants of others are more important than her own.

It is not accidental that Ferber sets this story in the windy city of Chicago. Although the protagonist appears strong in character, she lacks the ego strength to withstand the buffeting winds of others, who pull her in different directions than she would choose. Hannah's actions are motivated by shoulds, not wants.

Her will appears to be absent or overtaken by the needs of others. From birth, Hannah reacts to others' forceful demands. Her mother is a quick-tongued character who often leaves young Hannah to mind the house in her absence. Later, she dutifully marries a man of whom her father approves and denies her physical attraction to the man of her choice. When Hermie, her son, does not pay back his tuition as promised, Hannah foregoes her retirement plans and works several more years to make up his debt. She never asserts her will to ask for the money, nor does she speak of her feelings. In the last few years, she struggles against the domination of a self-centered daughter.

Hannah may be viewed as the product of the society and times in which she lived; pleasing and caring for others were the most acceptable characteristics of womanhood in the early 1900s. She is a reactor, rather than an initiator, of life events. Only in the absence of others' directives does she take an assertive stance, as is evident in her behavior as a businesswoman. Even then, her actions are acceptable in the eyes of society because of her widowhood.

Hannah does not remarry for fear that she will be burdened with a host of new responsibilities. Nor has she ever experienced pleasure or fun in a relationship with a man. In her sixties, she turns away a second time from Clint Darrow. She cannot envision a relationship that might satisfy some of her needs. Men have always taken more from Hannah than they have given; they remain a threat to her individuality.

When Hannah is either by herself or with her peers, she can be herself and experience her individuality unclouded by others' images of an aging woman. Instinctively, Hannah knows that the essence of her individuality is untouched by age. It is worth noting that the protagonist retains her maiden name throughout the story. Hannah's marriage was one to which she was resigned, not committed. She has remained as stiff and solitary as the gown in which she was married—"so stiff it could stand alone."

It is hardly surprising that Hannah's children play such a dominant role in her life. She sees them as extensions of herself. Perhaps this is why she knows no limits or boundaries in what she gives them. However, as Hannah gives up more and more of her free time, twinges of remorse grow into feelings of angry rebellion. Hannah must choose between meeting her own needs and meeting the needs of her family. In order to live her life, she must value her own needs as much as she does the needs of others, and she must take responsibility for her feelings. Hannah needs enough self-esteem to believe that she is valuable not only for what she does, but what she is.

The resolution of Hannah's conflict is incomplete as the tension grows between what Hannah perceives as selfishness and selflessness. The story reaches its climax when, after a full day of helping Marcia shop, Hannah goes back to her daughter's home for dinner. Although she longs for the peace and quiet of her own room, she feels she cannot decline the invitation.

Meanwhile, her grandchild Joan has gotten one of her frequent sore throats. Marcia is upset that she will be forced to give up the next day at the country club. In a fit of anger, the ten-year-old shouts at her mother, "Giving up is easy for you. You're an old lady."

Joan's words hit a nerve. As the opening mirror incident suggested, Hannah cannot bear to think of herself as old, and she is torn between the image of herself as the young girl at the altar and the old woman in the mirror. Coming full circle, the story concludes with another mirror incident. This time, Hannah sees her struggle with Marcia reflected back in Marcia and Joan's argument. Just as there is a generation gap between Hannah and Marcia, a gap exists between Marcia and the next generation.

Joan is centered on her own needs, as are all children. She is not concerned about her mother's feelings or what her mother must give up. Ironically, this mirrors the indifference of Marcia to her mother's needs. In witnessing this, Hannah could be experiencing the sweetness of revenge. Instead, she wants to protect her daughter from the onslaught of demands that she herself has experienced.

The final scene also may be viewed symbolically. The parent and self-serving child may be seen as conflicting counterparts within Hannah's psyche. Hannah's sacrificing mother always wins over her free-spirited child. Hannah tells Marcia that she will stay with her grandchild so her daughter and son-in-law can have a good time at the country club. At that moment, when Hannah sacrifices her plans for Marcia's sake, she becomes old. An aged person, as the child points out, gives up. When Hannah gives in, she allows herself to be identified by the child's definition of old age.

This provocative short story encapsulates the struggles of the aging with great sensitivity. Clearly, lifelong struggles, instead of abating with age, often continue with greater force than ever. A person's struggle to maintain and develop individuality does not stop. There is a continuous need to set one's priorities and follow one's path, regardless of the expectations and pressures of others in society. The Hannah Winters of the world struggle against giving up and giving in. Like all of us, Hannah is struggling with life's challenges up until the very last moment.

Questions for Discussion

1. What is the significance of Ferber's choice of the name Hannah Winter for the main character?

2. How does the mirror at the beginning of the story validate or diminish Hannah's image of herself? Do the older person's inner image of self and outer image usually match? Other people also become mirrors that reflect back an image. How do the other characters distort Hannah's image of herself?
3. Mothers are sometimes accused of "smotherlove"—that is, constricting the growth of their children to meet their own needs. In reverse, a grown child may do this to a parent. Why does Hannah's daughter do this to Hannah?
4. Should a mother's love be unlimited? When do responsibilities to children end? Or do they?
5. What stops Hannah from taking responsibility for and acting on her feelings?
6. What do the terms "selfishness" and "selflessness" mean in terms of Hannah's situation?

Annotated Bibliography

Print

Albee, Edward. *The American Dream*. New York: Signet, 1959.

This one-act play is a satirical fantasy that comments on the values of the American family. Grandma, the protagonist, represents the older person who is subjected to cruelty by an insensitive society. She is tormented by her daughter's constant threats to take her to the nursing home. Grandma is the scapegoat of her daughter's frustration, and she retaliates with wit and intelligence. Grandma's feisty character is juxtaposed by her son-in-law, a passive invalid in a wheelchair. He represents the emasculated male, tolerated only because of his wealth. Grandma finds herself living in a world that has substituted artificial values for real ones. Albee attacks the vacuousness of the American dream through Grandma, whose wisdom is ignored. Grandma is triumphant at the play's conclusion, when she devises a plan to escape her impossible situation.

Berry, David. *The Whales of August*. New York: Dramatists Play Service, 1984. (Film: *The Whales of August*. Active Films. 1987.)

Two sisters have different attitudes toward aging. Whereas Libby focuses on the presence of death as the escort in waiting, Sarah bustles with the excitement of daily events, regardless of how small and insignificant. The play poses the question that every older person must answer: Does one live out one's last years planning how to live or how to die? Sarah also must confront the question of what her responsibilities are to her older sister, as well as to herself. The importance of reacting to change with adaptation rather than fear is an underlying theme. The need to experience all of life, regardless of approaching death, moves Sarah to make a final decision. She chooses a path that validates her individuality as she pursues a new and daring adventure.

Buck, Pearl S. "The Old Demon." In *Great Modern Short Stories*, edited by Bennett Cerf. New York: Vintage, 1955.

"The Old Demon" tells the story of an elderly Chinese matriarch, Mrs. Wang, and the ancient river that has blessed and cursed her family for generations. It has kept them alive and, on occasion, taken life away. When the Japanese attack, Mrs. Wang refuses to run with the others. Fortified by courage and love, she takes a stand against the enemy. In a heroic, defiant gesture in the face of disaster, Mrs. Wang relies on the old demon river to preserve what is left of her family and destroy the Japanese troops. Mrs. Wang illustrates the older generation's wisdom in her adherence to traditional values and her reliance on the power of nature for survival.

Calisher, Hortense. *Age*. New York: Weidenfeld and Nicolson, 1987.

In *Age*, the story of a passionate elderly couple as they approach death, Calisher deals sensitively with the themes of love, sexuality, and the impending loss of one's life partner. Preoccupied with the fear of one partner being left alone, Gemma and Rupert decide to write secret diaries, which constitute the novel itself. The purpose of the diaries is to comfort the partner left behind. Through the characters depicted, Calisher illustrates the manner in which a person may greet old age and impending death. We meet older persons who flirt with death, submit meekly, commit suicide, or—like Rupert and Gemma—accept the inevitable with a mixture of fear and courage. At the novel's conclusion, the couple decide to trade diaries and share their secrets while they are still able to do so.

Capote, Truman. *I Remember Grandpa*. Atlanta, Ga.: Peachtree, 1987.

I Remember Grandpa depicts the relationship between a young boy and his grandfather in West Virginia. The story illustrates the theme of intergenerational love and the inevitability of change. When Bobby's parents leave the Allegheny Mountains for a better life in the big city, Bobby must say good-bye to his grandfather despite ambivalent feelings. Grandpa asks Bobby to return one day and promises to tell his grandson a wonderful secret when he does. However, Bobby is an adult before he understands what Grandpa's secret was. Capote sensitively expresses the pain of separation while acknowledging a relationship that separation and death cannot sever.

Cather, Willa. "Old Mrs. Harris." 1932. Reprint, in *Obscure Destinies*. New York: Random, 1974.

In "Old Mrs. Harris," Cather contrasts the cultural attitudes toward aging held by two social groups—southern whites (as represented by the Templetons) and German-Jews (as represented by the Templetons' neighbors). This short story depicts the grandmother of the Templeton family (Mrs. Harris) and her proud struggle to maintain the facade of responsibility at the cost of her own comfort. No neighbors are allowed to visit Mrs. Harris when she is alone. Her daughter's worst fear is that the neighbors will think her mother is put upon by chores. Keeping up appearances is important. Observing her daughter's rules is lonely and difficult, but Mrs. Harris is a model of self-sacrifice. The distance between the generations is depicted by the strained relationship of Mrs. Harris and her daughter. Mrs. Harris foregoes pride when she asks the neighbors for monetary assistance to enable her grandchild to attend college. This story examines pride, as well as its positive and negative consequences.

Dell, Floyd. "The Blanket." In *A Family Is a Way of Feeling*, edited by Marjorie B. Smiley. New York: Macmillan, 1966.

"The Blanket" focuses on the sad good-bye of a grandfather the evening before going away to live in a nursing home. This poignant story captures the sadness, loneliness, and pain of a family abandoning one of its members. Petey, the grandchild, grieves over his father's decision to send his grandfather away. (Petey's father will be remarrying and starting a new life in which the grandfather will be in the way.) Petey is the voice of conscience. He bitterly suggests that the blanket, Grandpa's going away gift, be cut in two; Grandpa will take one half and the other half will come in handy when Petey's father is old and it is his turn to be sent away. Resentment, guilt, and sorrow are interwoven in the powerful short story.

Fisher, Dorothy Canfield. "The Heyday of the Blood." In *Twenty Grand Short Stories*, edited by Ernestine Taggard. New York: Bantam, 1941.

An older professor tells his young assistant, whose depression has depleted his enthusiasm for living, the story of his 88-year-old "gran'ther," whose message is that life is meant to be lived and enjoyed to the fullest. The professor's gran'ther is a risk taker who refuses to allow the obstacles of ill health and concerned family stand in his way. When the county fair comes to town, Gran'ther sneaks away with his great-grandson. The very old man and the very young boy share a deep bond, as well as a yearning to be free. Together they relish every forbidden pleasure with absolute abandonment and delight in the moment. Guided by a zest for life, Gran'ther does away with the constraints of convention and stereotyped images of aging.

Foote, Horton. *The Trip to Bountiful*. New York: Dramatists Play Service, 1954. (Film: *The Trip to Bountiful*. Island Pictures. 1985).

An old woman (Mrs. Watts) wishes to spend her last days in Bountiful, where she grew up. Currently, she feels alienated, imprisoned, and unwanted in a small, two-bedroom apartment, which she shares with her son, Ludie, and his wife, Jessie Mae. She longs for a space of her own. Despite warnings and interference, Mrs. Watts finally sets out for the place of her birth to die. Foote sensitively illustrates the domination and infantilization of the older person by family and society in this play.

Freydberg, Margaret Howe. *Winter Concert*. Woodstock, Vt.: Countryman, 1985.

Freydberg successfully shatters any stereotyped conceptions of the complacent older person whose life tasks are completed. The spirits of her characters are young, striving, and still seeking personal fulfillment. *Winter Concert* depicts three aging couples and their love relationships during one winter in New England. Celeste and Cabe are two people in their sixties whose previous marriages have left wounded but seeking hearts. Lidi, in her seventies, is a poetess whose passion cannot be assuaged by her husband, Freddie. Tillie and Turk, in their eighties, enjoy passionate sexual intimacy in a fulfilling, illicit affair. Love, sexuality, and integrity are Freydberg's major themes.

Kavaler, Rebecca. "Depression Glass." In *Tigers in the Wood*. Champaign: Univ. of Illinois Pr., 1986.

"Depression Glass" illustrates the emotional distance between an elderly father and his adult daughter. The daughter's voice alternates with her father's, and we hear the inner monologues of two personalities who are worlds apart in thought and feeling. We also become aware of the contrast between private self and public image. The father presents incomplete bits and pieces of his past, which further alienates his daughter. Only we are privy to his true feelings. When his daughter's friend admires his antique depression glass, he recalls a childhood memory that haunts him. Bittersweet memories momentarily dull the loneliness of an old, misunderstood man.

Lardner, Ring W. "The Golden Honeymoon." In *Fifty Great Short Stories*, edited by Milton Crane. New York: Bantam, 1952.

When Charley and Lucy go on a trip to celebrate their fiftieth wedding anniversary, they are sure that their love has withstood the test of time. They are happy for the companionship they have in each other and for the leisure time in which to enjoy it. However, when they accidentally meet Lucy's sweetheart from 52 years earlier and his wife, they are confronted by another test of time. The two couples become friendly and engage in a succession of competitive games, in which the tension rises. Beneath the competitiveness and jealousy is the insecurity that prompts Lucy and Charley to ask each other whether they regret the choice made 50 years earlier. The story illustrates the permanency and security of love and marriage that have withstood the pressures of time.

Lavery, Emmet G. *The Magnificent Yankee*. New York: French, 1946.

Supreme Court Justice Oliver Wendell Holmes, Jr., was a powerful and colorful character appointed to the Supreme Court in 1902 by President Roosevelt. This play focuses on Holmes' personal relationships, which are highlighted as he celebrates his eightieth birthday. Holmes is a role model of dignity, optimism, and productivity in his old age. Lavery captures the warmth and loyalty of Holmes' relationship to others, as we see the interplay between him and his wife, Fanny, his colleague, Brandeis, and his "boys," the legal aides who have been dedicated to him for years. We cannot help but admire Holmes, the magnificent Yankee, for being as capable and committed to social change at age 80 as he was at 40.

O'Connor, Flannery. "Everything That Rises Must Converge." In *Family: Stories from the Interior*, edited by Geri Chavis. St. Paul, Minn.: Graywolf, 1987.

Julian and his mother's relationship is embittered by dependency and sacrifice. Julian is a frustrated writer who resents all that his mother has done for him. He feels imprisoned by guilt over his mother's sacrifices. Julian would like to withdraw from his aging mother, but she desires to remain close. Thus, Julian feels obligated to accompany his mother downtown to her reducing classes at the YMCA, which she takes to lower her blood pressure. During the bus trip, Julian's irritation builds with every word his mother utters and every gesture she makes. When his mother attempts to give a black child a penny, an angry confrontation brings unexpected results.

Olsen, Tillie. *Tell Me a Riddle*. New York: Dell, 1981. (Film: *Tell Me a Riddle*. Filmways. 1980.)

Tell Me a Riddle depicts a 47-year-old marriage torn apart by differences and illness. The story focuses on the heartbreaking compromises spouses may be forced to confront in old age. Eva, the main character, wants to live out her remaining years in her own home, not forced to "move to the rhythm of others." Her husband would prefer to live in his union's retirement haven. An unexpected illness forces the couple to make unwelcome decisions. As Eva struggles against her progressive illness and growing dependency, her husband becomes the unwanted caretaker, berated for a lifetime of decisions and behaviors. Their children watch in frustration as the marriage deteriorates. In his efforts to make her last months happy, Eva's husband sacrifices his life's savings, while both of them fight feelings of loss and the betrayal of impending death.

Thompson, Ernest. *On Golden Pond*. New York: Dramatists Play Service, 1979. (Film: *On Golden Pond*. Universal Films. 1981. 109 min.)

On Golden Pond tells the story of a couple who have lived well and who want to savor their remaining years together. Norman and Ethel's love and desire to protect each other is the central theme. They sustain a rich relationship despite illness and aging. Bridging the generation gap is an alternate theme. Old patterns and ways of relating to others are challenged in Norman's confrontations with his daughter, her fiancé, and Billy, the young teenager who comes to visit. Thompson suggests that living means being open to new ways of thinking, which rigidity, stubbornness, and prejudice do not permit. This poignant and witty play illustrates that growing is a necessary aspect of growing older.

Tulloch, Janet G. *A Home Is Not a Home (Life within a Nursing Home)*. New York: Seabury, 1975.

In this novel, Tulloch illuminates aspects of nursing home life in a series of disturbing episodes. We are introduced to the home through the eyes of Joady, an invalid forced to enter the home because of an unnamed physical handicap. Although younger than most of the residents, Joady too is in the process of dying. All must cope with loss, dependency, and deterioration in an artificial environment. On a daily level, there is a continuous need for love and compassion, as well as a striving for dignity. For Joady and the other residents, survival requires accepting and adapting to the limitations of her new friends within the confines of a home that can never truly be a home.

Welty, Eudora. "A Worn Path." In *A Curtain of Green, and Other Stories*. New York: Harcourt, 1969.

Phoenix Jackson, an elderly black woman, journeys through the desolate countryside of Mississippi to the city of Natchez to attain medicine for her ailing grandson. Love and self-sacrifice, courage in the face of insurmountable difficulties, and reliance on others are emerging themes. Phoenix must overcome the vicissitudes of nature and the condescension of white people who consider her a charity case. Although small and very old, she uses her persistence and fortitude to help her triumph over circumstance. On her journey, necessity forces her to ask others' assistance. However, spurred on by the importance of her mission, Phoenix never loses her dignity and proud composure.

Wiesel, Eli. *The Oath.* New York: Random, 1973.

The Oath is a powerful story, confronting existential questions regarding the meaning of life, suffering, and war. It tells of Azriel, an elderly survivor of the Holocaust, who attempts to keep a young man from committing suicide. He tries numerous arguments without success before he realizes that his own story of disillusionment may provide meaning. Decades before, Azriel took an oath that he would never reveal the story of how his village was destroyed. He has been a wanderer ever since, never able to escape the horrors of his experience. He has struggled with the guilt of the survivor, his acceptance of destiny, and his fear of death, as well as life. The old man battles the young man's pain with his own as he breaks the oath to save a life.

Film

Cocoon. Twentieth Century-Fox. 1985. 117 min.

Cocoon, directed by Ron Howard, is a delightful science fiction fantasy, in which the residents of a Florida nursing home have the opportunity to turn back the clocks. The residents, played by Wilford Brimley, Don Ameche, and Hume Cronyn, trespass and bathe in the pool of a nearby estate. The pool is a veritable fountain of youth, owned by visiting aliens from Enterra, a planet where the inhabitants never get sick, never get old, and never die. The film confronts us with some age-old questions. Shouldn't people be adventurous and lead productive lives regardless of age? Do people have the right to cheat nature when they feel it has cheated them? Is there anything people will not do to attain immortality?

Dad. Universal Films. 1989. 110 min.

Dad, a powerful film directed by Gary David Goldberg and based on William Wharton's novel, is about reconnecting with family and saying what needs to be said before it is too late. Jack Lemmon and Ted Danson play the father (Jack Tremont) and son (John) who deal with difficult questions about the reciprocal nature of the parent-child relationship. Having seen the child through to adulthood, can the parent expect similar care in old age? When Jack's wife suffers a heart attack, he becomes confused and helpless. John comes for an extended visit to help

Jack regain his former vitality. With compassion and devotion, John helps his father stand on his own again. The story suggests the importance of treasuring the best in a relationship, without being overwhelmed by fear of its loss.

Driving Miss Daisy. Warner Bros. 1989. 115 min.

Directed by Bruce Beresford, this film portrays the friendship that develops between an elderly Jewish woman (Miss Daisy, played by Jessica Tandy) and an aging black chauffeur (played by Morgan Freeman). The setting is Georgia in the late 1960s. When Miss Daisy's son decides that she is no longer capable of driving on her own, he hires a chauffeur for her against her wishes. Infuriated by her son's domination and striving to maintain her independence, Miss Daisy indignantly rejects the new chauffeur. Eventually, she is won over by his good humor and patience. With tenderness and wit, the film explores dimensions of a relationship that goes beyond given roles. Despite differences in station and color, Miss Daisy and her chauffeur are bonded in an unexpected special friendship. The film beautifully illustrates the difficulties encountered as an older person becomes more dependent, as well as the importance of companionship in later years.

Harold and Maude. Paramount Films. 1971. 92 min.

Two individuals, one old (Maude, played by Ruth Gordon) and one young (Harold, played by Bud Cort), are drawn together by their fascination with death. They meet one day in a graveyard when both are attending a funeral just for the fun of it. Harold is a troubled young man whose only interest in life is death. Maude, who is 79, has a lust for life that is infectious. The film reminds us that age has little to do with enjoying life; it is one's attitude that is most important. Maude teaches young Harold how to live. Although Harold's mother has set him up with different girls, he is interested only in Maude. Maude is a staunch individualist who shatters stereotypes of aging with behaviors and attitudes that are unconventional, humorous, and sometimes shocking. On her eightieth birthday, Maude exercises her right to die before her vitality and health decline. *Harold and Maude* makes a strong statement about living life with integrity and on one's own terms.

Harry and Tonto. Twentieth Century-Fox. 1974. 115 min.

Harry and Tonto, directed by Paul Mazursky, tells the story of Harry, a gutsy 72-year-old (played by Art Carney), and his quest to find a place where he belongs. After wreckers destroy his apartment building, Harry and his cat, Tonto, have no place to live. When staying with his son's family proves intolerable, Harry and Tonto hit the open road. On the road, they befriend a young hitchhiker. The common bond between young and old is evident as both seek to find a place to be themselves. Harry looks up an old flame, who is now in a nursing home. His nostalgic memories of the past blend with his adventures in the present as he meets a variety of colorful characters. Harry's resiliency and calm acceptance of other people's ways enable him to meet harsh circumstances with humor and dignity. He relishes the past without clinging to it and understands the importance of living for today.

I Never Sang for My Father. Columbia Pictures. 1971. 92 min.

Directed by Gilbert Cates, this poignant film portrays a father-son relationship and all the thoughts and feelings that go unspoken between them. The story begins when the old man's life is ending, although he will not admit it. The 81-year-old man (played by Melvyn Douglas), formerly the mayor of the town, is now forgotten and spends much of his time falling asleep in front of the television. He is proud, stubborn, and demanding. The son (played by Gene Hackman) has difficulty meeting his father's needs. His own wife died a year before, and at the age of 44 he has decided to marry a woman who lives in California. With the death of his wife, the father becomes totally dependent on his son. The son works through his ambivalence to offer his father a place in his new home, but the father rejects this and all other alternatives. Tragically, the difficulties between father and son remain unresolved at the time of the old man's death. The film suggests that death ends a life, but not a relationship. Long after the father's death, the son wonders what could have been done differently.

About the Authors

Charles Ansell took his doctorate in education at Columbia University. In addition to having a private practice in Sherman Oaks, California, he is on the faculty of the Cambridge Graduate School of Psychology in Los Angeles and serves as a consultant at outpatient mental health clinics. He is a former president of the California Psychological Association and was editor of its publication for many years. He has appeared in the op-ed pages of the *Los Angeles Times* and the *New York Times*, and has authored chapters in books on his favorite themes—psychology, art, and religion.

John Brander was educated in Great Britain, South Africa, and the United States and has an M.A. from the University of San Francisco, an LL.M. from Georgetown University, and a B.Sc. from the University of Wales–Cardiff. He is a practicing attorney and a widely published poet and short story writer, here and abroad. Currently, he is the editor of *CQ* (*California State Poetry Quarterly*) and the co-editor of *The Webs We Weave*, an anthology of Orange County (Calif.) poetry.

Geri Giebel Chavis has an M.A. and Ph.D. in literature and language and an M.A. in counseling psychology and is a certified poetry therapist. She is chairperson of the English department and a professor of literature, and family studies and women's studies at the College of St. Catherine. She also is a therapist at the Hamm Clinic in St. Paul and has been actively involved in the field of poetry therapy and bibliotherapy, serving as vice president and board member of the National Association for Poetry Therapy and associate editor of the *Journal of Poetry Therapy*. Her book, *Family: Stories from the Interior*, was published in 1987 by Graywolf Press.

Norman J. Fedder, distinguished professor and director of graduate studies in theater at Kansas State University, holds a Ph.D. from New York University and is a member of the Kansas Theatre Hall of Fame. A widely produced playwright and registered drama therapist, he teaches playwriting, creative drama, and American ethnic theater and leads workshops in these fields throughout the nation. He is coordinator of the Drama Network of the Coalition for the Advancement of Jewish Education and director of the Theatre of Values, which presents plays of his authorship concerning Jewish religion, history, and culture.

Samuel T. Gladding, Ph.D., assistant to the president and professor of counseling at Wake Forest University in Winston-Salem, North Carolina, is a widely published poet. He is editor of the *Journal for Specialists in Group Work*, former president of Chi Sigma Iota (a counseling academic and professional international honor society), and author of numerous publications, including *Counseling: A Comprehensive Profession*; *Group Work: A Counseling Specialty*; and *Counseling and the Creative Arts*.

Marian I. Goldstein is a registered poetry therapist and a counselor in the women's program at the Carrier Foundation, a private psychiatric hospital in Belle Mead, New Jersey. She holds an M.A. in psychology from the New School for Social Research and is affiliated with Caldwell College as a lecturer. She has published articles in *Arts in Psychotherapy*, the *Journal of Poetry Therapy*, and the *American Journal of Social Psychiatry*. Her poetry has been published by a number of small presses.

Kenneth Gorelick, M.D., is a board certified psychiatrist and a registered poetry therapist. He received his medical and psychiatric training at Harvard Medical School. Since 1979, he has been chief of continuing medical education at the D.C. Commission on Mental Health Services, formerly Saint Elizabeth's Hospital, in Washington, D.C. He is associate clinical professor of psychiatry at George Washington University School of Medicine and is on the editorial board of the *Journal of Poetry Therapy*. He has served two terms as president of the National Association for Poetry Therapy, 1987 to 1991.

Peggy O. Heller holds a master's degree in social work from Catholic University of America. She has been a staff bibliotherapist at the Psychiatric Institute in Washington, D.C.; has served as a consultant in poetry therapy at Mt. Vernon Hospital in Alexandria, Virginia; and has lectured at Catholic University. Currently, she consults for Dominion Hospital's Abuse and Dissociation Disorders Recovery Program and maintains a private practice. She also is vice president of the National Association for Poetry Therapy and edits for creative arts therapy journals.

Owen E. Heninger, M.D., is a graduate of the New York Medical College and is a board certified psychiatrist. His work has appeared in the *Journal of Poetry Therapy*, *Arts in Psychotherapy*, and the *American Handbook of Psychiatry*. He also is director of continuing medical education and president of the board of directors of the Poetry Therapy Institute, assistant clinical professor at the University of Southern California School of Medicine, and in private practice in Whittier, California.

Aaron Kramer's many books of poetry include *Rumshinsky's Hat*, *On the Way to Palermo*, *Carousel Parkway*, and *Indigo*. He has translated Heine, Rilke, and the 1989 anthology *A Century of Yiddish Poetry*. His scholarly works include *The Prophetic Tradition in American Poetry* and *Melville's Poetry*. For many years, he co-edited *West Hills Review: A Whitman Journal*. Since 1956, he has worked extensively with poetry therapy for the handicapped. He has produced more than 70 radio broadcasts and has recorded for Folkways Records and the Library of Congress. He received his Ph.D. at New York University and has taught at Dowling College since 1961.

Arthur Lerner holds doctorates in counseling and literature from the University of Southern California. He is professor emeritus at Los Angeles City College, a pioneer in poetry therapy, and author of four books of poetry. He also edited *Poetry in the Therapeutic Experience* and authored *Psychoanalytically Oriented Criticism of Three American Poets: Poe, Whitman, and Aiken*. He is founder and director of the Poetry Therapy Institute, was director of poetry therapy at Woodview-Calabasas Hospital in Calabasas, California, between 1971 and 1986, was president of the National Association for Poetry Therapy between 1983 and 1987, and currently is director of poetry therapy at Van Nuys Hospital in Van Nuys, California.

Ursula R. Mahlendorf holds a Ph.D. in German literature and an M.A. in English literature from Brown University and has been teaching undergraduate and graduate courses in literature and psychology at the University of California–Santa Barbara for more than 30 years. She has published widely on such subjects as male and female creativity and its psychology and literary representation in such journals as *American Imago*, *Modern Austrian Literature*, *German Quarterly*, *Psychoanalytic Review*, and *American Journal of Social Psychiatry*. Her book, *The Wellsprings* *of Literary Creation: An Analysis of Male and Female Artist Stories from the German Romantics to American Writers of the Present*, was published in 1985 by Camden House of Columbia, South Carolina. She also has co-edited a special issue of the *American Journal for Social Psychiatry* (1987) with Arthur Lerner.

Marjorie Marks-Frost has been a free-lance journalist and book reviewer for ten years, principally for the *Los Angeles Times*. A graduate of the University of California–Los Angeles, she also has been a business and media analyst for the corporate planning department of Times Mirror Company. She has served on the board of PEN Center in U.S.A. West for four years and currently is manager of the *Los Angeles Times* book prizes.

Jay Martin is the Leo S. Bing professor of American literature at the University of Southern California, as well as a graduate of the Southern California Psychoanalytic Institute; a faculty member of the department of psychiatry at the University of California–Irvine Medical School; and a psychoanalyst in private practice. He has written more than 100 articles and reviews and twelve books, the most recent of which is *Who Am I This Time? Uncovering the Fictive Personality*, published by Norton in 1988.

Nicholas Mazza, diplomate in clinical social work, is an associate professor at the Florida State University School of Social Work. He holds Florida licenses in clinical social work, marriage and family therapy, and psychology. He also is the editor of the *Journal of Poetry Therapy* and has lectured and published extensively on crisis intervention and treatment, family social work practice, and the use of the arts in clinical practice.

Ronald W. Pies, M.D., was graduated from Cornell University and did his psychiatric residency at Upstate Medical Center in Syracuse, New York. His interests include the relationship between poetic and schizophrenic language; the relationship between literature and psychotherapy; and the use of poetry in the therapeutic process. He is the author of a chapbook of poetry, *Lean Soil*, and a book on psychotherapy for the general public, *Psychotherapy Today: A Guide to Current Therapeutic Approaches*, published by Manning-Skidmore-Roth in 1991. He teaches at Tuft University School of Medicine in Boston.

Sherry Reiter received her master's degree in social work from Yeshiva University in New York and her master's degree in educational theater and creative arts therapies from New York University. She is a registered poetry and drama therapist and teaches poetry and drama therapy for the helping professional at Hofstra University. She also conducts groups for the Kingsboro Psychiatric Institute and the Jewish Board of Children and Family Service. She is director of the Creative Righting Center in Brooklyn.

Charles M. Rossiter, Ph.D., C.P.T., is the director of the Albany Training Program in Poetry Therapy and a consultant in poetry and poetry therapy to various schools, libraries, growth centers, prisons, and mental health facilities. His research has appeared in dozens of academic journals, and he co-authored the text *Communicating Personally*. His most recent collections of poetry are *Thirds* and *The Man with Two Days' Stubble*. He is producer and host of "Poetry Motel," New York State's poetry television program, and serves as president of the Poetry Motel Foundation and as a board member of the National Association for Poetry Therapy.

Author-Title Index

Prepared by Julie Mueller